CURRICULUM DEVELOPMENT FOR THE MENTALLY HANDICAPPED

Alaine Lane, ed.

Longman

New York & London

Curriculum Development for the Mentally Handicapped

Longman Inc.
95 Church Street
White Plains, N.Y. 10601

Associated companies:
Longman Group Ltd., London
Longman Cheshire Pty., Melbourne
Longman Paul Pty., Auckland
Copp Clark Pitman, Toronto
Pitman Publishing Inc., Boston

Library of Congress Cataloging in Publication Data

Curriculum development for the mentally handicapped.

   Bibliography: p.
   1. Mentally handicapped children—Education—
Curricula—Addresses, essays, lectures. 2. Curriculum
planning—Addresses, essays, lectures. I. Lane, Alaine.
LC4603.3.C87   1986   371.92'84   86-158
ISBN 0-582-28660-3
ISBN 0-582-28661-1

86 87 88 89 9 8 7 6 5 4 3 2 1

SPECIAL EDUCATION SERIES

Administration of Special Education
Agnosia
Anorexia Nerovosa and Eating Disorders
Aphasia
Autism—Revised ed.

Brain Injury

Career and Vocational Education for the
 Handicapped
Child Psychology
Counseling Parents of Exceptional Children
Curriculum Development for the Gifted
Curriculum Development for the Learning
 Disabled
Curriculum Development for the Mentally
 Handicapped
The Classroom Teacher and the Special Child

Deaf Education
Down's Syndrome
Dyslexia

Educable Mentally Handicapped

Foundations of Gifted Education

Human Growth and Development of the
 Exceptional Individual

Identification and Evaluation of Exceptional
 Children
Individualized Educational Programs
Instructional Media and Special Education
Introduction to Audiology and Hearing Science

Language and Writing Disorders

Mainstreaming—Revised ed.
Mental Retardation

Microcomputers and Emotional and Behavioral
 Disorders
Microcomputers and the Gifted Child
Microcomputers and Individualized Educational
 Programs
Microcomputers and Learning Disabilities
Microcomputers and the Mentally Handicapped
Microcomputers and Special Education
Muscular Dystrophy
Motor Disorders

Perception and Memory Disorders
Physically Handicapped Education
Pre-School Education for the Handicapped
Psychology of Exceptional Children

Reading Disorders

Severely and Profoundly Handicapped Education
Special Education and Mathematics
Special Education—Revised ed.
Special Olympics
Speech and Hearing
Student Teaching and Special Education
Stuttering

Three Models of Learning Disabilities
Trainable Mentally Handicapped

Visually Handicapped Education
Vocational Training for the Mentally Retarded

Ways and Means

Reference Texts

Autism
Learning Disabilities
Mentally Handicapped

CONTENTS

GLOSSARY
OF
TERMS

auditory perception The ability to interpret or organize the sensory data received through the ear.

clinical teaching An approach to teaching that attempts to tailor-make learning experiences for the unique needs of a particular child.

cognitive style An individual's characteristic approach to problem solving and cognitive tasks.

comprehensive diagnosis Examination of the causes, complications and consequences of a problem; includes, but not limited to, an educational, physical, neurological, psychological, social, speech and hearing, and language evaluation.

developmental imbalance A disparity in the developmental patterns of intellectual skills.

down's syndrome Named for Dr. John Langdon-Down, who first identified it in 1886, this condition is caused by an extra number 21 chromosome. This disorder occurs in all degrees of retardation severity. Those affected have similar physical characteristics.

educable mentally retarded Those individuals whose IQ falls between 50 and 70.

frustration level A degree of task difficulty which a child is incapable of performing at a given time.

generalization The process of deriving or inducing a general concept or principle from particulars.

hydrocephalus Pressure on the brain and skull from cerebral-spinal fluid.

mainstreaming The placement of handicapped students into educational programs with normal functioning children.

neurological examination An examination of sensory or motor responses, especially the reflexes, to determine whether or not there are localized impairments of the nervous system.

psychomotor Pertaining to the motor effect of psychological processes.

severe retardation Those persons whose IQ falls approxi-

mately between 0 and 29.

social learning Increasing a child's competence in making relevant decisions and exhibiting appropriate behavior.

trainable mentally retarded Those individuals whose IQ falls between 30 and 49.

transactional relationship One in which the learner has a role in instigating learning, in determining its direction, and in terminating any learning situation.

trisomy 21 The most common form of Down's Syndrome in which there is a trisomy of three individual number 21 chromosomes where there should be one pair. All of the cells of this individual will have 47 chromosomes.

visual impairment The physical loss of part or all of useful vision.

visual perception The identification, organization, and interpretation of sensory data received by the individual through the eye.

PREFACE

All too often the education system has discriminated against both the physically and mentally handicapped child. There have been times when they were considered only parcels to be kept out of the way, not educated. Education for the mentally handicapped was hampered by disdain for the inability of those children who could not measure up to the prescribed norms of intelligence deemed necessary for success in the educational system of the United States.

In 1975, P.L. 94-142, the Education for all Handicapped Children Act, was passed into law by Congress. The passage of the law was encouraging, but the rules and regulations stated in the law were only concerned with minimum requirements. The law could be revised as need dictated, and those revisionary powers resided with the individual states. Each state has the right to define what cutoff point will be used when determining which children will be considered mentally retarded. Even though most states do use an I.Q. cutoff point, the delivery of services is uneven from state to state. Large amounts of money have been poured into the education of the mentally retarded by the Federal Government, but use by the states has produced both good and bad programs.

Presently, a great deal of research is being carried out with a view toward providing guidelines which all states can adopt to even out the quality of applicable programs available to all mentally retarded people. The current view, and the one espoused by public law, is that every child, including the retarded, has the right to the best education that can be provided. All people have a potential for development, no matter how limited, and it is the responsibility of education to provide that opportunity. Research has demonstrated that intervention in the lives and education of the retarded produces growth that would otherwise have been impossible. This reader provides a sampling of some of the latest and best research aimed at making the lives of the retarded richer and more fulfilling.

Curriculum Planning and Evaluation

The exact nature of a curriculum is very difficult to identify, except to say that it is the planning stage of any educational effort. The relationship between the planning and the implementation of the plan is not as clear cut as educators would like. Experienced teachers, who are also good at their jobs, will take from a curriculum what best suits their teaching style, and the needs of the students. Good teaching depends only to some degree upon the plan, but to a larger degree upon the style of the one who implements the plan. Attempts to quantify a curriculum, in terms of how much a child learns when that particular plan is used, tend to eliminate the need to also examine the ambient atmosphere in which that learning took place.

Finding the best way in which to teach a group of mentally handicapped children has been the subject of countless experimental studies and articles. The goal has always been to narrow the field to a manageable number of alternatives, so that the concerned educator could provide the best possible method for the students involved. Curriculum development must necessarily rely upon research findings that examine how particular populations learn. The literature in the area of mental retardation reveals that there are almost as many findings as there are experiments. The findings are all reasonable, but are so diverse as to make the design of a sound curriculum a very difficult task. The curriculum designer, who examines the literature, is faced with the problem of bringing together results that have been obtained from widely differing populations. There are even instances where it is difficult to actually identify the population from which the data was gathered.

The population designated as mentally retarded is diverse, and difficult to quantify exactly. There are mildly retarded individuals — also called educable — moderately or trainable mentally handicapped, severely mentally handicaped and profoundly mentally handicapped. Within one identifiable disability there are four groups with markedly different abilities, and so there must be completely different programs developed for their education. Much of the research focuses on the first two groups because they can learn the most from educational intervention, and ultimately benefit society in some capacity. There is, however, much effort expended in an attempt to teach the last two groups of the mentally handicapped.

There is no question that it is important to have a global plan of the goals of any given program. The curriculum should do the following: (a) specify goals for each learning level; (b) specify instructional strategies; (c) identify activities to meet the needs of students of differing abilities; (d) provide a variety of methods for the evaluation of student progress. As in all segments of education, it becomes the task of the professional to design, use and evaluate the tools which make quality education possible. The readings contained in the following section indicate some of the best efforts, as well as some of the difficulties, in coping with the idea of a "best" possible education.

Curriculum Development for the Severely Handicapped Student

DIANE M. BROWDER   KATHY L. STEWARD

Lehigh University   Greenbrier Elementary School

Diane M. Browder is Asst. Professor with the School of Education, Lehigh University, Beth-lehem, Pa. 18015; Kathy L Steward is a teacher of severely/profoundly handicapped with the Greenbrier School, Charlottesville, Va. 22901.

Abstract

The functional or community adaptation approach to curriculum development for the severely handicapped is described using the curriculum characteristics (1) philosophy and research support, (2) content and sequence, and (3) individualization. This curriculum model is further clarified through a wheel design, a complete curriculum example, and guidelines for I.E.P. development.

Curriculum Development for the Severely Retarded Adolescent or Adult

One challenge of curriculum development is selecting from all possible skills those that are priorities for a given type of student. Meeting this challenge can be especially difficult when developing a curriculum for severely handicapped students because of their skill deficits. To develop any curriculum, the educator needs to consider a stated educational philosophy and incorporate information from research, 2) provide content and a longitudinal sequence for the content, and 3) flexibility for individualization (Doll, 1982).

Philosophy and Research

Adopting an educational philosophy first can make the curriculum task easier. The chosen philosophy will help determine priorities for inclusion of skills in the final content. The philosophy of normalization can guide curriculum development for the severely handicapped. Normalization is the utilization of culturally normative means to prepare a person to live in the mainstream of society (Wolfensberger, 1972). By adopting this philosophy, the educator assumes that the best placement for the severely retarded person is the community and that all instruction should enable the student to obtain this goal. Brown, Nietupski, & Hamre-Nietupski (1976) have called the goal of community living the "criterion of ultimate functioning" and advocate using this criterion to plan and evaluate educational programs for the severely handicapped.

Given this criterion, the next step is to identify the skills that are essential for community living. General guidelines can be obtained from research on characteristics of mentally retarded adults who succeed in community placements and on skill deficits of those who are reinstitutionalized. These critical skills include, for example: time telling, self help, housekeeping, meal preparation, money management, telephone use, handling emergencies, using community agencies, obeying laws, using leisure time and friendships (Crnic & Pym, 1979; Katz & Yekutiel, 1974; Nihira & Nihira, 1975; O'Connor, 1976; Schalock & Harper, 1978). These skills can be clustered under four life domains that form the "subjects" for this curriculum including; vocational, domestic, community and recreational skills (Brown, Branston-McClean, Baumgart, Vincent, Falvey, & Schroeder, 1979).

Content and Sequence

The content and sequence for this community living curriculum will have several characteristics. First, this curriculum will be designed for individual students based on their actual environments. Since jobs, homes, and communities differ, no prescribed content will meet the needs of all students. Second, the scope and sequence will be influenced by the student's current chronological age and by the current and future least restrictive environments for the student. For example, a severely retarded fifteen year old student might currently live with her parents and potentially live in a community group home after completing her public education at age 21. This student's curriculum will need to prepare her to function in her current family home and begin to prepare her for group home living.

A third characteristic of the content and sequence is that it focuses on the student's eventual exit level performance. That is, the teacher selects as priorities for instruction those skills needed to survive as an adult and breaks these skills down to those expected at the student's current chronological age. For example, an adult will need independent housekeeping skills. A fifteen year old might be expected and taught to help with family housecleaning by vacuuming or doing the laundry.

This breakdown of skills has been called a "topdown" or community adaptation approach to curriculum development (Brown, Branston, Hamre-Nietupski, Pumpian, Certo, & Gruenwald, 1979; Guess & Noonan, 1982). A contrasting approach to curriculum development is the developmental model. In this approach, the special educator utilizes normal child development as the content and sequence for instruction. The philosophical basis for this approach is derived from theories of normal child development and especially from the cognitive theories of Jean Piaget (Bricker, Siebert, & Casuso, 1980). The disadvantages of the developmental model of curriculum development have been described by Guess & Noonan (1982). The most serious problems of the developmental curriculum model are that: 1) empirical data has not supported the theory that severely handicapped persons follow normal developmental sequences and, 2) the content generated by this model often includes infantile skills that are inappropriate for adults (e.g., mouthing objects). Until recently, the use of developmental curriculum models for the severely handicapped have been the traditional approach. Rather than teaching the severely retarded adult a preschool curriculum, the "top down" or community adaptation approach selects adult skills and materials and uses systematic instruction and material adaptations to make mastery of these skills feasible. Materials and skills that are immediately useful to a person and that are required in normal daily living are "functional" (Brown, et al., 1976; Whitney & Striefel, 1981). Because a "top-down" curriculum approach emphasizes instruction in useful skills and materials it can be called a functional curriculum.

The sequence, then, is based on a student's current and future least restrictive placements. The teacher first considers adult priorities and then notes the student's current age expectations for these skills. The content is delineated from the four domains of vocational, domestic, community and recreational skills. Brown, et al., (1979) have described the breakdown of these domains into instructional skills. However, the application of Brown's model can be extremely difficult for the teacher whose training has been solely in the traditional developmental model of curriculum development. Unlike the developmental model, the functional curriculum cannot be directly derived from existing assessment devices. Instead, the teacher must be able to develop both the content and sequence of the curriculum. The illustration of curriculum development to follow expands the work of Brown, et al., (1979) by 1) defining the levels within the model, 2) providing a complete example of one student's curriculum using a wheel design, and 3) describing the process of translating the curriculum into an Individualized Education Program (I.E.P.).

Content Development

A wheel design, as shown in figure one, illustrates a "topdown" curriculum model. The student occupies the center of the wheel. The first level which consists of *domains* is divided into four parts.

The *domestic domain* includes all those abilities related to the care of the home or household, as well as those pertaining to her personal care. Those abilities usually defined as self-help would fall into this domain. The *leisure recreational domain* encompasses all the skills needed to enjoy time away from work. Curricular areas traditionally labeled as socialization and physical fitness could be placed in the leisure recreational domain. The *vocational domain* is defined as those abilities which enable the

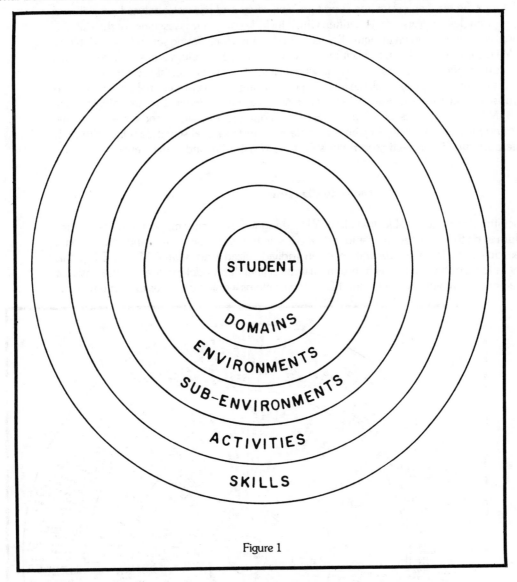

Figure 1

student to maintain a regular occupation thus making her capable of economic solvency. The *community domain* includes those abilities which enable a person to share and participate in the services, facilities and opportunities available to persons in her locality. This domain also includes the shared responsibilities of laws and codes of conduct of the community. These general definitions provide the flexibility necessary for this model's use for individual students. Some important skills are required across all domains and might be included in each. For example, language, motor skills, and functional academics would be listed as needed within each activity.

Environments occupy the second level of the wheel. These are geographic areas, physical structures, public and private facilities which are located within the four domains. For example, environments within the leisure recreational domain may include a recreation center, outdoor track, dormitory and employees lounge.

Sub-environments or specific areas within an environment make-up the third level of the wheel. Examples of sub-environment in a vocational site such as a sheltered workshop may include a work station, bathroom, lunch area, lounge and transportation vehicle.

Activities are located on the fourth level of the wheel. They are those competencies required to function successfully within each sub-environment. Long term objectives found in an Individualized Educational Plan (I.E.P.) format can be easily adapted to the activity level of the wheel. At this level many activities can cross domains. For example, eating activities could occur in all four domains. Generalization training of basic eating skills would require a specific intervention program for different environments.

Skills constitute the fifth level and are specific tasks or components of the activities. Short term objectives can be written for each skill. If the wheel were extended to a sixth level, each skill could be task analyzed. Once the teacher has written short term objectives and has task analyzed the skills, an instructional program (lesson plan) can be written which includes ongoing assessment of the skills.

A functional curriculum, shown in Figure 2, has been designed for a young severely retarded boy named Mike. Mike currently resides in an institution in Virginia. This curriculum is designed to help his transition to a group home in a nearby city. As the wheel illustrates, every possible activity and skill is not included. Rather, at the activity level, the teacher begins establishing instructional priorities based on: 1) skills most critical to the transition to a less restrictive environment, 2) chronological age expectations, 3) Mike's preferences, and 4) activities most frequently used within and across domains. Further prioritizing may be necessary to plan a feasible daily instructional schedule. Once the skills listed are mastered, new skills and activities can be substituted on the fifth and sixth level of the wheel.

Individualization

The curriculum described for Mike was individually designed. A teacher might find some strands of the curriculum to be the same for other students who live in the same community and similar home environments. However, like the preparation of an Individualized Educational Plan (I.E.P.), this curriculum needs to be described for each student. If written first, this model can then be the basis for the I.E.P. development. When developing this I.E.P., the *domains* would be used as the *content areas*

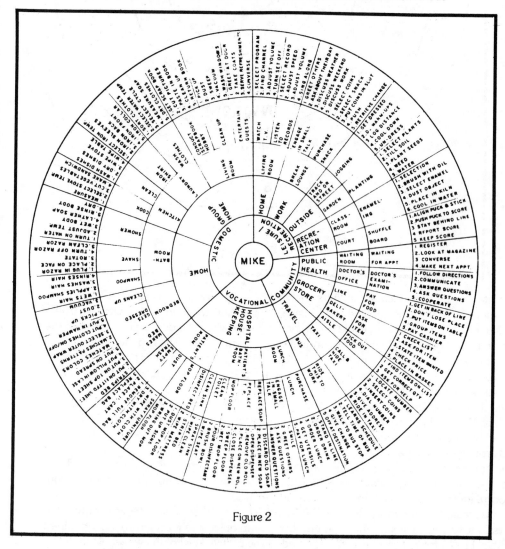

Figure 2

rather than the traditional developmental areas (e.g., self help, fine motor, etc.). To ensure that traditional skills have been included in functional activities, these skills may be coded across domains as illustrated in Table 1. This cross coding may be essential to identify the skills for ancillary services such as occupational or speech therapy. An example of cross coding would be the identification of instruction in "fine motor". This skill might be taught in all of the I.E.P. content domains (e.g., domestic — use of can openers; community — opening push doors; vocational — use of screw driver; recreational — grasp of box game piece).

Implications of a Functional Curriculum

Using an individually designed functional curriculum for the severely handicapped student has several implications for special education programs that may require changes in current practice. First, educational assessment cannot rely solely on standardized instruments or developmental checklists. The educator must also rely on inventories and task analyses of the specified skills and on assessment of the *environment* as well as the student. Another implication is that instruction will be focused on specific useable skills rather than on concepts or tasks requiring generalization to other materials and settings. For example, to teach the concept of size the teacher would *not* select construction paper circles and using tabletop instruction, ask the student to point to "big". Instead, skills requiring size discrimination that are needed most by the student would be taught using their natural times, setting, and materials. For example, the teacher would instruct the student to sort screws by size in the workshop where she works, to select the largest container of milk while shopping for the family, and to give the smaller form to the receptionist at the health clinic. By carefully choosing, teaching, and testing the skills, the teacher might help the student acquire the concept of size that would generalize to untaught tasks as well as a repertoire of functional skills. During any one lesson, the teacher might include instruction on several skills and concepts since the focus of instruction is the *functional activity* (Holvoet, Guess, Mulligan, & Brown, 1980).

Table 1

**Example of Cross Coding Traditional Skill Areas
in Functional Domain Areas for I.E.P. Development**

DOMAINS

DOMESTIC	VOCATIONAL	RECREATIONAL	COMMUNITY
Preparation of Tuna Casserole • • • •	Coffee Break Activities • • • •	Bowling • • • •	Visit to Public Health • • • •
- Recipe (PA)	- Restroom (SC)	- Phone (C)	- Personal data (C)
- Can Opener (FM)	- Coffee Machine (PA, CG)	- Score (PA)	- Wait to be called (C, SS)
- Use of Oven (PA)	- Peer interactions (SS, C)	- Bowling (GM)	- Interact with Doctor (C, SS)
- Mixing (FM, CG)		- Snacks (SC, PA)	- Undress/Dress (SC)
		- Restroom (SC)	
		- Peer interactions (SS, C)	

TRADITIONAL SKILLS	CODE
Self Care	SC
Communication	C
Fine Motor	FM
Gross Motor	GM
Cognition	CG
Preacademics	PA
Social Skills	SS

Another implication of this curriculum model is that all instruction cannot take place within the four walls of the classroom. To teach bus riding, use of the public health clinic, bowling, grocery shopping, and so on, the educational program must move into the community. This community based program will require new teacher skills in organization and community relations. However, by teaching the severely retarded adults community living skills in their own communities and gradually fading the teacher's help, successful independence can be assured.

References

Berkson, G., & Landesman-Dwyer, S. Behavioral research on severe and profound mental retardation (1955-1974). *American Journal of Mental Deficiency,* 1977, 81, 428-454.

Bricker, D., Seibert, J., & Casuso, V. Early intervention, In J. Hogg & P. Mittler (Eds.), *Advances in mental research.* New York: John Wiley & Sons, 1980.

Brown, L., Branston-McClean, M. B., Baumgart, D., Vincent, L., Falvey, M., & Schroeder, J. Using the characteristics of current and subsequent least restrictive environments in the development of curricular content for severely handicapped students. *AAESPH Review,* 1979, 4, 407-424.

Brown, L., & Branston, N. B., Hamre-Nietupski, S., Pumpian, I., Certo, N., & Gruenwald, L. A strategy for developing chronological age appropriate and functional curricular content for severely handicapped adolescents and young adults. *Journal of Special Education,* 1979, 13, 81-90.

Brown, L., Neitupski, J., & Hamre-Nietupski, S. Criterion of ultimate functioning. In M.A. Thomas, *Hey, don't forget about me!* Reston, Va.: CEC, 1976.

Doll, R. C. *Curriculum improvement: Decision making and process.* Boston: Allyn & Bacon, Inc., 1982.

Gold, M. Researach on the vocational habilitation of the retarded: The present, the future. In N. Ellis (Ed.), *International review of research in mental retardation,* Vol. 6. Academic Press: New York, 1973.

Guess, D., & Noonan, M. J. Curricula and instructional procedures for severely handicapped students. *Focus on Exceptional children, 1982, 14,* 1-12.

Holvoet, J., Guess, P., Mulligan, M., & Brown, F. The individualized curriculum sequencing model (11): A teaching strategy for severely handicapped students. *Journal of the Association for the Severely Handicapped,* 1980, 5, 337-351.

Whitney, R., & Striefel, S. Functionality and generalization training the severely and profoundly handicapped. *Journal of Special Education Technology,* 1981, 4, 33-39.

Wolfensberger, W. *Normalization: The principle of normalization in human services.* Toronto: National Institute on Mental Retardation, 1972.

Multivariate Approaches to the Evaluation of Programs for Mildly Mentally Retarded Persons

JEREMY D. FINN
State University of New York at Buffalo

Multivariate analysis usually connotes a set of complex statistical models. It can also represent a way of thinking about research in which behavioral outcomes are seen as having multiple facets and resulting from multiple antecedents. Three areas of research on mentally retarded children that need conceptual multivariate analysis were identified: (a) the characterization of learners, (b) the description of process features of an instructional setting, and (c) the depiction of change. Examples were provided, drawing on a recent National Academy of Sciences report. Finally, statistical developments were described that are appropriate to the data that these conceptualizations yield.

The application of "multivariate analysis" is often one of the recommendations in empirical studies in special education and elsewhere. Yet is seems that such questions as "Which multivariate methods? Applied in what ways? What will they tell us that is different?" are usually kept secret in the mind of authors and left to the imagination of readers. This presentation carries a two-fold message. First, multivariate analysis is not only a set of complex and less-than-obvious statistical procedures or computer programs, but represents a way of conceptualizing research problems. In this paper I have attempted to identify areas of research and evaluation, particularly in the study of mildly mentally retarded children, that could benefit from a multivariate perspective. Two, there have been a number of statistical developments over the past decade that make it easier to deal with complex multivariate data without forcing research designs into one of a few prohibitively simple molds. These methods should be used whenever the natural "multivariateness" of a problem requires them.

The identification of issues requiring multivariate analysis is made easier by the recent appearance of the National Research Council report *Placing children in special education: A strategy for equity* (Heller, Holtzman, & Messick, 1982). The authors pointed to the many ambiguities in the definition and identification of "mild mental retardation." As a result of these complexities, problems involving the most appropriate placement for a child sometimes seem unresolvable; school curricula are frequently developed anew in each school, district, or state; and results of studies in

An earlier version of this paper was presented as an invited address to Division 33 at the annual convention of the American Psychological Association, Washington, DC, August 1982. The author is grateful to Kathleen Reidy for assistance in finding and summarizing the many articles reviewed as background material. Requests for reprints should be sent to Jeremy D. Finn, Faculty of Educational Studies, 408 Christopher Baldy Hall, Amherst, NY 14260.

which segregated EMR classes are compared to resource rooms or mainstreaming, for example, are notoriously contradictory (see Heller, 1982).

Given these conditions, the Office for Civil Rights may be justifiably concerned with racial disproportion in EMR classes. For example, the National Research Council report confirmed that the approximately 600,000 identified EMR students in American public schools in 1978–1979 consisted of 2.5% of all minority students and 1.1% of nonminorities. At the same time, the magnitude of racial differences in EMR programs varies dramatically. Statewide average EMR placement rates for minority students range from less than 1% to over 9%, whereas statewide averages for white students do not exceed 2.5% anywhere in the country.

This variation is not surprising in view of the many different procedures for identifying children for EMR placement. Fifteen states do not specify IQ ranges that qualify a child for such placement, 25 states include adaptive behavior as part of the definition whereas others do not, and interdistrict differences in definitions and procedures are significant. The Council's finer analysis of placement rates revealed that minority–white differences varied as a function of district size, percentage of minority enrollment, size of the current EMR program in a district, as well as the particular minority group itself. For example, although nationwide EMR rates for students of Hispanic origin and nonHispanic whites are both about 1%, this summary statistic conceals tremendous variation in EMR rates for Hispanics, from districts in which they are heavily overrepresented in EMR classes to others in which they are significantly underrepresented. (The complete breakdown of special-education placements is given in Finn, 1982).

These findings, some of which are common knowledge among special educators, may be symptomatic of ambiguity in our understanding of which children "should" be classified as EMR and the types of instructional programs to which they "should" be exposed. I do not propose to resolve these ambiguities. I am suggesting, however, that multivariate conceptualizations and multivariate methods of data analysis in our research and program evaluations will give us a better understanding of the underlying issues. The following are three areas, based on the major conclusions of the National Research Council report, that require further multivariate development.

Characterizing the Learners

Among its conclusions, the National Research Council report indicated that we rely too heavily on IQs both for assessing learning difficulties and for research on EMR children. To determine whether this is the case in published research, we reviewed entries in the *Journal of Special Education, American Journal of Mental Deficiency*, and *Mental Retardation* for the 8-year period from 1975–1982 and chose those articles in which the subjects were school-aged EMR children and whose authors examined the effectiveness or differential effectiveness of educational settings (e.g., special class, mainstream) or specific treatments (e.g., reading program) on outcomes related directly to schooling (e.g., achievement, social behavior). Of the 20 studies identified, 14 contained descriptions of the functioning of the children only by giving IQ levels and/or whether they were enrolled in an EMR program; in 3 others the investigators discussed adaptive behavior as well, and only 3 others (2 by the same author) gave baseline achievement scores.

The employment of IQ alone has limited utility for educational prescriptions and may detract attention from the enormous variability among children in prior learning or more specific functional needs. According to Heller et al. (1982): "Functional needs may be classes of academically relevant skills (e.g., reading comprehension, vocabulary, mathematical concepts or computations), cognitive processing skills (e.g., generalization, self-monitoring), adaptive and motivation skills (e.g., impulse control, social skills), or physical problems that hamper learning" (pp. 98–99).

In order to determine the types of children who benefit most from an instructional strategy, investigators must characterize each subject of a study by a multivariate profile of functional needs. The summing of subscales, forming of composite scores, or substitution of a different global index such as IQ may neglect important differences among individuals. Analyzing the scales separately focuses on specific aspects of the data and generally reduces the replicability of an investigation.

The profiles of functional needs may serve either as the independent variables of an investigation, the dependent variables, or both. If they are viewed as the independent variables in predicting some other outcomes (e.g., length of institutionalization or performance in school) then blockwise multiple regression enables one to relate the entire profile of functional needs, or subsets of antecedents, to one or more dependent variables. Blockwise analysis treats the predictor variables as comprising one or more subsets, each of which is tested for its contribution to regression above and beyond prior subsets, and may be performed using any of several commonly available computer programs such as MUL-TIVARIANCE (Finn, 1980) or certain combinations of options on SPSS (Nie, Hull, Jenkins, Steinbrenner, & Bent, 1975).

Like stepwise regression, the results of blockwise regression analysis are dependent on the order of subsets that must be established prior to the analysis. In contrast, stepwise techniques used to find the best possible predictor empirically from among all those available, then the second best, and so on, do not confirm to standard probability statements; these increase the number of Type-I errors and reduce the replicability of the conclusions. Such procedures should be used only with extreme caution in any case, but do not maintain the integrity of sets of predictors and cannot be used in a blockwise analysis.

If the profiles are seen as the dependent variables of an investigation, multivariate analysis techniques are widely accessible and should be used. Techniques such as multivariate analysis of variance have the advantage of allowing investigators to view the outcomes as a whole rather than as isolated or uncorrelated responses and ultimately enhance the replicability of the findings by controlling statistical error rates (see Bock, 1975; Finn & Mattsson, 1978).

In our review of published studies, 13 of 20 contained multiple dependent variables—indeed this was the most common situation—but only 2 used any multivariate data methods. More typically, multiple interrelated univariate tests were made and presented. For example, in the evaluation of special day schools for EMR pupils (Myers, 1976), three different settings were compared in terms of average achievement on three scales of the Wide Range Achievement Test, self-concept, and social adjustment. The results included 13 univariate F ratios for these variables and a complex pattern of results in which some were apparently significant and others were not. These measures could be grouped naturally into two subsets—achievement and personality measures—from which multivariate tests would provide a smaller number of more definitive statements about setting differences. The multivariate tests would control the experiment-wise error rates that are likely to be much inflated in the 13 nonindependent F ratios. In a multivariate approach, follow-up analysis

would reveal the individual measures and combinations of measures that discriminate among the settings so that detailed descriptive information is also available.

Although many researchers are familiar with multivariate analysis of variance, multivariate multiple regression analysis is also an important tool to add to our set of statistical models; i.e., it is possible to use this model to test the relationship of one or more predictors ("x" variables) to the set of response measures; that is an extension of simple or multiple regression analysis to multivariate outcomes ("y" variables) and would be particularly appropriate to an expanded characterization of learners. For further information, see Finn and Mattsson (1978, chapter 2).

Characterizing the Setting

Multivariate descriptions of the educational setting are essential in characterizing instructional programs. The National Council Research Report presented a reconceptualization of the mainstream-resource room–separate class issue and pointed in this direction. Their review confirmed that research comparing the three settings has not yielded consistent outcomes. With respect to academic achievement, Heller et al. (1982) stated:

As in the earlier round of research, findings concerning mainstreaming have been inconclusive. Some studies show positive effects for programs administered in separate classrooms, but there are negative effects as well. Many studies have included one or more measures of social adjustment. . . . In more recent work . . the results are more contradictory (p. 79).

The report concluded that it is not the administrative setting per se that determines how children perform, but instead features of the instructional process. The authors reviewed recent work on instructional dimensions at both the classroom and school level and noted that the list of effective features converged on a set of descriptors of "direct instruction." These included, for academic outcomes, "high content overlap between learning activities and criterion (test) tasks; built in formal assessment techniques; increased time on academic tasks; teacher pacing; and the use of motivating management systems" (p. 81). For social outcomes, such features as providing competent models, having children rehearse social skills, and providing feedback may have promise. These processes, in principle, may be implemented in any of a variety of settings.

In the National Research Council report, the process dimension "performance expectations" was discussed separately. The authors concluded that "a classroom full of children bearing the label "mentally retarded" does not typically seem to evoke very high expectations, and therefore, *the academic demand on them may be reduced* [italics added]" (p. 84). If performance expectations affect the opportunities offered to EMR children and, as a result, some children's performance is lessened, then this factor should be investigated by incorporating expectations measures in our process analysis.

Only 7 of the 20 studies reviewed provided sufficient information so that outcomes could be related to instructional process. The more common procedure was to

decrement is attributable to proximity to shop and homemaking classrooms or to the part-time/full-time teacher and student teacher composition of the class or whether other social and academic processes are more important determining factors.

From a methodological perspective, it is not sufficient to compare mainstreamed groups with special-class groups, institutional residences with community residences, or any two or more administrative settings as if the processes that distinguish them are concealed in opaque black boxes. If the settings evoke different responses, why do they do so? If not, it may be that the settings are not distinct in the features that are most important to cognitive or social

focus on administrative characteristics. As a typical example, Budoff and Gottlieb (1976) informed readers that a special class setting was "located on a ground floor . . . adjacent to the shop and homemaking classrooms . . . taught by a full-time teacher, with the assistance of a student teacher . . . another experienced special-education teacher worked with half the class for 1 hour each day in the school shop. The student-teacher ratio . . . was approximately 7 to 1" (p. 4). They employed an elegant analysis and discovered that, after 1 year, segregated-class students had lower morale and less internal control than did students in integrated settings. Unfortunately, because social processes that may affect morale or locus of control—or the authors' other outcomes—were not measured, one can only wonder whether the

outcomes.

Statistically, measures of instructional process dimensions should augment simple group membership variables. This means that instead of using analysis of variance to compare group means, analysis of covariance—the model having both categorical and measured independent variables—may be more appropriate. Analysis of covariance allows investigators to ask whether there are group differences in attainment or other outcomes and, if so, are those differences attributable to the measured process variables. If the answer is yes, the program may be more readily exported to other settings to take advantage of its positive features.

Examining Change

There have been developments in

methods for analyzing growth or change over time that are important for research and evaluation with mildly retarded youngsters. The National Research Council report noted that too little attention is given to criteria by which EMR children may exit from special education, perhaps under the assumption that these individuals are permanently disabled. The research reflects a more optimistic perspective. In 13 of the 20 articles reviewed, investigators gave direct attention to change in school outcomes over time, at least through the inclusion of pretest and posttest scores and frequently by measures at three or more time points. The methods of statistical analysis varied widely, from presentation of means and graphs (e.g., Fink & Sandall, 1978; Matson, Esveldt-Dawson, & Kazdin, 1982) to complex analysis of variance models for change (e.g., Budoff & Gottlieb, 1976; Lally, 1981), but were not always selected appropriately.

For example, analysis of covariance is commonly applied to compare posttest scores holding constant pretest differences. This technique is useful in randomized experiments to increase the sensitivity of the analysis to treatment effects. Randomized experiments are difficult to arrange, but the feasibility of assigning students or classes to experimental treatments is demonstrated in 6 of the 20 studies reviewed (Budoff & Gottlieb, 1976; Campbell, Moffat, & Brackett, 1978; Gottlieb, Gampel, & Budoff, 1975; Peleg & Moore, 1982; Vandever, Maggart, & Nasser, 1976; Zucker & D'Alonzo, 1981), and the conclusions relating independent to dependent variables in these studies are stronger as a result. If an experiment has more than two measurement points, an extension of analysis of covariance to the conditional analysis of repeated measures is available (Bock, 1975).

When comparing intact groups (e.g., low-IQ and average-IQ children; low-IQ children with and without deficiencies in adaptive behavior; and children already placed in different settings, such as those mainstreamed or those placed in a separate class, institution, or community housing), investigators simply cannot equate for initial differences by holding constant pretest scores or other background variables through analysis of covariance. Ultimately, the use of covariance as a partial or complete substitute for random assignment is doomed to failure because group differences at the end of the study can always be attributed to factors that were outside the investigator's control. If groups begin with different average levels of adaptive behavior, then differential outcomes may

result from the reactions of other individuals as much as the characteristics of the subjects themselves. In many "natural experiments," better-functioning individuals are placed in new or less restrictive settings, and differences in outcomes can be attributable to a host of correlated selectivity factors.

To make best use of nonexperimental data, investigators should (a) describe the initial differences as completely as possible, including the criteria and procedures by which the groups were originally formed; and (b) analyze the amount of change that has occurred over a defined period of time by comparing pretest, posttest, and/or follow-up measures directly for the groups being investigated. This technique will detect not only differences in the amount or rate of change but also whether there has been any change at all. Thus, for example, although low-IQ children may conclude an experimental period just as far behind the average group as they were initially, there may have been significant growth in both groups that should be documented.

A variety of models for analyzing repeated measures data (i.e., for measures taken at several occasions) are becoming more accessible. Program packages such as SPSS (Nie et al., 1975), BMDP (Dixon, 1981), and SAS (Freund et al., 1981) are extending their repeated measures features, whereas MULTIVARIANCE (Finn, 1980) remains the most extensive program for this purpose. Texts and reference materials are appearing regularly, if slowly (e.g., Bock, 1975; Finn, in preparation; McCall & Applebaum, 1973; Poor, 1973). These models are not restricted to the comparison of pre- and posttest, but generalize to repeated testings before, during, or after a specified time period. They can reveal whether the rate or amount of change continues, decelerates, or stops. Also, they allow for a direct comparison of change among groups, so that conclusions about group differences are not limited to the comparison of analyses performed separately for each subsample as is sometimes done (e.g., Richardson, Oestereicher, Bialer, & Winsberg, 1975).

There are both univariate and multivariate analysis of variance models for growth, of which the former have been covered in graduate statistics courses under the rubric "within and between-subjects analysis" (Lindquist, 1953). The phrase "within subjects" was used to indicate that the same individuals were measured repeatedly to study the differences among the subjects' responses; each subject served as his or her own control. These models, however, are cumbersome and complex, and, in the absence of easy-to-use computer programs, may have done more to discourage than to facilitate the appropriate analysis of change. Furthermore, the models were thought to require strong assumptions about the data that are difficult or impossible to meet, namely, the standard deviations (*SD*s) of the measures at each time point must be equal, and if there are more than two measurement points, the correlations of all pairs of measures (e.g., pre with post, pre with follow-up, post with follow-up) must be equal.

More recent statistical developments have shown that the pattern of equal *SD*s and equal correlations is only one pattern out of a broader set for which the univariate within-and-between-subjects analysis is valid. In general, the variances and covariances of the measures must be "spherical," a condition that cannot be detected through inspection alone but requires a mathematical test. Experience indicates, however, that data that do not conform to the more specific conditions frequently do not have sphericity defined more generally.

Multivariate analysis frees us from these restrictions by treating the responses at two or more occasions to be multiple dependent variables. As such, they may have any pattern of *SD*s and correlations. This is particularly important for time-structured data because variability usually increases as individuals age, and more distal time points usually have lower correlations than do points close in time. The multivariate models generalize readily to doubly multivariate data, in which several different measures (e.g., vocabulary and comprehension) are taken at each time point.

I will not describe how multivariate models for repeated measures operate, except to reiterate that they are particularly useful for the types of data gathered in studies of special student groups; the analyses are performed readily by computer programs available at most university centers. Because they use matrix algebra, some programs can also perform trend analysis in which the time intervals are not equal and analysis of variance for designs with unequal numbers of subjects in the groups. Thus, an exact analysis may be obtained for the more natural situation in which *N*s are unequal without discarding data, guessing missing values, or calculating the approximate "unweighted means" solution.

In summary, our thinking about mildly or educably retarded children needs to be expanded to understand the many diverse profiles of functional needs that these individuals represent. This can be reflected in research and evaluations by using a more detailed set of measures to represent each individual and by using corresponding multivariate statistical techniques. Also, the "black box" of educational programs must be opened, and measures of instructional process included, together with simple group membership. Recent developments provide a broad set of statistical models that go hand-in-hand with improved conceptual models to improve our understanding of the interactions of retarded children with their environments.

References

Bock, R. D. (1975). *Multivariate statistical methods in behavioral research.* New York: McGraw-Hill.

Budoff, M., & Gottlieb, J. (1976), Special-class EMR children mainstreamed: A study of an aptitude (learning potential) × treatment interaction. *American Journal of Mental Deficiency, 81,* 1–11.

Campbell, J., Moffat, K., & Brackett, L. (1978). The effect of language instruction on the math skills of retarded children. *Mental Retardation, 16,* 167–169.

Dixon, W. J. (Ed.). (1981). *BMDP statistical software.* Berkeley: University of California Press.

Fink, W. T., & Sandall, S. R. (1978). One to one vs. group academic instruction with handicapped and nonhandicapped preschool children. *Mental Retardation, 16,* 236–240.

Finn, J. D. (1980). *MULTIVARIANCE: Univariate and multivariate analysis of variance, covariance, regression and repeated measures. Version 6.* Chicago: National Educational Resources.

Finn, J. D. (1982). Patterns in special education placement as revealed by the OCR surveys. In K. A. Heller, W. H. Holtzman, & S. Messick, (Eds.), *Placing children in special education: A strategy for equity* (pp. 322–381). Washington, DC: National Academy Press.

Finn, J. D. (1983). *The analysis of repeated measures data.* Book in preparation.

Finn, J. D., & Mattsson, I. (1978). *Multivariate analysis in educational research: Applications of the MULTIVARIANCE program.* Chicago: National Educational Resources.

Freund, R. et al. (1981). SAS for linear models. *A guide to the ANOVA and GLM procedures.* Cary, NC: SAS Institute.

Gottlieb, J., Gampel, D. H., & Budoff, M. (1975). Classroom behavior of retarded children before and after integration into regular classes. *Journal of Special Education, 9,* 307–315.

Heller, K. A. (1982). Effects of special education placement on educable mentally retarded children. In K. A. Heller, W. H. Holtzman, & S. Messick (Eds.), *Placing children in special education: A strategy for equity* (pp. 262–299). Washington, DC: National Academy Press, 1982.

Heller, K. A., Holtzman, W. H., & Messick, S. (1982). *Placing children in special education: A strategy for equity.* Washington, DC: National Academy Press.

Lally, M. (1981). Computer-assisted teaching of sight-word recognition for mentally retarded school children. *American Journal of Mental Deficiency, 85,* 383–388.

Lindquist, E. F. (1953). *Design and analysis of experiments in psychology and education.* Boston: Houghton-Mifflin.

Matson, J. L., Esveldt-Dawson, K., & Kazdin, A. E. (1982). Treatment of spelling deficits in mentally retarded children. *Mental Retardation, 20,* 76–81.

McCall, R. B., & Applebaum, M. I. (1973). Bias in the analysis of repeated-measures designs: Some alternative approaches. *Child Development, 44,* 401–415.

Myers, J. K. (1976). The efficacy of the special day school for EMR pupils. *Mental Retardation, 14*(1), 3–11.

Nie, N., Hull, C. H., Jenkins, J., Steinbrenner, K., & Bent, D. (1975). *SPSS: Statistical package for the social sciences* (2nd ed.). New York: McGraw-Hill.

Peleg, Z. R., & Moore, R. F. (1982). Effects of the advance organizer with oral and written presentation on recall and inference of EMR adolescents. *American Journal of Mental Deficiency, 86,* 621–626.

Poor, D. D. S. (1973). Analysis of variance for repeated measures designs: Two approaches, *Psychological Bulletin, 80,* 204–209.

Richardson, E., Oestereicher, M. H., Bialer, I., & Winsberg, B. G. (1975). Teaching beginning reading skills to retarded children in community classrooms: A programmatic case study. *Mental Retardation, 13*(1), 11–15.

Vandever, T. R., Maggart, W. T., & Nasser, S. (1976). Three approaches to beginning reading instruction for EMR children. *Mental Retardation, 14*(4), 29–32.

Zucker, S. H., & D'Alonzo, B. J. (1981). Time compressed speech and the listening comprehension of educable mentally retarded students. *Mental Retardation, 19,* 177–179.

Concerns About Instructional Materials for Severely Handicapped Students

ARLENE SCHOONHOVEN[1]

Program Coordinator, Instructional Materials
Office of the Los Angeles
County Superintendent of Schools
9300 E. Imperial Highway
Downey, CA 90242

Teachers of severely handicapped students face more problems in finding appropriate instructional materials for their learners than do any other group of teachers. Although some of the problems are the same as those faced by all teachers, the severity of the problems are intensified for the teacher of the severely handicapped individual. In addition, teachers of the severely handicapped person have problems which are unique. Both the severity and the unique nature of the problems are cause for concern.

Before beginning a discussion of the concerns faced by teachers of the severely handicapped in locating and selecting appropriate instructional materials, the term "severely handicapped" as used in this discussion, must be defined. The incidence of severely handicapping conditions is low. The children labeled "severely handicapped" often exhibit similar characteristics, such as severe and profound retardation and multiple handicaps, including physical disabilities, deafness, and blindness.

"Concerns About Instructional Materials for Severely Handicapped Students," Arlene Schoonhoven, *Journal of Special Education Technology*, Vol. V, No. 1, Winter 1982. Copyright 1982 by Utah State University.

Other characteristics that often occur are stereotypical behavior and nonverbal or poor language skills. Children labeled autistic, deaf-blind, or severely emotionally disturbed are usually placed in this category. Common to all the children is the difficulty they have in learning. This may be due to poor attending skills, the inability to generalize learning, the inability to learn abstract concepts, difficulty with short-term memory, and impulsive behavior (Klein, 1979). Individually or as a group, these children are often untestable and present a challenge to those who would teach them. This is not to say that the child who is deaf, blind, or very involved physically does not have a severe handicap; he or she does. This discussion will be concerned only with the population as defined above.

AN HISTORICAL PERSPECTIVE

Because PL94-142 mandates a free and appropriate education for every child, more children with severe disabilities are now in schools than ever before. As more of us began to work with these children, we discovered that we, as professionals, knew little of what these children could learn. (But we have learned that they can learn more than we expected!) As educators gained more experience in teaching the severely handicapped, various approaches were developed. Traditionally most of these children were placed in institutions where they were protected and were provided with total care. An assumption was made that severely handicapped children were incapable of learning, and little attempt was made to teach them. As more of the learning process was understood, attempts were undertaken to teach these individuals. As teachers began to teach, the children learned slowly, but they learned! Again, an assumption was made that the retarded child developed and learned in the same way that the normal child did--only more slowly. As a result, the curriculum used to teach the retarded learner was a "watered-down" one based on the same developmental sequence as that of the young normal child. The materials available to implement the curriculum were very often the same as those used in preschool or primary grades. Lower-level tasks were emphasized to the detriment of higher-level tasks (Winschel, 1978). In the 1970s there was a movement away from large institutions toward community residential facilities. This movement along with the principle of "least restrictive environment" (Brown, n.d.) have combined to change the approach to the education of the severely handicapped student. Currently most curricula for the severely handicapped student are derived from normal developmental models pioneered by Bayley, Gesell, Alpern and Boll, and Uzgiris and Hunt (Brown, 1980). The developmental approach holds that the mentally retarded child goes through the same developmental sequence that the normal child does, but he or she does so at a slower rate. The traditional curricular-content domains of this approach are language/cognitive development, social/emotional development, gross-motor/fine-motor skills, and self-help skills (Brown, 1980; Klein, 1979). Most of the instructional materials currently in use were developed from this frame of reference. Similar to the developmental approach, but with a different emphasis, is the cognitive model of which Piaget is an example as are the Ordinal Scales by Uzgiris and Hunt (Guess, 1982).

As more severely handicapped individuals entered the community, the need for them to develop basic skills became imperative. Researchers applied the principles of behavior modification to training the severely mentally retarded and were successful using this method. As the behavioral approach was developed, the teacher relied heavily on task analysis and the principles of behavior management. Tasks were broken down into the necessary skills required. Each skill was then analyzed and again broken down into small, sequential, incremental steps until the child could perform the task. Teachers utilizing this approach need task analyses and materials to teach the skills and to serve as reinforcers. Programs providing step-by-step instructions and the necessary task analyses were and are being published.

THE CURRENT VIEW

In the attempt to find better ways of teaching these students, some new, but similar, approaches have been and are being developed. The names vary a little (e.g., community adaptation, normalization, functional living, and ecological and holistic approaches). These approaches often use the principles of behavior modification, but common to all is the belief that the educational programming for a student should prepare the student to function as independently and effectively as possible in a variety of least restrictive and natural environments. Phrases such as "criterion of ultimate functioning," "partial participation," "ecological inventory," and "chronologically age-appropriate" have become key words (Falvey, 1980). Because there is evidence that the severely handicapped learner may not develop in the same way as the normal child, developmental scales are used only as guidelines. White (1980) indicates that a student's program is appropriate if it reflects the behavioral demands of his/her potential future placement. The curricular-content domains of this approach differ from the traditional in that the domains are domestic, vocational, recreational/leisure, general community functioning, and interaction with non-handicapped persons (Brown, 1980). This approach with its emphasis on teaching functional, chronologically age-appropriate skills necessary for successful interactions in domestic, community, and vocational settings will have an impact on the instructional materials used. Whatever material is used must be chronologically age-appropriate, and most of the materials will be found in the student's natural environment. To teach shoe-tying, the child's own shoes would be used instead of lacing boards; to match one-to-one, socks would be used instead of chips and colored circles (Bates, 1981). As we can see from the previous discussion, the teacher must decide on the approach to be used before the selection of materials can begin.

A major concern of teachers is whether or not the material would work for their students, especially if the product must be purchased. Ashcroft (1979) stated that 75% to 90% of the average student's time is structured around instructional materials. Yet most classroom teachers are unaware that only about 1% of all instructional materials sold have been systematically tested with children and then revised on the basis of the results of that field test. Furthermore, on the average, less than 1% of a school's budget goes to the purchase of instructional materials. A major problem is the expense involved in the process of designing, packaging, producing, and publicizing new materials, because commerical publishers must answer to their shareholders for a profit. Teachers often fail to ask for the field-test data and are unaware that educational products, like any other products, are packaged to create a need to buy and to appeal to the buyer--the teacher (Bleil, 1975; Larsen, 1978). Until teachers demand learner-verified materials, many publishers will continue to publish materials without field testing them in order to cut costs.

A priority need identified by the National Needs Assessment of Educational Media and Materials for the Handicapped (1980) was for new and improved materials. One particular area identified by teachers of severely handicapped individuals was independent student-use materials designed to provide needed practice. When one considers how little time a teacher actually has to provide one-to-one instruction, one can see how necessary the independent-use material to practice appropriate tasks is. There is also an identified need for materials to be used by parents with their children to provide additional reinforcement. Stowitschek (1980) indicates that the interaction between teacher, materials, and the learner is critical.

In the past researchers have developed some excellent materials which have been highly successful in controlled settings but have not worked well in the classroom. It behooves researchers, who are currently involved in product development, to remember that the average classroom teacher has little equipment, little time away from the classroom for training, minimal staff support, and few funds. The need for appropriate materials is great, and research is needed to develop both new products and strategies utilizing the newest technologies which can be replicated in the average classroom. Without this research invaluable resources will be lost to the classroom teacher. The average teacher does not have the time, expertise, or money to develop these resources independently.

For the severely handicapped student, the choice of materials is small, and often inappropriate. All materials for these students should have some common characteristics. Elder (1978) indicates that materials should be functional, easily discriminated by the student, and tailored specifically to the skill being taught. Materials must be created that are concrete, manipulative, indestructible, untearable, unchewable, and feasible. The materials should also be motivating and reinforcing for the student. Research suggests that some stimulus material is so dull that the student's curiosity is never aroused (Gaylord-Ross, 1980).

Products for use with severely handicapped students represent a very thin market for the commercial publisher. The high cost of development results in the publication of fewer products, and marketing costs are exacerbated by the thin market. Both factors dictate that materials for severely handicapped students be more expensive than materials for other students. To help alleviate this problem the federal government in 1978 infused considerable money into special education. Large publishers were becoming interested in product development for severely handicapped students (Shackelford, 1978). This is no longer true. Special education is now facing decreasing funds and cutbacks. Neither large nor small publishers can afford to develop products for a thin market with decreasing funds. If commercial publishers cannot afford to develop and publish new products, and if the federal government will not assist in the matter, we must then consider having commercial publishers publish teacher-made products. But there is a problem with this. Hurley (1979) indicates that only about 10% of the new products considered by a publisher are teacher-mades. Of all teacher-made products submitted, about 95% are rejected! Teachers understand the educational needs of their students better than the marketers do but are least prepared to write sound curricula (Larson, 1978). A grave concern, then, is the question of who will develop the needed materials.

A major concern of this author has been the problem of identifying appropriate instructional materials for teachers, including those who teach the severely handicapped individual. There have been specific types of materials for which the author has received many requests. Some of these requests have been for pictures of concrete objects without distracting details, very low reading-level materials that teach and utilize functional survival vocabulary in a mature format, low-level recreational reading material with topics that are relevant to the severely handicapped adolescent or adult, simple puzzles appropriate for the older student, manipulative and multisensory materials for the younger child, and a list of others. There is also a need for inexpensive electronic devices which can be used for sensory stimulation and activation (Finkle, 1980).

CONCLUSION

Direct materials support for exceptional students is critical, but this support is at its lowest level (Stowitschek, 1980). In this period of decreasing financial resources, we may need to reassess our approach to the use of media and materials. Teachers will have to become cognizant of all available resources and learn to use these resources efficiently. If product development is going to become increasingly difficult, we need to consider other options. Training will have to be given to teachers to assist them in improving their skills in the selection, evaluation, adaptation, and development of instructional materials. Most of all, commercial publishers, researchers, and teachers will have to work together to develop needed, appropriate, and well-designed materials.

REFERENCES

Ashcroft, S.C. Research and evaluation: new directions. *Journal of Special Education Technology*, 1979, *2*(4), 1-5.

Bates, P., Renzaglia, A., & Wehman, P. Characteristics of an appropriate education for severely and profoundly handicapped students. *Education and Training of the Mentally Retarded*, 1981, *16*, 142-149.

Bleil, G. Evaluating educational materials. *Journal of Learning Disabilities*, 1975, *8*, 19-26.

Brown, L., Falvey, M., Baumgart, D., Pumpian, I., Schroeder, J., & Gruenewald, L. *Strategies for teaching chronological age appropriate functional skills to adolescent and young adult severely handicapped students*. Vol. 9, P. 1). Madison, Wisconsin: University of Wisconsin and Madison Metropolitan School District, 1980.

Brown, L., Nietupski, J., Lyon, S., Hamre-Nietupski, S., Crowner, T., & Grunewald, L. *Curricular strategies for teaching functional object use, nonverbal communication, problem solving, and mealtime skills to severely handicapped students*. (Vol. 7, P. 1) Madison, Wisconsin: Madison Metropolitan School District, 1977.

Elder, J. Technology of education for the severely handicapped: The future. *Journal of Special Education Technology*, 1978, *1*(2), 32-34.

Falvey, M., Brown, L., Lyon, S., Baumgart, D., & Schroeder, J. Strategies for using cues and correction procedures. In Sailor, W., Wilcox, B., & Brown, L. (Eds.), *Methods of instruction for severely handicapped students*. Baltimore: Paul H. Brooks, 1980.

Finkle, L. Teaching the severely/profoundly handicapped: The need for media in the institutions. *Journal of Special Education Technology*, 1980, *2*,(3), 40-47.

Gaylord-Ross, R. A decision model for the treatment of aberrant behavior in applied settings. In Sailor, W., Wilcox, B., & Brown, L. (Eds.), *Methods of instruction for severely handicapped students*. Baltimore: Paul H. Brooks, 1980.

Guess, D., & Noonan, M. J. Curricula and instructional procedures for severely handicapped students. *Focus On Exceptional Children*, 1982, *14*, 5.

Hurley, K. M., & Hallenstein, K. Teacher-made materials: A publisher's view. *Journal of Special Education Technology*, 1979, *2*(4), 69-72.

Klein, N., Pasch, M., & Frew, T. *Curriculum analysis and design for retarded learners*. Columbus: Charles E. Merrill, 1979.

Larsen, L. Some problems facing producers and developers of media and materials for the severely handicapped. *Journal of Special Education Technology*, 1978, *1*(2), 13-24.

Rago, W. V., & Cleland, C. C. Future directions in the education of the profoundly retarded. *Education and Training of the Mentally Retarded,* 1978, *13,* 184-186.

Sailor, W., Wilcox, B., & Brown, L. *Methods of instruction for severely handicapped students.* Baltimore: Paul H. Brooks, 1980.

Shackelford, W. Synergy: May the "combined and correlated force" be with us. *Journal of Special Education Technology,* 1978, *1*(2), 38-43.

Stowitschek, J., Gable, R., & Hendrickson, J. *Instructional materials for exceptional children: selection, management, and adaptation.* Germantown, MD: Aspen Systems Corporation, 1980.

Vale, C. *National needs assessment of educational media and materials for the handicapped.* Columbus: LINC Resources, Inc., 1980.

White, O. Adaptive performance objectives form versus function. In Sailor, W., Wilcox, B., and Brown, L. (Eds.), *Methods of instruction for severely handicapped students.* Baltimore: Paul H. Brooks, 1980.

Winschel, J., & Ensher, G. Educability revisited: Curricular implications for the mentally retarded. *Education and Training of the Mentally Retarded,* 1978, *13,* 131-138.

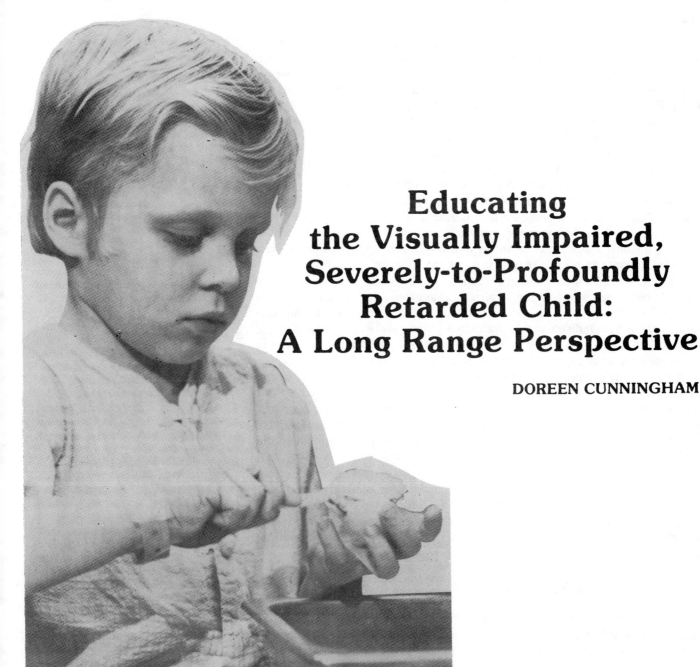

Educating the Visually Impaired, Severely-to-Profoundly Retarded Child: A Long Range Perspective

DOREEN CUNNINGHAM

Doreen Cunningham is at the Maryland School for the Blind. She is teaching supervisor for multiply handicapped students at the Wolfe Center.

ABSTRACT: This article deals with the past, present, and future trends in the education of the visually impaired, severely-to-profoundly retarded population. Traditional developmental orientation toward program planning is explored. Present trends calling for use of a functional curriculum, particularly with the chronological adolescent, is reviewed. Within the framework of life goals, a narrowing of the range and scope of individualized programming is proposed as the direction for the future.

"Educating the Visually Impaired, Severely-to-Profoundly Retarded Child: A Long Range Perspective," Doreen Cunningham, *Education of the Visually Handicapped*, Vol. XV, No. 3, Fall 1983. Copyright 1983 Heldref Publications, a publication of the Helen Dwight Reid Educational Foundation.

The Traditional Orientation

In the past, the education of the visually impaired, severely-to-profoundly retarded child has been based upon a developmental orientation. The result has been, as the chronological age of the child increased, that a twenty-year-old adolescent, for example, has been treated as a two-year-old toddler (Brown, 1980). Particularly with one's oldest clientele, this is neither valid nor appropriate. Lacking within this orientation is the provision of appropriate experiences for young adults who will be asked to function upon graduation in an adult, not a child's, world. Furthermore, there is no acknowledgment of the fact that, though successful skill acquisition has been minimal until this point, the twenty year old will be approaching a new skill in light of twenty years of life experiences, while the two year old has been building upon only two years of life. Finally, the normal two year old is able to assimilate new information in all areas of development simultaneously. Training the twenty-year-old, profoundly retarded adolescent in the same manner results in bombarding him with more input than he can successfully integrate and organize for use in his environment.

Using the traditional developmental orientation, the child is assessed regarding the skills he has acquired thus far, in such areas as gross and fine motor development, self-help skills, etc.; he is then compared to the normal child at the same chronological age. Individualized educational programs are developed, and the child is then taught those skills he is found to be lacking, in the same order in which the nonhandicapped child would have learned them. Unfortunately, the child is also taught these skills *in the same way* one would teach a two year old. This results in the use of materials not normally used by nonhandicapped persons at that same chronological age, use of activities in which the nonhandicapped persons of similar age would not normally engage, and teaching in settings which are not naturally conducive to the performance of those skills in the daily life of the nonhandicapped person. For example, a developmentally appropriate skill such as learning to correctly position objects in relation to each other may be targeted. The objective in and of itself may be valid, but to ask an adolescent to learn that concept by putting together a four-piece, colorful Sesame Street puzzle is clearly inappropriate. Moreover, under such conditions, the student will never acquire the self-respect and dignity necessary for integrated functioning in the normal adult community.

The Advent of the Functional Curriculum

Within the functional approach to curriculum development, the same objective cited above may also be targeted, with several important differences. In a functional curriculum, that objective will be chosen only if the client will need to apply that concept in a group home or work activity center upon graduation. This is in sharp contrast to teaching the concept simply because every nonhandicapped two and one-half year old is learning it. The student is taught the concept because it is a functional skill; its application will frequently be demanded in natural domestic, vocational, and community environments. He now will learn the concept through such activities as fitting sheets to his bed, placing cold cuts between two slices of bread, or changing a light bulb. He uses the same materials with which the nonhandicapped person of a commensurate age would interact during the normal course of a day's activities, across a variety of settings. Finally, teaching within a functional orientation does not take place strictly within the classroom. The student will learn to make his bed in a bedroom or make a sandwich in a kitchen. Teaching occurs in the natural environment; in a variety of least restrictive environments in which he is being prepared to function (Brown, 1979).

Use of a functional curriculum offers several advantages. Certainly, it requires an analysis of potential future living and working environments (Arkell, 1982). A rationale for choosing to teach a particular skill is necessarily built into this orientation, with a direct connection to the child's projected future living arrangements. In doing so, one takes a concrete step toward the reduction of the "bombardment" effect described earlier. Finally, one has now ensured inclusion of generalization of learned skills into the teaching process. By teaching skills in their natural environment, the student is no longer expected to acquire a set of skills and information which will *eventually* be useful to him at work, home, or in social situations (Schedgick, 1978). Generalization cannot be assumed; the student must be taught a skill's practical application through rehearsal of the use of that skill in its natural environment.

The Long Range Perspective

The question "what do we teach?" is answered within the functional orientation to curriculum development. Only those skills which are projected to be used frequently by the student in future settings are emphasized. They are to be taught in the environment in which the activity is naturally performed—i.e., cooking in a kitchen, bedmaking in a bedroom, etc. The materials used are those which the non-handicapped older adolescent and young adult would use—i.e., typical family tableware, rather than play eating utensils toddlers would use in learning to set a table.

Brown (1980) describes one process by which the specific content of a functional curriculum may be determined. Program areas should be divided according to the primary aspects or domains of adult life—domestic, vocational, recreational, general community living (such as use of public transportation systems), and interaction with nonhandicapped persons. The student's current living environment and possible future least restrictive environments should be identified. The student's current skill level, as well as input from the parents or guardians regarding functioning level at home, should be ascertained. Given the above information, targeted skills can then be prioritized according to any number of factors such as people preferences, the functional nature of the skill, the number of times the performance of that skill will be required in an environment, etc.

Processes such as the one described above, however, continue to present a wide range of potential programming areas for any individual student. While all the skills identified within this framework may indeed be necessary for successful functioning along a continuum of least restrictive environments, not all students can acquire the volume of appropriate skills needed by the age of twenty-one. This is particularly true of the blind, profoundly retarded child. McGee (1981) describes a similar population as individuals who may require a highly structured and individual setting outside of the family throughout their life span. There are individuals within the visually impaired, profoundly retarded population who not only do not have the potential to gain independence in even one living domain, such as vocational, but will require maximum supervision on a twenty-four-hour basis throughout their life span. Given the slow rate of learning exhibited by this population, the rehearsal time required for successful acquisition of any skill, the need for repetitious performance of learned skills to maintain those skills, and the limited life span available to the educator to impart these skills, teaching skills in all program areas to all students simultaneously will simply not be effective.

It does not appear to be enough, for example, given the aforementioned constraints, to identify all possible environments within which the graduate may conceivably find himself placed, and simply begin teaching within that framework. Rather, a professional team must project a more specific goal from the onset of the child's formal training, to be modified over time in light of the child's continued growth and development. Prioritization of program areas would then be based on those skills most essential to active and successful participation in the targeted future settings. In so doing, one narrows the range and scope of programs. This allows one to increase the depth and intensity of training provided to students, thereby facilitating the likelihood of successful and practical learning experiences. Without such a narrowing in program goals, one must either settle for having perhaps only partially prepared the student for successful participation in the setting in which he actually finds himself placed, or continue to request the additional staff, the cost of which current education budgets cannot withstand. As neither of the latter alternatives seems feasible, intensive training in a restricted number of areas at one time, selected on the basis of a defined life goal, must be considered.

The concept of a life goal, as used here, will be defined as those day and evening settings in which the child, at age twenty-one, given his projected level of dependence on, or independence from, significant others in his environment, is likely to be successful and/or accepted for placement. The development of a life goal should be based on at least the folllowing: the student's current skill in manipulating a variety of materials in his interactions with his environment; his rate of learning new skills as exhibited thus far; his acquisition of skills necessary to independent care of personal physical needs, such as eating; his overall work or learning behavior; and the type of community-based program recommended to meet the student's projected future needs. Certainly, the team must meet on a regular basis, actively seek to gather the most current available information regarding the student, and review or revise life goals in light of the new information on at least an annual basis.

Life goals must be as specific as possible based on available data regarding the student's performance and must be formulated with full knowledge of the entry criteria for community programs. It is not, for example, sufficient to identify a work setting as day community placement involving production-oriented manipulation of materials, or that the goal for all graduates from this population is to secure a placement in a sheltered workshop. If it is projected that a student, in all reality, will not develop sufficiently to match or exceed minimum criteria for entry into a sheltered workshop, this information should be reflected in a life goal. Successfully teaching that student, through advanced behavioral technology and extensive investment of time, to correctly assemble bicycle brake components will not adequately prepare the student to function in the environment in which he will actually be placed. This student may more appropriately be considered for a day activity center, in which case such centers should be identified, the daily activities used in that setting assessed, and an individual curriculum be developed to prepare the student for successful entry and participation in that level work environment. This process should begin from the time the child enters school. If the child is orthopedically involved to the extent that he will always be totally dependent upon a caretaker to meet his daily nutritional and personal hygiene needs, that should be a guiding factor in projecting his life goal and in determining specific program content. Certainly, voluntary relaxation of muscle tone, cooperation with hygiene routines, and a method of communication all become priority program areas. Programming must start with an honest appraisal of the student's future prospects regarding community placement. Given the expensive investment in time and training required in teaching these students to travel independently and function within even a self-contained, sheltered environment, for example, it becomes even more imperative that one provides those learning experiences most representative of the setting in which the student will be placed.

Educators will also need to expand their role as a service provider to include actively seeking and securing both living and vocational placements for their students as the successful culmination of a future-oriented, reality-based, and functional educational program. Only by narrowing the range and scope of programs, thereby increasing the depth and intensity of training provided, can one hope to prepare adequately this population for a successful and constructive life experience.

REFERENCES

Arkell, C. Functional curriculum development for multiple involved hearing impaired students. *Volta Review*, 1982, *84*, 198–208.
Brown, L., Branston, M., Hamre-Nietupski, S., Pumpian, I., Certo, N. & Gruenewald, L.,

A strategy for developing chronological-age-appropriate and functional curricular content for severely handicapped adolescents and young adults. *The Journal of Special Education*, 1979, *13*(1), 81-90.

Brown, L., Falvey, M., Vincent, L., Kaye, N., Johnson, F., Ferrara-Parrish, P., & Gruenewald, L. Strategies for generative comprehensive, longitudinal and chronological-age-appropriate IEP's for adolescent and young adult severely handicapped students. *The Journal of Special Education*, 1980, *14*(2), 199-215.

McGee, J. & Menolascino, F. Life goals for persons of severe disabilities: A structural analysis. *Viewpoints in Teaching and Learning*, 1981, *57*(1), 14-20.

Scedgick, B. & Deschapelles, A. Curriculum for severely handicapped: Focuses on the generalization process. *Education and Training of the Mentally Retarded*, 1978, *13*(4), 389-392.

Serving Handicapped Young Children: *Six Imperatives*

Phillip M. Wishon

Phillip M. Wishon, Ph.D., is Assistant Professor, Early Childhood Education, East Tennessee State University, Johnson City.

The Education for All Handicapped Children Act (P.L. 94-142), that was passed by Congress in November 1975, has been the catalytic agent and has provided direction to the efforts of educators and others who provide services to handicapped young children. Whatever its future, the issues that the law made manifest have ignited our consciousness and will influence our efforts on behalf of young handicapped children for a long time.

The essence of P.L. 94-142 is the provision of a free public education for handicapped children. Turnbull, Strickland, and Brantley (1978) outline six major principles of the act that relate to the appropriateness of the educational services required: zero reject, nondiscriminatory testing, individualized education programs, least restrictive environments, due process, and parent participation.

Delivery of purposeful learning opportunities for young handicapped children cannot be guaranteed legislatively, however. P.L. 94-142 is not likely to become the redemptive legislative agent it has been commonly perceived to be until our teaching becomes genuinely attuned to the letter and spirit of the act in practice and attitude.

This article outlines a series of six imperatives designed to provide educators and other child advocates with a backdrop against which they may implement strategies for serving handicapped young children. Collectively considered, these imperatives may provide child and family advocates with a framework for clarifying their plans for helping handicapped children and their families.

Recognize the individual's potential

Even profoundly handicapped children's behaviors change as they grow. However subtle these behavioral changes might be, it is important that attempts be made to channel these changes in directions that promise the most benefit to the child.

Often when we observe handicapped children we concentrate on the problems that might exist. We have been trained to look at children with pathological eyes. We should begin to focus more on the positive aspects of the child as we generate a prognosis. What powers does the child have? What strengths? Torres (1978) suggests that child advocates initiate diagnostic services by determining the things the child *can* do and at what level of performance. Will (1980) believes that society must acknowledge its obligation to nurture the significant fulfillment of even the limited potential of exceptional children.

In planning for services required by handicapped children, we must be more sensitive to the overall quality of life an individual experiences. Programs should be designed to meet children's affective needs as well as providing educational and therapeutic services. Child caregivers not only teach, prepare and serve snacks, manage behavior, plan activities, oversee toileting and body care, and attend to special care requirements, but they also soothe children's feelings, express affection, and work to improve the children's self-concepts.

Affirm the importance of early intervention

Bloom (1964) estimates that at least 50 percent of an individual's intelligence at age 17 is developed by age 4, 80 percent is developed by about age 8. At approximately age 5, at least such personality characteristics as intellectual interest, dependency, and aggression are predictable into adolescence. Early intervention with a variety of purposeful and individually prescribed learning events can help assure that young children will derive the most benefit from the powers they have at birth.

The effectiveness of early intervention has been demonstrated. Umansky (1980) reports that longitudinal data from 14 early intervention projects reveal that all of the programs had a positive and resilient effect on the children's lives (Consortium for Longitudinal Studies 1978). Children in one project, for example, when compared to controls, demonstrated greater social and intellectual maturity as measured by fewer school failures, and greater achievement, better attitudes toward school, and lower delinquency rates (Schweinhart and Weikart 1979).

Early intervention may prevent more serious conditions from developing. For example, if ignored, achievement differences between "normal" and developmentally delayed children widen over time. Consider the early psychomotor development of cerebral palsied (c.p.) children. Insistence from the beginning that young c.p. children learn to sit on the floor with their legs crossed may help prevent the children from adopting the less desirable pattern of sitting with their weight distributed on the insides of their ankles and knees. Likewise, scooting behavior may be avoided if caregivers work with young children to help them crawl.

Early intervention may also help to moderate the emotional trauma within the family following the birth of a handicapped child. Most intensive-care nurseries encourage parents to feed and hold their high-risk infant to help establish a bond between parent and child. Social workers, nurses, physicians, and others can help parents overcome feelings of guilt or anger, and these professionals can assist the family in adopting strategies that strengthen family life and enable all family members to live as normally as possible.

Dmitriev (1974) defines a high-risk infant as "one who, for socioeconomic, health, or genetic reasons faces developmental delay" (p. 55). We must reach children with suspected handicaps as soon as possible and provide appropriate services to those children throughout their early years.

Many advances have been made in reducing infant distress in the past ten years. For example, portable respirators, and blood gas monitoring to determine oxygen levels have increased survival rates of infants affected by respiration distress. Catheters can be inserted into the intestines of infants with underdeveloped digestive systems in order to provide proper nourishment. Kruse (1980) documents that almost all children with PKU, *if* placed on a specially prescribed diet as newborns, grow up with normal or near normal intelligence.

Brazelton (1969) underlines the significance of early intervention by stressing the importance of valuing and protecting every moment of an infant's existence. Especially among the very young, the preciousness of every day of life must be appreciated and nurtured.

Emphasize prevention

Broman, Nichols, and Kennedy (1975) found the strongest predictor of mental retardation at four years of age to be maternal education (among prenatal and neonatal variables). Each year about 1 million teenage girls become pregnant—two-thirds of whom deliver a child. The suicide rate of pregnant teenage girls is about nine times greater than their nonpregnant counterparts. As many as one-half of at-risk infants have parents who abuse drugs, alcohol, etc. Family life education is an important component of even very young children's learning as we work toward eliminating at-risk births.

Among the other factors that are known to contribute to infant risk are indications of neglect or disinterest, a potentially harmful environment, anxious or insecure parents, and parent obesity or chronic illness.

Maintain family integrity and vitality

Parents of handicapped children frequently express feelings of isolation, uncertainty, and guilt. The myriad of problems with which they are faced can be overwhelming. Family members are often unsure of their roles, unaware of their rights, and unaware that help exists. They sometimes express unrealistic expectations about the progress the handicapped child might make. Feelings of inadequacy, despair, or rejection, which are sometimes revealed, may interfere with the ability of some family members to take proper care of the child. These feelings are legitimate, and such families are best served when these attitudes are recognized and confronted openly and compassionately by family members and by supportive family advocates such as teachers or social service workers.

Marital problems, employment difficulties, and substance abuse problems are some of the factors that frequently complicate the family. Often friends and relatives of family members form a "pity-party," the results of which accentuate the depth of the problems rather than help to resolve them. All of these factors impair the effectiveness of the family's attempts to provide every member with opportunities that promise both individual and collective integrity.

Differences in feelings and identity between the primary caregivers and their handicapped young children often make satisfactory attachment between them highly improbable. Sometimes parents of handicapped children are unwilling or feel unable to accept the responsibility of providing the services and attention the children need. Because some parents cannot adjust to changes in their life style that providing for a handicapped child sometimes requires, it is not uncommon to find a high percentage of handicapped chil-

dren in foster homes or with grandparents.

Threats to the establishment of viable family units must be clarified and resolved. Social service agencies attempting to resolve family difficulties should accept the concerns of each family member as having worth, suggest ways that quality time be spent daily with the nonhandicapped children in the home, help the family to understand its rights and obligations, and help family members to become aware of the resources that are available to serve them.

Underscore the worth and dignity of the individual

There are times when many handicapped children appear to learn from the attitudes of teachers and age-mates that it is not important how well they do academically. Feeling patronized at times, handicapped children are often frustrated in their attempts to engage as equals in activities with those who are not handicapped. We dignify the achievements of the handicapped when we challenge them to meet performance standards that are reasonable and not condescending.

The stigma of being handicapped is conveyed in the classroom in a variety of ways. When we raise our voices too loudly, speak more slowly than is necessary, stand above or apart from the handicapped, pull and drag them by their arms, etc., we communicate to young handicapped children that they are not one of us. Likewise, in some centers, handicapped children find themselves isolated, constrained, and confronted with architectural barriers. The inability to negotiate passageways, use toilet facilities, or acquire supplies without assistance diminishes one's efforts to be self-sufficient.

An individual's worth does not vary with one's intelligence or some performance competency. Instead of offering purely clinical or therapeutic episodes, we should begin planning transactional relationships with handicapped children— interchanges that respect the contributions they can make to our lives. Learners may be said to have transactional integrity when they are afforded opportunities to positively influence what topics are presented and what instructional strategies

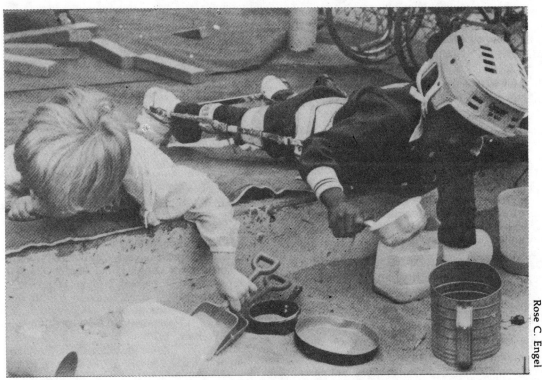

Rose C. Engel

In planning for services required by handicapped children, we must be more sensitive to the overall quality of life an individual experiences.

are employed. Spodek (1972) describes the transactional relationship as "one in which the learner has a role in instigating learning, in determining its direction, and in terminating any learning situation" (p. 52).

We should watch for and avoid experiences for children that generate a life void of those qualities that give life human dignity. Genuine caring must be demonstrated and handicapped children must be given opportunities to make choices and to succeed and fail realistically.

Provide comprehensive services

Child advocates find themselves overwhelmed at times by the compelling range of services required by many handicapped young children. Areas of development for which comprehensive assessment, counseling, and treatment are commonly required include speech and language development, cognition, biochemical and physiological viability, visual and auditory perception, nutritional balance, psychological stability, and psychomotor development. Services that provide support for young children in terms of who they are as people—ego support—should be included. We must apply ourselves above all to the primary proposition that

every child is an individual eminently worthy of our respect, understanding, and acceptance. Bettelheim (1979) stresses that if we want to educate children as people, we must know where they come from, who they are, and where they wish to go. We must "reach children as the persons they are at present in order to guide them to where they should go" (p. 34).

In addressing ourselves to the challenge of providing comprehensive services, the critical paths we choose must involve multidisciplinary strategies (Allen, Holm, and Schiefelbusch 1978). Interagency cooperation stands out as the most promising approach for addressing the singular range of needs expressed by so many young children. Strategies for service delivery arrived at through a consensus of pluralistic philosophies most nearly assure that all important concomitants will be considered.

The transcendent task before us is to assist handicapped young children in becoming individuals who are as fully functioning and expressive as possible. Through our sensitivity to this cause and our enduring commitment to it, we elevate the quality of our lives and those of young handicapped children.

References

Allen, K. E.; Holm, V. A.; and Schiefelbusch, R. L., eds. *Early Intervention—A Team Approach.* Baltimore, Md.: University Park Press, 1978.

Bettelheim, B. "Education and the Reality Principle." *American Educator* 3, no. 4 (Winter 1979): 34.

Bloom, B. S. *Stability and Change in Human Characteristics.* New York: Wiley, 1964.

Brazelton, T. B. *Infants and Mothers.* New York: Dell, 1969.

Broman, S. H.; Nichols, P. L.; and Kennedy, W. A. *Preschool IQ: Prenatal and Early Development Correlates.* New York: Wiley, 1975.

Consortium for Longitudinal Studies. *Lasting Effects After Preschool.* Washington, D.C.: Administration for Children, Youth and Families, Office of Human Development Services, Department of Health, Education and Welfare, 1978.

Dmitriev, V. "Motor and Cognitive Development in Early Education." In *Behavior of Exceptional Children: An Introduction to Special Education,* ed. N. G. Haring. Columbus, Ohio: Merrill, 1974.

Kruse, S. *Preventing Mental Retardation: Metabolic Disorders.* Nashville, Tenn.: ARC Publishing, 1980.

Schweinhart, L. J., and Weikart, D. P. *Perry Preschool Effects in Adolescence.* Paper presented at the biennial meeting of the Society for Research in Child Development, San Francisco, March 1979.

Spodek, B. *Teaching in the Early Years.* Englewood Cliffs, N.J.: Prentice-Hall, 1972.

Torres, S. T. *A Primer on Individualized Education Programs for Handicapped Children.* Reston, Va.: Foundation for Exceptional Children, 1978.

Turnbull, A. P.; Strickland, B.; and Brantley, J. C. *Developing and Implementing Individualized Education Programs.* Columbus, Ohio: Merrill, 1978.

Umansky, W. "Influencing the Social and Emotional Capabilities of Young Children." *Practical Applications of Research* 2, no. 3 (1980): 4.

Will, G. F. "The Case of Phillip Becker." *Newsweek* 95, no. 15 (April 14, 1980): 112.

Assessment and Identification

The definition of intelligence has always puzzled reseachers and educators. If an actual definition could be arrived at, it would be easier to both measure and modify it. The present state of the research presents a number of plausible ideas concerning intelligence. One theory espouses the idea that intelligence is a unitary function, another says that it is a generalized function. Intelligence can also be seen as a group of relatively separate abilities. The human mind is still a mystery, and is not likely to be fully understood for years. Given our present lack of understanding, educators must find some way to classify children in order to place them in the appropriate educational setting. This is especially true of individuals who have some deficit in their demonstrated ability to learn. The mentally handicapped comprise a diverse group that does not lend itself to easy classification. There are three main categories into which the mentally handicapped fall. They are; educable mentally handicapped, trainable mentally handicapped, and severely and profoundly mentally handicapped.

The first group, the educable mentally handicapped often are not diagnosed as having a problem because the disability is not easily discerned, especially at an early age. These children are slower to walk, slower to feed themselves and slower to talk than most normal children. Once identification is made, a child with a mild disability can learn to read and do arithmetic up to the sixth grade level, and can acquire the requisite skills to hold a job, and to conform with the norms of society. It is most important that early identification be made in order for these individuals to reach their potential.

The trainable or moderately mentally handicapped exhibit noticeable delays in motor development, especially in speech. These individuals can learn simple communication skills, elementary health and safety habits, and simple manual skills. Although they are not capable of progressing to functional use of reading or mathematical skills, under protective conditions, they are capable of performing simple tasks. The moderately mentally handicapped participate in simple recreation, can travel alone in familiar places, but are usually incapable of complete self maintenance.

The severely and profoundly mentally handicapped are grouped together here for easy identification, even though there is some discussion in the field as to whether they should be considered as two distinct groups. All of these individuals suffer from gross retardation, and have minimal capacity for functioning in sensori-motor areas. The severely involved group may be kept at home in some cases, while there is no question that the profoundly retarded group must receive nursing care in order to survive. The severely retarded group usually walks, while the profoundly retarded probably will not. Both groups are too retarded, in most instances, to benefit to any appreciable degree from continued training and must remain under constant, supervision during their entire lives.

The last two groups, the profoundly and the severely retarded, are the easiest to identify in a cursory examination. They exhibit the most obvious evidence of a problem, and so are seen by specialists at an early age. In many cases the original diagnosis may be incorrect because of the confusion of mental with physical disability, but as soon as a correct diagnosis is made, proper care is given.

The first two groups are more difficult to identify. The moderately mentally handicapped, though not immediately identified, are seen as having problems early in life. The group called educable or mildly retarded presents the most difficult screening and identification problem. There are numerous tests now available to test children when they enter school, and they all focus on more than one area of intelligence and development. In order for a testing device to provide replicable results, it must examine as many areas of a child's learning and maturation as possible. Without replication, no test can be given serious consideration for placing children in special educational settings. Tests for mental retardation must be designed to test very young children, from ages two and a half to five and a half years. The four most common areas of examination are gross motor development, fine motor development, conceptual development and communication ability. A child who fails to reach criterion in any one of these areas should be re-examined, but should not be referred for special education. A child who does not reach criterion in three areas, is a good candidate for special consideration.

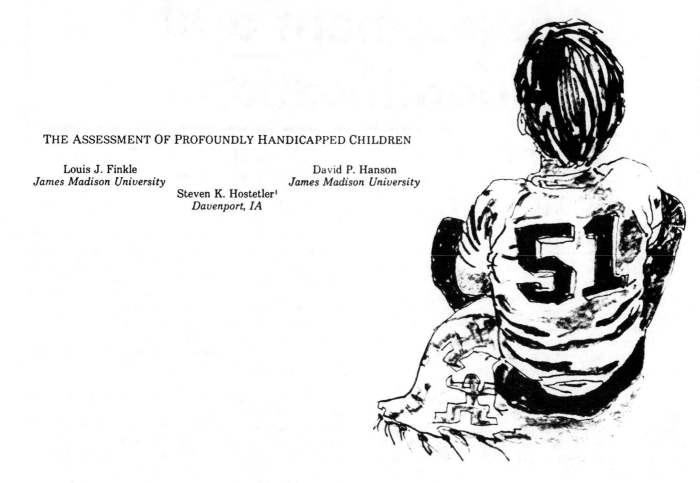

THE ASSESSMENT OF PROFOUNDLY HANDICAPPED CHILDREN

Louis J. Finkle
James Madison University

David P. Hanson
James Madison University

Steven K. Hostetler[1]
Davenport, IA

ABSTRACT

The authors talk about school psychology and the assessment of profoundly handicapped children from their personal experiences in two fields: special education and school psychology. Each author has practical experience relevant to current trends in these fields.

As a direct result of P.L. 94-142, many school psychologists are taking on new ventures — assessing profoundly handicapped children to fulfill the psychological component of an evaluation. The profoundly handicapped are those persons who exhibit extreme deficits in communication, locomotion, personal and social skills to such an extent that specialized instructions, materials, and behavior modification are necessary to supplant traditional academic instructions usually required for learning. There is no doubt that such an experience is challenging to many school psychologists and may be frightening to others. Some fears can be rationalized as temporary feelings of uncertainty due to lack of familiarity with severe and profoundly handicapped children and to the need for knowledge and specific competencies to initiate new techniques to make these evaluations. The authors would like to suggest the following systematic process (See Figure 1) as a model that has been successful over the past eight years with many profoundly and multi-handicapped children[2]. Steps 1 through 3 can be used to assess program entry goals for individualized educational plans (IEP). Step 4 provides for ongoing progress assessment. In addition, it is imperative that the school psychologist secures accurate information regarding the child's medical and developmental history prior to initiating any assessment. It is assumed that proper observation and interview strategies will take place before entering the flowchart schema.

During the past two decades, evaluations of handicapped children, class placements and exclusions sometimes were determined primarily on the basis of an index known as the intelligence quotient (IQ). Many specialists believed that the IQ represented an indication of the summative ability of a child (Budoff and Hamilton, 1978). This approach has led to occasional problems arising from such a singular focus, e.g., faulty diagnosis, misplacement, and exclusion. At present, IQ is accepted as just one of many factors relating to a child's potential learning rate, development, and behavior (Faris, Anderson, and Greer, 1976).

	FIGURE 1 Systematic Process Prior to Full-Time Placement
STEP 1	1. Initial referral to a school psychologist. 2. Initial screening of the child. 3. Recommend lesson plans based on screening information.
STEP 2	4. Initiate an interim program. 5. Evaluate the interim program. 6. Use teching site also an assessment site.
STEP 3	7. Select the most appropriate complete assessment techniques. 8. Assess the child.
STEP 4	9. Assist the teacher/parent in designing a formal IEP. 10. Re-evaluate on a planned basis.

Additional factors must be taken into consideration in the assessment process besides IQ tests (see Figure 2). A *single* instrument should never be used alone to assess and/or place a child in special education programs. Other procedures must also be involved.

A functional knowledge and understanding of successful, efficacious programming for the profoundly handicapped is a necessity to the evaluator. As noted by Sontag (1977) and Clark and Clark (1973), when we approach the assessment of a handicapped child, we should consider its applicability or appropriateness for that specific individual child, the milieu within which the child functions, and the broad range skills or current functioning level of that child. Flexibility and openness are two key ingredients for the evaluator. Unlike normal children, profoundly handicapped children exhibit behaviors, both cognitive and emotional, which often seem incomprehensible (Berkson and Landesman-Dwyer, 1978). Keeping in mind the assessment information itself will become a guide in determining directions taken in an educational setting, psychologists should also consider the applicability of the assessment toward such educational planning (White and Liberty, 1977). Both the severity and multiplicity of handicapping conditions affect the assessment procedure and consequent educational programming. The way the assessment is completed, the findings, and the potential long-range outcomes, are greatly influenced by both the nature of the handicap(s) and the assessment approach.

Meier (1976), a proponent of the team approach, e.g., school psychologist, teacher, parent, and other relevant persons, feels this method will effect a more comprehensive assessment and educational program for each child being evaluated. The team approach provides a greater degree of comprehensiveness than would be the case if each person were to suggest opinions separately. A concerted effort should be made by the team to reach agreement as to direction, impetus, and alternative strategies for the profoundly handicapped child. Such agreement will enhance prospective growth in the educational skills and adaptive behavior of a profoundly handicapped child.

STEP I: INITIAL SCREENING

The evaluation of a profoundly handicapped child often requires a comparatively long period of time. Step 1, Screening, may take 1 to 2 hours; Step 2, Preliminary Assessment, may take 2 to 10 hours; and Step 3, A Complete Behavioral Assessment, may take 2 to 4 weeks. It is recommended that Step 1 be done prior to entrance into a public school setting if possible. Assessments should not be attempted during the first week or two of school. Thus, the child should be provided ample opportunity to interact with the school environment and explore the settings in which he or she will be expected to perform (Forcade, Matey, and Barnett, 1979). Ideally, such interaction with the school environment and screening could take place over the summer months.

These activities can be initiated *prior* to a lengthy, costly, complete behavioral assessment, i.e., Step 3 and are as follows:

1. *Provide for initial screening of each child.*

    The *Denver Developmental Screening Test* published by Ladoca Project and Publishing Foundation, Denver, Colorado, is probably the most common screening device used with handicapped children. It is an individual test which can be administered inexpensively in about 1 hour or less depending on the child and the examiner.

If screening a large number of children is necessary, the *Developmental Indicators for the Assessment of Learning (DIAL)* published by DIAL, Inc., Highland Park, Illinois, is a mass screening device requiring several examiners to work simultaneously on a large group of children.

2.   *Use screening (information) results to begin the teaching process.*

After preliminary screening results are known, a remediation/teaching manual, Utilizing Psychodiagnostic Data (Finkle, 1977), is available for parents, teachers, and school psychologists. The manual contains specific lesson plans which allow parents/teachers to train their handicapped children in the broad skill areas assessed by some screening devices. The implementation of these lesson plans can continue up to and including the days in which the children will be assessed formally (Step 3).

The screening instruments and the *UPD Manual* and/or other references should enhance the child's interim educational program, Step 2.

STEP II: INTERIM PROGRAM

Using an interim lesson plan, the teacher can help the child learn the significant activities which were derived from screening data, e.g., the child can become familiar with significant

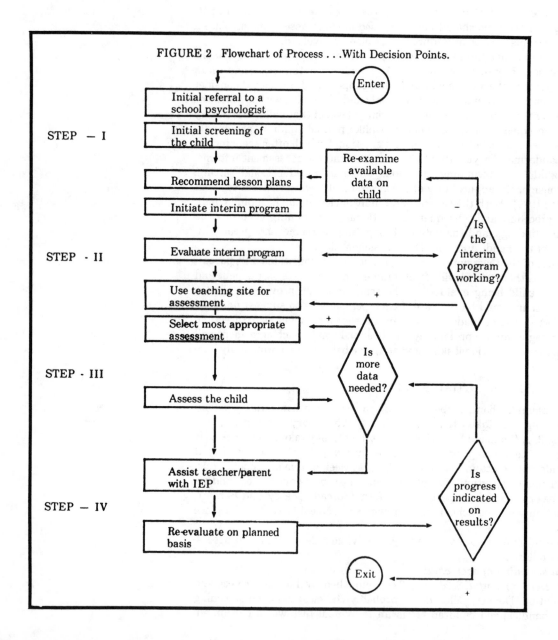

FIGURE 2   Flowchart of Process . . .With Decision Points.

others in the environment such as teacher, other children, aide, school psychologist, etc. During this initial or interim period, some important observations are in order. The school psychologist should try to note answers to questions about these factors:

Attention —	What attracts the child? For how long? What occupies the child's time?
Movement —	How does the child propel the body? What is the extent of help needed, if any?
Handedness —	Is manual dominance evident? Are there co-active hand movements?
Compensation —	Are there compensatory behaviors present? What are they? Can they be more effective?
Deficits —	What are deficit behaviors?
Reinforcers —	What appears to be highly reinforcing? What reinforcement strengths are needed?
Tonicity —	What is the child's general health and strength?
Endurance —	Does fatigue set in early?

Answers to these questions provide further information about the child, and may point out some of the shortcomings of the interim program. For instance, it would hardly be appropriate to concentrate on teaching an individual to walk, when it is discovered that she/he has not yet learned to stand unassisted. At this point adjustments can be made in the interim program to compensate for gained information. On the other hand, evaluation of the interim program may indicate that satisfactory measures have already been taken with regard to the child's abilities. It is at this juncture that formal assessment may be initiated.

STEP III: FORMAL ASSESSMENT

When the child has become accustomed to the people in the room, enjoys the surroundings, and responds attentively to the school psychologist, it is time to initiate a formal assessment, Step 3. There are several formal assessment procedures currently being used with profoundly handicapped children throughout the nation (See Figure 3). These techniques are those most favored by author Finkle in his work in assessment. For an expanded list of assessment instruments, the reader may want to refer to Switzky's chapter on "Assessment of the Severely and Profoundly Handicapped," in Sabatino and Miller (1979). All techniques have unique strengths and weaknesses which prevent them from being the only or best approach for the assessment of profoundly handicapped persons.

FIGURE 3. Formal Assessment Programs

- A.A.M.D. Adaptive Behavior Scale (1975 Revision)
- Behavioral Characteristic Progression (BCP) (1974)
- Callier-Azusa Scale (1977)
- Learning Accomplishment Profile (LAP (1974)
- Performance Objectives of Preschool Children (POPC) (1974)
- Portage Guide to Early Education (1976)

In addition to the use of formal assessment packages, psychologists should also take careful note of certain key behavioral activities. Keeping in mind that the purpose of administering an exacting assessment, Step 3, is to provide a comprehensive framework from which the child's educational program will emerge, evaluation of some essential behavioral activities must be included (Sailor and Haring, 1977). It is of utmost importance to evaluate the quality, extent, and degree of functioning as well as deficits in specific key areas. Observation of these essential behavioral activities should not be too difficult for school psychologists who are usually trained well in observational techniques. These activities are listed in Table 1.

Table 1.   Behavioral Activities/Observations

Feeding/Eating/Drinking
Components:
— ingesting through the mouth.
— liquids, colloidals, solids.
— swallowing reflex.
— dribbling, vomiting, regurgitation.

Toileting
Components:
— incontinent aids, self-containment of
feces/urine.
— toilet use, wiping, flushing.
— hygenic behaviors.

Dressing/Undressing
Components:
— dependent, custodial, adaptations.
— semi-dependent.
— independent, selection, care.

Nasal Passage
Components:
— clear, clean, absence of dried mucus.
— nasal control, bloody, runny.
— social cleanliness.

Oral Passage
Components:
— gum disease.
— teeth conditions and palate abnormalities.
— tonsil abnormalities.
— tongue intactness/flexibility.

Self-Awareness
Components:
— knows name.
— pays attention to stimulus.
— identifies body parts.
— identifies members of the family/ward/unit.
— recognizes home or sleeping area.

Visual Motor Skills
Components:
— pursuit of visual stimuli.
— small muscle coordination.
— large muscle reflexive (defensiveness).
— discriminating behaviors.

Gross Motor Skills
Components:
— locomotion.
— mobility, ambulation with aids.
— orientation to physical surroundings.
— agility.
— balance.

Pre-Articulation (Readiness for Speech)
Components:
— lateral, medial, vertical jaw movements.
— lip control.
— tongue thrust.
— teeth (as facilitator of sounds).

Primary Mode of Language (However Primitive)
Components:
— gestural.
— sounds (gutteral).
— pointing.
— body usage (blinking, motor reflex, etc.).

Attention
Components:
— autistic.
— strong stimulus needed.
— facility to shift attention.
— tracking (visual and/or auditory).
— recognition of verbal stimulus.

Posture
Components:
— scoliosis.
— upright, horizontal (prone).
— myelomeningocoele.
— embryonic fetal position.

The formal assessment of a profoundly handicapped child encompasses much more than is tapped by the WISC-R, Standford-Binet, Illinois Test of Psycholinguistic Abilities, or any other device which is widely used in public school testing (Berkson and Landesman-Dwyer, 1978). Often such instruments may be of little value with the profoundly handicapped. Even the recommended assessment techniques listed in Figure 3 vary widely in their components and procedures.

SOME CONCLUSIONS AND CAVEATS

One might say that profoundly handicapped children constitute the second most challenging group of humans to assess. (Deaf-blind, rubella children are the most difficult, in the author's opinion[2].) The profoundly handicapped do not readily respond to one's immediate suggestions, commands, and gestures. They are often immobile, unattentive, disfigured, unpredictable, self-destructive, unresponsive, and lack comprehensible language. They do constitute a challenge to those who elect to interact with them. Sometimes, just when one decides that they are "untestable, unteachable, or hopeless," they respond by displaying the behavior which has been taught them for days or months! One asks what can be so rewarding as witnessing the child's first smile, or word like "milk", or a step forward, or dual response of "yes" or "no", or perhaps the swallowing of a semi-solid food?

If teaching is the name of the game, then assessment must dtermine its directions. The school psychologist's interest, attention, and dedication are vital to successful assessment. However, there are some limits which psychologists need to consider before testing a profoundly handicapped child. These include ethics, training, and prior experience.

First, it would be unethical for a psychologist to accept referral of a child with handicapping conditions which are beyond the scope of one's competencies to deal with such factors (NASP, 1978). Consultation with someone experienced in working with and testing such children is surely indicated.

Secondly, many school psychologists have no formal training and/or coursework relating to severely, profoundly, or multihandicapped children. Psychologists should seek such training. Coursework should include methods of assessing, handling, teaching, and maintaining multihandicapped chldren. A portion of that training must necessarily deal with the medical complications affecting physically deviant bodies.

Thirdly, prior experience with such children is often possible to obtain if it is integrated into the various practica of students studying in school psychology. The Socratic method of gaining direct experience, i.e., the master-student-situation triad, can be an effective means of gaining experience.

The assessment of profound/multiply handicapped children is an exciting experience if the results of such evaluative efforts yield a chance for future learning for the child. By blending good procedures with valid assessments, a well-rounded, formal training program, and prior supervised experiences, there is no reason why a school psychologist could not comfortably proceed with the evaluation of persons who happen to be profoundly and/or multiply handicapped. □

REFERENCE NOTES

[1]Dr. Louis J. Finkle is a consultant in special education. His previous experiences are with the John F. Kennedy Center for Mental Retardation, the Governor Morehead School for the Blind, and the Cloverbottom Hospital and State Institution (Nashville, Tennessee).

Dr. David P. Hanson is professor of school psychology at James Madison University and his experience is in training school psychologists and special educators. Prior to his experience as a trainer, he was a public school teacher, and school psychologist .

Steven K. Hostetler, M.Ed.,is a former school psychology student at James Madison University with previous experience in youth care and as a coordinator of a citizen advocacy program for mentally retarded persons. He is now employed at Miss. Bend A.E.A.

[2]This model was derived from Dr. Finkle's experiences at George Peabody College for Teachers, John F. Kennedy Center for Mental Retardation, the Governor Morehead School for the Blind, and Cloverbottom Hospital and State Institution in Nashville, Tennessee. It was implemented with children exhibiting profound retardation and/or deaf-blindness in Northern Texas.

REFERENCES

Behavior Characteristics Progression (BCP). Palo Alto, CA.: Vort Corporation, 1974.

Berkson, G., & Landesman-Dwyer, S. Behavioral research on severe and profound mentally retarded (1955-1978). In Readings in Special Education. Guilford, Connecticut: Special Learning Corpora tion, 1978.

Budoff, M., & Hamilton, J.L. Optimizing test performance of moderately and severely mentally retarded adolescents and adults. American Journal of Mental Deficiency, 1976, 1, 225-231.

Faris, J.A., Anderson, R.M., & Greer, J.G. Psychological assessment of the severely and profoundly retarded. In R. M. Anderson and J.C. Greer (Eds.) Educating the severely and profoundly retarded. Baltimore, MD.: University Park Press, 1976.

Finkle, L. J. Utilizing psychodiagnostic data (UPD). Sioux City, South Dakota: ADAPT Press, Inc., 1977.

Forcade, M.C., Matey, C.M., & Barnett, D.W. Procedural guidelines for low incidence assessment. School Psychology Digest. 1979, 3, 248-256.

Meir, J.H. Development and learning disabilities: Evaluation and prevention in children. Baltimore, MD.: University Park Press, 1976.

Nihira, K., Foster, R., Shallhaas, M., & Leland, H. Adaptive behavior scale. Washington, D.C.: American Association on Mental Deficiency, 1975.

Sailor, W., & Haring, N.G. Some current directions in education of the severely/multiply impaired. AAESPH Review, 1977, 2, 3-23.

Sanford, S.R. Learning accomplishment profile (LAP). Winston-Salem, North Carolina: Kaplan Press, 1974.

Schirmer, G.J. (Ed.) Performance objectives of preschool children (POPC). Sioux Falls, South Dakota: ADAPT Press, 1974.

Shearer, D. The Portage guide to early education. Portage, WI.: Cooperative Education Service Agency No. 12, 1972.

Sontag, E. (Ed.) Educational programming for the severely and profoundly handicapped. Reston, VA.: Division on Mental Retardation, Council for Exceptional Children, 1977.

Standards for the Provision of School Psychological Services. National Association of School Psychologists, 1978.

Stillman, R. The Callier-Azusa scale. Dallas: Callier Center for Communications Disorders, 1977.

Switzky, H.N. Assessment of the severely and profoundly handicapped. In D.A. Sabatino & T.L. Miller (Eds.) Describing learner characteristics of handicapped children. New York: Grune and Stratton, 1979, 415-463.

White, O. & Liberty, K. Behavioral assessment and precise measurement. In N. Haring & R. Schiefelbusch (Eds.) Teaching special children. New York: McGraw Hill, 1976.

The Development of a Visual Acuity Test for Persons with Severe Handicaps[1]

PAMELA J. CRESS

University of Kansas

JANIS L. JOHNSON

Prince William Sound Community College

CHARLES R. SPELLMAN

University of Kansas

ANDREA C. SIZEMORE

University of Mississippi

RICHARD E. SHORES

Vanderbilt University

Charles R. Spellman, Ed.D., Research Associate, University of Kansas, Bureau of Child Research, Parsons, KS 67357; Janis L. Johnson, M.Ed., Prince William Sound Community College, Valdez, AK; Pamela J. Cress, M.S., Program Director, University of Kansas, Bureau of Child Research, Parsons, KS; Andrea C. Sizemore, Professor, Dept. of Special Education, University of Mississippi, Oxford, MI; Richard E. Shores, Ed.D., Research Associate, University of Kansas, Bureau of Child Research, Parsons, KS, Chairman, Department of Special Education at Peabody College, Vanderbilt University, Nashville, TN.

Abstract

Vision screening services are provided in almost all school programs for regular students. However, many special education students are unable to benefit from these screening programs do to their inability to perform on the screening tests commonly used. The Parsons Visual Acuity Test (PVAT) described in this article has been developed for use with difficult-to-test individuals who have previously been labeled untestable. Tests of validity produced significant correlations between the PVAT and the Snellen E. During field testing visual acuity threshold measurements were obtained on over 90% of the population who were previously considered untestable. The studies reported support use of the PVAT as an alternative screening procedure for indentifying difficult-to-test persons who are in need of a professional eye examination.

[1] The activities described in this paper were partially supported by a grant from the Department of Education, USOSE Grant #G007901961, Bureau of Education for the Handicapped. The views expressed herein do not necessarily represent the official position of that agency.

Vision screening services are provided in almost all school programs for regular students to detect visual impairments and to refer students who need professional care. Unfortunately, persons with severe handicaps are seldom screened due to many factors (e.g., uncooperative behavior, difficulty in following directions, poor attention span, etc.). Available data indicate that the incidence of visual impairments in the population may be as high as 75-80% (Fletcher & Thompson, 1961; Woodruff, 1977 & Ellis, 1979). An effective vision screening program should be implemented for persons of all ages with severe handicaps.

Subjective acuity tests are the single most effective tool available to screeners to determine the need for professional vision care (Blum, Peters, Bettman, 1959). Most subjective acuity tests require the person being screened to answer questions about the test stimuli, e.g., "What letter is this?" Such tests depend upon the cooperation of the person being screened and therefore, are often inappropriate for young children, children with behavior problems, and illiterates (Duke-Elder, 1965). Many handicapped persons are not able to respond to the verbal instructions nor perform the responses required by most visual acuity assessment procedures. The screener may be measuring the handicapped person's failure to discriminate between stimuli rather than measuring his/her visual acuity. Often the inability of persons with handicaps to perform on standard acuity tests prevents them from being referred for further examinations.

The Snellen E test is the most widely used screening device for non-readers. However, it may not be an appropriate test for many persons with severe handicaps in locating and responding to stimuli at a distance (in the case of the Snellen chart, 20-feet) and in making directional discriminations. Other acuity tests have been developed to yield similar information (visual acuity scores), but require less difficult responses from persons being screened. For example, some tests now include a match-to-sample technique (Lippmann, 1969; Faye, 1968). These tests are fairly simple to learn to administer and can be administered quickly with a cooperative person who has a match-to-sample discrimination repertoire. Unfortunately, data concerning the accuracy of these tests and a criterion for referring students who need professional care have not been documented.

Described in this article is a procedure that has been demonstrated to be effective in assesing visual acuity in persons with severe handicaps. Known as the Parsons Visual Acuity Test (PVAT) (Cress, Spellman, DeBriere, Sizemore, Northam, & Johnson, 1981) the test, though more difficult to learn to administer and requiring more testing time than the tests described above, includes a program to train the persons being screened in the specific discrimination necessary to measure their visual acuity. The purpose of this paper is to provide information regarding the developement of the PVAT.

Description of the PVAT

The PVAT is designed for persons with handicaps who are capable of a simple operant response. The response may include movement of the head, button press, eye blinks, etc. The response most often used is a pointing response. Materials are presented in a three-choice discrimination format in which the figures are line drawings of a hand, cake, and bird. Initially the person being tested is asked to point to the hand. If a correct response is not immediately forthcoming a physical guidance procedure may be used to train the pointing response. The PVAT procedures include: a pretest, discrimination training program if needed, and, finally, a visual acuity test. Following is a brief description of the assessment procedure. (See Spellman, DeBriere, Cress, 1980 for a more detailed description of the procedure.)

Pretest

In the pretest the person being screened is presented with an auditory cue (i.e. "Point to the hand") and required to respond to the three-choice form discrimination on the pretest card (see Figure 1). For persons who are unable to make a pointing response, but who have an operant "yes/no" response (head nod, button press, etc.), the tester makes the pointing response to each figure and the person being screened indicates when the hand has been touched. Nine trials are presented with the hand changing position on each card. Criterion for passing the pretest is 8/9 correct responses to the hand figure.

If a student fails the pretest using an auditory cue and a point response, a second pretest is administered using a match response. This response involves matching a 2" × 2" printed card figure with the same figure on the pretest card. The tester asks the person being screened to "match hand" and continues pretesting in the same manner as the auditory/visual pretest.

Discrimination Training

Persons who acquire the necessary motor response but continue to discriminate unreliably are

Figure 1.   Sample pretest card.

given discrimination training. The discrimination training programs are similar to the discrimination programs of Terrace (1963), Sidman & Stoddard (1966), and Dorry & Zeaman (1975) in that they are errorless training programs. One program consists of 30 cards (3 stimulus cards at each of 10 stages of intensity). Figure 2 provides a sample of selected trials. The stimulus being trained (the hand figure) is always at full intensity (black) and the other two figures gradually become darker, beginning with a very light gray and ending in black. Another discrimination training program uses a stimulus shaping approach (see Figure 3) in which the full figure of the hand appears at each step and the other two figures are formed by gradually introducing segments of the bird and cake. The stimulus shaping program is currently being investigated as an alternative to the intensity fading program.

Visual Acuity Threshold Test (Near-point testing)

Once a person demonstrates a reliable discrimination response (8/9 on the pretest), visual acuity threshold testing can proceed. Testing is first conducted at near-point (both eyes and each eye separately) while the person being screened maintains forehead contact with a headrest which is 13 inches from the stimulus card. Cards with the three figures decreasing in size from 20/250 to 20/20 are presented. Pointing to the hand remains the correct response throughout the testing. Criterion for determining the person's visual acuity threshold is four correct responses out of six or fewer trials on one threshold size and three errors on the next smaller size. Figure 4 provides samples of selected sizes of the Threshold Test; the two smallest sizes (20/20 and 20/30) are not illustrated since further reductions in size would render them indistinguishable.

Far-point Testing. For far-point testing, a +3.00 diopter lens is used to opitcally simulate the 20-foot distance. This simulation enables far-point testing to occur without a change in the test environment or in the response of the person being screened. Far-point testing is conducted for each eye separately.

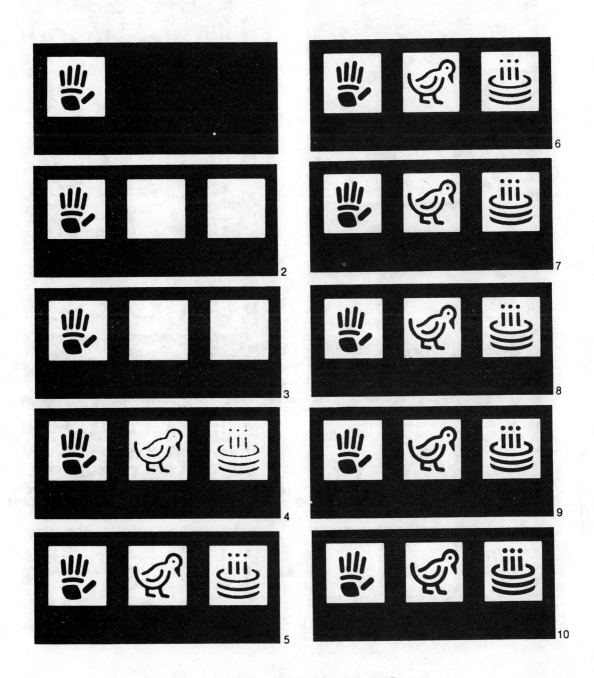

Figure 2.   Selected trials from the Intensity Fading Program.

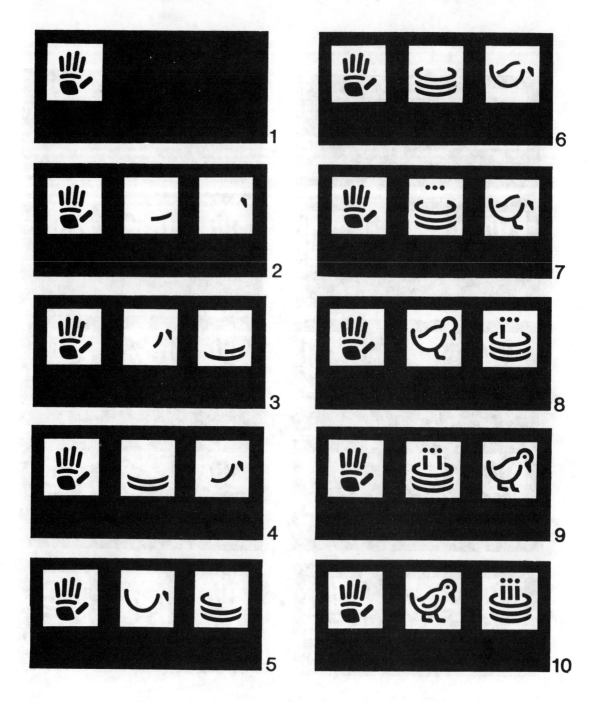

Figure 3.   Selected trials from the Stimulus Shaping Program.

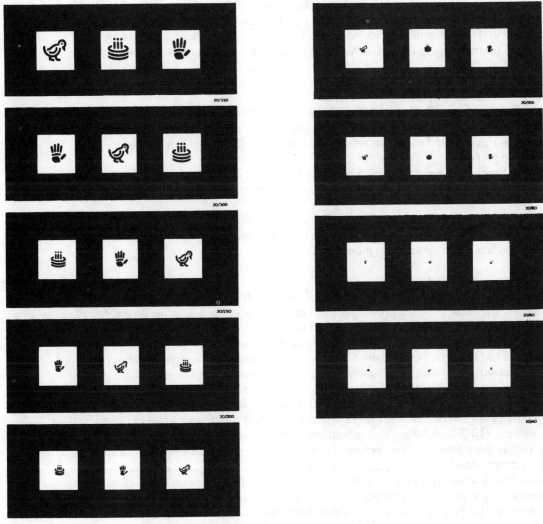

Figure 4.   Selected trials from the Threshold Series.

Assessment of Validity

Three studies were conducted to assess the validity of the PVAT and are described below.

First Study

Subjects. Forty non-handicapped school aged children ages 5-18 with known refractive errors served as subjects. Each subject had had an optometric examination and had been prescribed glasses within the preceeding six months. Spherical refractive errors ranging from +3.50 to −6.50 diopters, with cylinder refractive errors ranging from zero (plano) to −3.75 diopters.

Procedures. Subjects' far-point acuities were assesed using two procedures, the Snellen E test at 20 feet and the PVAT. Standard procedures were used in administering the Snellen E Test (National Society for the Prevention of Blindness, 1976). Procedures for administering the PVAT were those found in the PVAT instruction manual (Spellman, et. al., 1980).

Results. The PVAT identified 78% of the students with myopia, while the Snellen E identified 81% of the myopic students (N=27). The remaining students (N=13) were diagnosed by the optometrist as mild hyperopes. The Snellen identified three of these students while the PVAT identified only one.

Second Study

Subjects. Subjects included 33 non-handicapped elementary school children in grades kindergarten through sixth who had successfully passed standard bi-yearly vision screening tests.

Procedures. Procedures were identical to those used in the first study.

Results. The results indicated that the PVAT identified seven children who scored above 20/40 while the Snellen E identified one child who scored above 20/40 (this subject was not one of the seven identified by the PVAT). The results indicated a need for a retesting procedure to reduce the over-referral rate. Current procedures for the PVAT suggest retesting all subjects who score 20/40 or 20/60.

Third Study

Subjects. Subjects were 27 school aged residents of the Parsons State Hospital and Training Center who were categorized as having educable and trainable mental retardation. Subjects were selected from those with mild and moderate retardation who were able to perform on the Snellen E test for comparative purposes.

Procedures. Procedures were identical to those used in the first and second study. Additionally, the PVAT was re-administered to all subjects on a separate date to gain an estimate of test-retest reliability.

Results. The test-retest scores for all subjects indicated a significant correlation $(r = .83)$ between first and second PVAT testing. Additionally, the experimental far-point procedure correlated significantly with Snellen E 20-foot far-point procedure $(r = .65)$.

Field Test

Subjects. Subjects for the field test were 527 children ages 6-21 years with varying levels of mental retardation. These subjects had previously been judged untestable (i.e., other attempts had been made to screen these subjects for visual acuity but they were not successfully screened due to uncooperative behavior, inconsistent performance, or, in general, the screener gave up).

Procedures. Field test data were gathered by testers at twelve sites in the United States. A total of 113 testers received three days of on-site training and supervision in the use of the PVAT procedures. Data on the 527 subjects were subsequently contributed by 50 testers.

Results. Most of the subjects (455 persons or 86.3%) were able to perform on the PVAT with little or no training (less than one 30-minute training session using the intensity-fading program). Seventy-two subjects (13.7% of the original group) were initially unable to perform the task and subsequently began the intensity fading program to learn the correct discrimination. Twenty-six (36.1%) of the subjects who entered the program were successful in learning the necessary discrimination (usually within 5 sessions), and then completed threshold testing. The remaining 46 subjects failed to demonstrate the required discriminative response. These results indicated that the PVAT procedures were effective in gaining visual acuity threshold measurements with 91.3% of the total population who were previously considered to be untestable. However, 8.7% or 46 subjects of the total population were not amenable to testing even with the PVAT procedures.

Discussion

The results of the three studies and the field test described in this paper indicate that the PVAT can provide visual acuity scores for a substantial portion of the population who were previously defined as untestable. This population includes persons with moderate and severe handicaps who are unable to perform on the standard vision screening tests discussed earlier. The results of these efforts support use of the PVAT as an alternative screening procedure for identifying difficult-to-test persons who are in need of a professional eye examination. Subsequent research has been conducted at Ferris State College School of Optometry (Richman, 1982) and by the University of Kansas School of Ophthalmology (Cibis, 1982), the results of which concur regarding the validity and usefulness of the PVAT in screening difficult-to-test populations.

The PVAT is not intended to replace the Snellen E Test for persons who are able to perform on that test. However, a substantial portion of the school population labeled as moderately and severely handicapped and preschool children with and without identified handicaps often cannot benefit from existing screening programs. The availability of the PVAT is an enabling step in the development of vision screening systems for the difficult-to-test.[3]

---

[3] Individuals and agencies who wish to establish a vision screening and follow-up program may write to the following address for more information about training and technical assistance: Parsons Vision Screening Project, Bureau of Child Research. University of Kansas, P. O. Box 738, Parsons, KS 67357. phone (316) 421-6550 X388.

References

Blum, H. L., Peters, H. B., & Bettman, J. W. *Vision screening for elementary schools: The Orinda study.* Berkeley: University of California Press, 1959.

Cibis, G. W. The validation of the Parsons Visual Acuity Test with children ages 18-48 months. *Ophthalmology* (in preparation).

Cress, P. J., Spellman, C. R., DeBriere, T. J., Sizemore, A. C. Northam, J. K. & Johnson, J. L. Vision screening for persons with severe handicaps. *The Journal of The Association for the Severely Handicapped,* 1981, 6, 41-50.

Ellis, D. Visual handicaps of mentally handicapped people. *American Journal of Mental Deficiency,* 1979, 5, 497-511.

Dorry, G. W. & Zeaman, D. Teaching a simple reading vocabulary to retarded children: Effectiveness of fading and non-fading procedures. *American Journal of Mental Deficiency,* 1975, 6, 711-716.

Duke-Elder, S. *The Practice of Refraction.* St. Louis: C. V. Mosby, 1965.

Faye, E. E. A new visual acuity test for partially-sighted nonreaders. *Journal of Pediatric Ophthalmology,* 1968, 5, 210-212.

Fletcher, M. C. & Thompson, M. M. Eye abnormalities in the mentally defective. *American Journal of Mental Deficiency,* 1961, 66, 242-244.

Lippman, O. Vision of young children. *Arch Ophthal,* 1981, 2, 763-775.

National Society for Prevention of Blindness. *A guide for eye inspection and testing visual acuity of school age children,* 1976.

Richman, J. E. Personal Communication, 1982.

Sidman, M. & Stoddard, L. T. Programming perception and learning for retarded children. In N. R. Ellis (Ed.), *International review of research in mental retardation* (Vol. 2). New York: Academic Press, 1966.

Spellman, C. R., DeBriere, T. J. & Cress, P. J. *Instruction Manual for the Parsons Visual Acuity Test.* Bernell Corporation: South Bend, Indiana, 1980.

Terrace, H. S. Discrimination learning with and without errors. *Journal of the Experimental Analysis of Behavior,* 1963, 6, 1-27.

Woodruff, M. E. Prevalence of visual and ocular anomalies in 1968 non-institutionalized mentally retarded children. *Canadian Journal of Public Health,* 1977, 68, 225-232.

A Survey of State Guidelines for Identification of Mental Retardation
William Frankenberger

Abstract: Results of a survey of state departments of public instruction regarding eligibility criteria for the diagnosis of mental retardation within the public schools are reported. It was found that states varied widely in their definitions and procedures for identifying mentally retarded children. Many states deviated from AAMD guidelines for diagnosis of mental retardation even though AAMD guidelines are included in the P.L. 94–142 definition. Implications of the varying criteria among states and the possible effects of the new AAMD definition are discussed.

Author: WILLIAM FRANKENBERGER, Ph.D., Adjunct Assistant Professor, Department of Psychology and Psychology Supervisor, Human Development Center, University of Wisconsin-Eau Claire, Eau Claire, Wisconsin 54701.

In 1975, P.L. 94–142, the Education for all Handicapped Children Act, was enacted by Congress. This legislation contained the requirement that each state education agency must submit a plan to the U.S. Commissioner of Education delineating procedures employed for the identification and educational programming of handicapped individuals (P.L. 94–142, Sec. 612). According to Meyen (1982), one reason for such plans was to reduce the wide array of responses made by states to earlier legislation. However, the rules and regulations for implementation of P.L. 94–142, published in the 1977 Federal Register, contained only minimum requirements which could be revised as need and experience dictated (Federal Register, 1977); thus the responsibility for specification of policies and procedures was again deferred to states.

One of the handicapping conditions included in P.L. 94–142 was mental retardation. The definition of mental retardation which was published in the 1977 Federal Register was based on the 1973 American Association on Mental Deficiency (AAMD) definition (Grossman, 1973) and stated:

> "Mentally retarded" means significantly subaverage general intellectual functioning existing concurrently with deficits in adaptive behavior and manifested during the developmental period, which adversely affects a child's educational performance.

However, the 1973 AAMD definition was interpreted by educators as excluding individuals

with IQ scores above 69 even though the 1973 and 1977 AAMD manuals suggested that such factors as standard errors of measurement be taken into consideration. As a result, special educators asserted that the 1973 definition eliminated special educational services for some children who really needed them (Payne and Patton, 1981).

The current study surveyed definitions of mental retardation developed by state departments of public instruction to determine if IQ, adaptive behavior, and academic achievement were specified and whether the published criteria conformed to AAMD classification guidelines (Grossman, 1973).

Method

Forty-five states responded to a request for their guidelines and/or standards for assessment of handicapped individuals.

State guidelines were initially reviewed and portions concerned with the definition, identification, and education of mentally retarded individuals were extracted. States' policies for identification of mental retardation were analyzed to determine which of the following types of evaluations were required: (a) IQ, (b) adaptive behavior, and (c) achievement. Results of the analysis were summarized in a matrix containing diagnostic requirements (IQ, adaptive behavior, achievement) on one axis and whether particular criteria were specified on the other axis.

States' criteria for measured intelligence were further analyzed. A summary table was developed to include AAMD levels (mild, moderate, severe, profound) and upper IQ limits for inclusion in each of the levels. Criteria stated as stan-

* An earlier version of this paper was presented at the 107th Annual Meeting of the American Association on Mental Deficiency, June, 1983, in Dallas, Texas. The author would like to thank the Human Development Research Committee for their assistance in collection of data for this work.

dard deviations below the mean were transformed into IQ scores based on a normal distribution with a mean of 100 and standard deviation of 15.

Results

Of the 45 states which participated in the survey, only 33 mention one or more of the following types of testing in their descriptions of diagnostic requirements for mental retardation: (a) IQ, (b) adaptive behavior, and (c) achievement, A summary of the types of evaluations employed and number of states that specify cutoff scores for mental retardation for each type of evaluation is included in Table 1.

Of the 33 states that mentioned IQ testing in the diagnosis of mental retardation, 30 states specified particular upper IQ limits. Thirty states mentioned adaptive behavior but only nine specified particular criteria. Only seven states mentioned measured academic achievement as a component in the diagnosis of mental retardation and of the seven, only four specified particular achievement criteria.

Upper IQ limits for AAMD levels and the number of states identifying each of the limits are presented in Table 2. A comparison of the recommended scores for mild retardation and 1973 AAMD guidelines reveals surprising variations. Of the 30 states which specify IQ criteria, only 15 employ the AAMD and P.L. 94–142 recommendation of two standard deviations below the mean or an IQ below 70. Most states deviating from the AAMD criterion suggest IQ cutoff scores above 70 (14 states). Even for those states recommending the higher criteria, there is little agreement. The range in IQ scores for diagnosis of mental retardation among states was 18 with a high of 85 and low of 67.

Fewer states presented IQ criteria for AAMD levels below mild retardation. Only 18 states (40%) presented criteria for moderate mental retardation. Of these, 11 adhered to AAMD guidelines. There was a great deal of variation among the remaining states.

For severe and profound levels of mental retardation, less than 20% of the states specified criteria and all but two states adhered to AAMD criteria.

Discussion

The results of this study reflect the effect of the 1973 AAMD definition on state guidelines mandated by P.L. 94–142. Consistent with the 1973 definition, many states included both measured intelligence (73%) and adaptive behavior (67%) within their mental retardation definitions and/or procedure. Academic achievement, which is not included in the AAMD definition, is infrequently (16%) included in state definitions even though it may be of paramount importance

TABLE 1
NUMBER OF STATES WHICH IDENTIFIED IQ, ADAPTIVE BEHAVIOR AND ACHIEVEMENT IN THEIR DEFINITION OF MENTAL RETARDATION

	Not Mentioned	Mentioned but Criteria not Specified	Criteria Specified	Total
IQ	12 (26.7%)	3 (6.7%)	30 (66.7%)	45
Adaptive Behavior	15 (33.3%)	21 (46.7%)	9 (20 %)	45
Achievement	38 (84.4%)	3 (6.7%)	4 (8.9%)	45

in determining a child's initial referral for testing (President's Commission on Mental Retardation, 1969). In fact, the importance of academic achievement for school children was articulated in the 1973 AAMD manual even though it was not included in the definition.

Most states which mentioned measured intelligence as an essential component of the diagnostic evaluation specified IQ cutoff scores above which a child should not be labeled mentally retarded. However, only a few states delineated cutoff scores indicative of deficits in adaptive behavior. This tendency not to specify criteria for adaptive behavior may be at least partially accounted for by the problems inherent in its measurement. For example, one state specifies that adaptive behavior scores must be in the lower 2% before a child could be identified as mentally retarded (Wisconsin, Chapter 115 1975). However, norm referenced adaptive behavior instruments have been quite rare, and current norm referenced instruments are not as sophisticated as those employed to measure intelligence (Payne and Patton, 1981). Thus even though a criterion is specified, the practical difficulties inherent in measurement are not addressed.

The examination of cutoff scores for IQ demonstrated that states employ varying diagnostic criteria in their definitions of mental retardation. In fact, the majority of states do not adhere to the AAMD guidelines which were incorporated in P.L. 94–142. In general, almost all states that deviate from the AAMD definition use IQ levels which are above those recommended by the AAMD. The propensity of states to employ IQ cutoff scores above the level recommended by the AAMD was also observed by Prout and Sheldon (1983) with regard to vocational guidelines.

The observed variability in states' definitions of mental retardation suggests certain implications. For example, there may be a lack of continuity of services provided mentally retarded children. It is conceivable that a child receiving special educational services in one state may not be eligible for the same services if the family moved to another state. It is also likely that the nature of

TABLE 2
STATES' DESIGNATIONS OF IQ LIMITS FOR LEVELS OF MENTAL RETARDATION

MILD (EMR) [a]70			MODERATE (TMR) [b]55			SEVERE [c]40			PROFOUND [d]25		
IQ	No. of States	%	IQ	No. of States	%	IQ	No. of States	%	IQ	No. of States	%
Not Specified	15	33.3	Not Specified	27	60	Not Specified	37	82.2	Not Specified	38	86.7
85	2	4.4	60	1	2.2	40	6	13.3	40	1	2.2
80	3	6.7	55	11	24.4	35	1	2.2	30	1	2.2
77	2	4.4	50	5	11.1	22	1	2.2	25	5	11.1
76	1	2.2	39	1	2.2		45			45	
75	6	13.3		45							
70	15	33.3									
67	1	2.2									
	45										

[a, b, c, d] 1977 AAMD levels (Wechsler IQs).

classes for educable mentally retarded (EMR) children will differ from state to state. An EMR teacher who moves from a state with an IQ cutoff of 70 to one with an IQ cutoff of 85 will certainly need to adjust his/her curriculum accordingly.

A second implication deals with institutional and political consequences of changing definitions of mental retardation. Blatt (1975) described the inherent problems and consequences of previous redefinitions of mental retardation when he stated:

> The most recent revision of the AAMD definition of mental retardation literally revolutionized the incidence, prevalence, and concept of mental retardation, all with the simple stroke of Herbert Grossman's pen (1973). The Grossman committee, sitting around a conference table, reduced enormously the incidence of mental retardation, never having to "see," or "dose," or deal with a client. (p. 414).

The 1973 definition which was included in P.L. 94–142 lowered the upper IQ limit for mental retardation from 84 to 69. However, according to Hallahan and Kauffman (1982) many educators continued to endorse the somewhat higher IQ cutoff of 75. This bias on the part of educators is reflected in the definitions of mental retardation for six (13%) of the states; these states proposed 75 as the upper IQ cutoff point. Perhaps compatibility between the educational and AAMD definitions may be achieved by the new AAMD definition of mental retardation (Grossman, 1983). The new definition continues to define "significant subaverage intelligence" as an IQ below 70 but emphasizes that this upper limit may be extended upward to 75, or beyond, depending on a variety of test and individual characteristics, especially in school settings (Grossman, 1983).

It appears the time has come for conformity in States' definitions of the handicapping condition of mental retardation. The IQ cutoff of 75 employed by educators is now consistent with the AAMD definition. This cutoff value would be a compromise between the conservative definition published by the AAMD in 1973 and criticized by educators as being too restrictive and the 1959 AAMD definition which could have allowed for up to 16% of the general population to be labeled mentally retarded. State committees currently involved in updating their definitions of mental retardation should be aware of current variations and strive toward a more precise and uniform definition.

References

Blatt, B. (1975). Toward an understanding of people with special needs. In J. M. Kauffman & J. S. Payne (Eds.) *Mental Retardation: Introduction and personal perspectives*. Columbus: Charles Merrill.

Federal Register. August 1977, 42 (163).

Grossman, H. J. (Ed.). (1973). *Manual on terminology and classification in mental retardation*. Washington, DC: American Association on Mental Deficiency.

Grossman, H. J. (Ed.). (1983). *Manual on terminology and classification in mental retardation*. Washington, DC: American Association on Mental Deficiency.

Hallahan, D. P., & Kauffman, J. M. (1982). *Exceptional children*. Englewood Cliffs, NJ: Prentice-Hall.

Meyen, E. (1982). *Exceptional children and youth*. Denver: Love Publishing.

Payne, J. S., & Patton, J. R. (1981). *Mental retardation*. Columbus: Charles Merrill.

President's Committee on Mental Retardation and Bureau of Education of the Handicapped. (1969). *The six-hour retarded child*. Washington, DC: US Government Printing Office.

Prout, H. T., & Sheldon, K. L. (1983). The diagnosis of mental retardation in vocational rehabilitation: State policies and their adherence to AAMD classification guidelines. *Mental Retardation*, 21, 59–62.

Wisconsin. (1975). Rules Implementing Subchapter IV of Chapter 115, Wisconsin Statutes. Bulletin No. 8357.

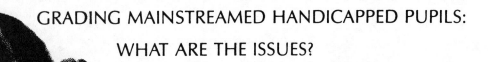

GRADING MAINSTREAMED HANDICAPPED PUPILS:

WHAT ARE THE ISSUES?

Dale Carpenter, Ed.D.
Larry B. Grantham, Ph.D.
Mary P. Hardister, B.S.Ed.
Western Carolina University, North Carolina

Grading mainstreamed handicapped pupils has caused considerable consternation for special and regular educators. Because grading practices relating to handicapped pupils have received little attention, this paper investigates the pertinent issues and gives examples. The major purpose is to avoid the confusion caused by arbitrary grading systems. Graders and consumers must be clearly identified, as must the messages intended by the grades. Choosing satisfactory grading formats is discussed. The issues are generalized to all children, including those without handicaps.

The challenge and demands of mainstreaming handicapped students have been clear in recent years; however, how to assess the progress of these students has not been so well defined. Grading demands much time from teachers, but has been accorded relatively little professional discussion. Few textbooks in special education offer more than a cursory treatment of grading issues or methods. Prospective special educators are seldom provided with a philosophy, theory, or unified procedure with regard to grading exceptional pupils. In this paper, the authors explore the issues in an attempt to bring grading "out of the closet." They attempt to demonstrate that grading practices, as they concern mainstreamed handicapped pupils, may be arbitrary, capricious, unfair, ineffective, and greatly misleading unless fundamental issues have been addressed. The article is intended as a statement of issues, not a statement of recommendation for particular grading policies.

WHAT ARE GRADES?

Terwilliger (1977) has called a grade "a symbol (letter, number, word, etc.) which represents a value judgment concerning the relative quality of a student's achievement of course objectives during a specified period of instruction" (p 22). Unfortunately, a grade doesn't mean the same thing to everyone. There is evidence that different groups perceive grades in conflicting ways (Cassidy, 1977; Hull, 1980; Middleton, 1982; Terwilliger, 1977). The crux of the problem is that each person viewing the grade of a pupil for a given time may perceive a different message than the one intended by the grader. For example, Marty, an EMR student, has worked hard this grading period but has made little progress. Her teacher gives her a B in reading. Marty thinks she should have received an A because she worked so hard. She asks, "What do I have to do to get an A?"

MESSAGES	RECEIVERS			
	Students	Parents	Teacher/Principals, ect.	Post-secondary schools/Employers
Competence				
Progress				
Effort				
Comparison with others				

Figure 1. Matrix of grading messages and receivers.

Marty's mother is pleased and a little surprised that she is making so much progress. Marty's nonhandicapped friend, Judy, remarks, "I got a C and I worked twice as hard as you did. All you have to do is baby work!" Who is right? What was the teacher communicating by the grade? Does it matter what the teacher meant if no one understands it?

WHO READS GRADES?

It is doubtful that any one symbol can communicate the intended message of the grader when a variety of purposes are possible (Terwilliger, 1977). Figure 1 illustrates the complexity of the problem. At least four major groups of consumers, with certain subgroups, look at grades with interest. Students, a primary group, expect grades to reflect something about performance in the class, and it has been shown that the class grade may have some effect on future performance (Yarborough & Johnson, 1980). Parents, the second group, often see grades as their only source of information concerning their offsprings' progress (Cassidy, 1977). School personnel, including teachers, principals, counselors, and others, comprise the third group. They rely on grades to provide them with an academic picture of the student. Finally, grades represent an indication of future performance to post-secondary institutions, such as colleges, trade schools, and potential employers (Middleton, 1982).

WHAT DO GRADES MEAN?

The problem might be drastically reduced if each group perceived grades in the same way. However, grades carry different messages. Usually four purposes, or more, are commonly intended and understood. Some grades are meant to be, or are perceived as, certification of competence or mastery of some sort of skills, knowledge, or abilities. In other words, an A in ninth-grade English might mean the student can read and write well on a ninth-grade level. In certain circumstances grades are intended to be indicators of progress during a period of time. For instance, a grade of A in ninth-grade English may mean that the student demonstrated considerably better skills, knowledge, or abilities at the end of the time than at the beginning. The grade shows that the individual improved. Then there are times when teachers assign grades on the basis of perceived effort. An A might mean only that the student visibly tried, without any statement concerning progress or competence. In this case, results of the effort are not communicated. In other contexts, grades are rankings of a pupil's performance in relation to others. A grade of A in ninth-grade English could mean that the pupil performed at a level higher than did those not receiving an A. Of course some grades are intended to convey a combination of the four major messages. A grade of A may mean that the pupil put forth much effort and showed progress, without regard to competence or comparison with others. On the other hand, a grade of A might mean that the pupil demonstrated mastery of the skill and was superior to others, although without trying or having improved much during the specified time.

This is certainly not an exhaustive list of grading purposes. Grades must also be considered in temporal contexts. The particular timing of certain grades may be messages in themselves. It is a common practice for teachers to attempt to use grades to motivate pupils. One teacher rarely assigns a B or better during the first grading period, reasoning that pupils will have nothing to strive for if they receive top grades the first time. Another teacher may frequently assign a high proportion of top grades during the first marking period to encourage and reward beginning efforts. Both teachers share the goal of improving performance by using grades in opposing ways. It is doubtful that pupils can discern the messages clearly when such diverse methods are employed. Certainly, grades can be intended to—and do— carry a variety of messages.

The four messages of competence, progress, effort, and comparison with others may all be valid, yet the communication vehicle frequently garbles the intent. If one considers that the teacher can intend at least one of four messages, 16 sender-receiver combinations are possible without multiple messages. Only four of these will be matches! It is possible that only 25% of the time will a receiver correctly comprehend the message that the sender intended unless explanations are available. The prospects for confusion and misunderstanding are boggling and frustrating. Imagine Paul Revere peering across the Boston harbor without knowing in advance the meaning of the signal lights! What alarm would have spread had there been three lights that night? Grades will not be useful unless the message intended is the message received.

HOW CAN WE MAKE GRADES CLEAR?

Suppose, then, that the teacher stated clearly that grades in a given class were an indication of competence and nothing else. Suppose, also, that the class had well-defined objectives. What would an A mean? How would it differ from a B? Would the situation be clearer if numbers were used? The problem takes on another dimension. In order for grades to have meaning, the scale or vehicle must effectively carry the consensus messages. In another example, if a pupil receives a 79 in a class where the grade is designed to indicate progress, what would it mean? Although more explanation is usually required, a variety of scales and vehicles are available (Bippus, 1981; Frierson, 1975; Mosier & Park, 1979; Terwilliger, 1977; Turnbull & Schulz, 1979). They range from the traditional letter and number grades to checklist systems, form letters, and other innovative reporting. School systems may attempt to report the messages of competence, progress, effort, and comparison as separate scales for a given class. This attempt could amount to four marks per class. Figure 2 demonstrates an attempt to convey four messages with three marks. In this scheme, *level* attempts to represent competency and comparison with others. A disadvantage of one mark conveying two messages is that competence is a mastery-type statement and comparison with others is a norm-referenced statement. One can tell at what level the pupil is reading, but one cannot be sure how well the student performs at that level in relation to others. The point is this—if a teacher assigns a grade and a receiver (e.g., a parent) understands the intent, it may still be unlikely that a single mark can convey the range of information intended and desired (Cassidy, 1977).

COMPARING PUPILS, GRADES, AND STANDARDS

What happens when a mainstreamed handicapped pupil joins a regular classroom? Is it fair to grade that pupil by the same standards as others? Is it fair *not* to grade that pupil by the same standards as others?

In the case of Marty, the EMR pupil, and her friend, Judy, one can see that Judy may have a valid complaint if she is compared with Marty, particularly if Marty becomes eligible for an award based on her B. Can we compare Marty's B with Judy's C? If Marty and Judy were in different classes, it may be apparent that the work required was not comparable; subsequently, the grades should not be comparable. But if Marty and Judy were in the same class, the issue becomes problematic. One of two or more situations probably exists. Marty and Judy may have different requirements in the class and may not be performing comparable tasks, or Marty and Judy have the same requirements. Neither situation leads to easy answers. Each must be explored further.

If Marty and Judy take the same class and have different requirements, their grades cannot be fairly compared. Unless explanations are provided, the likelihood of comparison by the four major receiver groups is high. Although Marty and Judy are physically in the same class during the same period of time, they are taking different classes with different requirements. It would be impossible to grade them

	Period 1	Period 2	Period 3	
Reading				
Level	3^1	3^2	3^2	3^1 means first half, third grade
Progress	B	C	D	A–F system, C is average
Effort	S	S	U	S is satisfactory U is unsatisfactory

Figure 2.   Report-card sample.

on the same scale. If the teacher reasoned that Judy's requirements were on a higher level than Marty's and that therefore Marty should not be able to earn a grade of more than C, for example, while Judy could possibly earn an A, would the problem be solved? No, since Marty and Judy are not taking the same class and cannot be compared, regardless of the well-intentioned but jerry-rigged handicapping system. The solution is not in comparison but in clearly stating that the objectives and requirements for Marty and Judy are not equivalent. Comparison is inappropriate.

If Marty and Judy take the same class and have the same requirements, it may seem reasonable that their grades should be open for comparison. Yet, mitigating factors may still prevent equitable comparison. Marty's handicap might hinder her ability to perform as well as Judy. She might meet objectives more slowly or with less proficiency. If Marty's handicap is determined to be no factor, they may justifiably be graded equally according to the established policy for grades. If Marty's handicap leads to reduced proficiency, should her ability have an effect on her grade? Should she be evaluated by the same standards as Judy? The answer in this case is in the purpose or message intended by the grades. Each purpose has its own dictates. As has been stated, one mark limits the range of messages that can be communicated. For these reasons, the purpose of each grade should be clearly stated.

Another issue arises when Marty and Judy are in the same class, have almost the same tasks, and perform at equivalent levels; however, Marty is aided by compensatory techniques. For example, she is allowed more time on tests or is given a multiple-choice test instead of filling in blanks. Perhaps Marty is merely given extra coaching in the resource room, but is expected to perform the same tasks in the regular classroom. Two assignments could easily be proposed. One could say that Marty's tasks in these cases are not the same as Judy's and thus the grades cannot be compared. Or one could argue that the difference in tasks is negligible, and that Marty's handicap entitles her to help. Furthermore, it may be argued that if her handicap is effectively compensated for to the point where it allows her to demonstrate proficiency, she should be considered separately and carefully. Each case can only be resolved satisfactorily if the purposes of grades are clearly explained.

IS SEPARATE-BUT-EQUAL FAIR?

These hypothetical examples foreshadow other issues posed by mainstreaming handicapped pupils. Teachers wonder if handicapped pupils should be considered in figuring class rankings upon graduation, because they are so important in decisions concerning admission to college. Some consider handicapped pupils ineligible for membership in honor societies or for other privileges granted on the basis of grades. Weighting classes by difficulty level may be proposed, but a satisfactory scheme is elusive. Whether minimum levels of proficiency in certain classes should be required before awarding credit remains another issue in an endless string of related problems.

Grading handicapped pupils, although troublesome, raises long-standing issues. All teachers, with or without handicapped pupils, are charged with pupils of different abilities. The teacher's mission is to adequately communicate an intended message or messages to the student and others about performance in a given time period. Success in fulfilling the grading mission is dependent upon teacher's understanding of the issues involved.

References

Bippus, S.L. A new look at progress reports. *NASSP Bulletin*, 1981, *65*, 109-111.

Cassidy, J. Reporting pupil progress in reading—parents vs. teachers. *Reading Teacher*, 1977, *31*, 294-296.

Frierson, E. C. *Grading without judgment: A classroom guide to grades and individual evaluation.* Nashville: EDCOA Publications, 1975.

Hull, R. Fairness in grading: Perceptions of junior high school students. *The Clearing House*, 1980, *53*, 340-343.

Middleton, L. Colleges urged to alter tests, grading for the benefit of minority-group students. *The Chronicle of Higher Education,* 1982, 23(21), 1, 10.

Mosier, D. B., & Park, R. B. *Teacher therapist: A text-handbook for teachers of emotionally impaired children.* Santa Monica: Goodyear, 1979.

Terwilliger, J. S. Assigning grades—philosophical issues and practical recommendations. *Journal of Research and Development in Education*, 1977, *10*(3), 21-39.

Turnbull, A. P., & Schulz, J. B. *Mainstreaming handicapped students: A guide for classroom teachers.* Boston: Allyn and Bacon, 1979.

Yarborough, B. H., & Johnson, R. A. How meaningful are marks in promoting growth in reading? *Reading Teacher*, 1980, *33*, 644-651.

PERFORMANCE OF HANDICAPPED STUDENTS IN A COMPETENCY TESTING PROGRAM

Robert C. Serow, Ph.D.
Kathleen O'Brien, M.Ed.
North Carolina State University

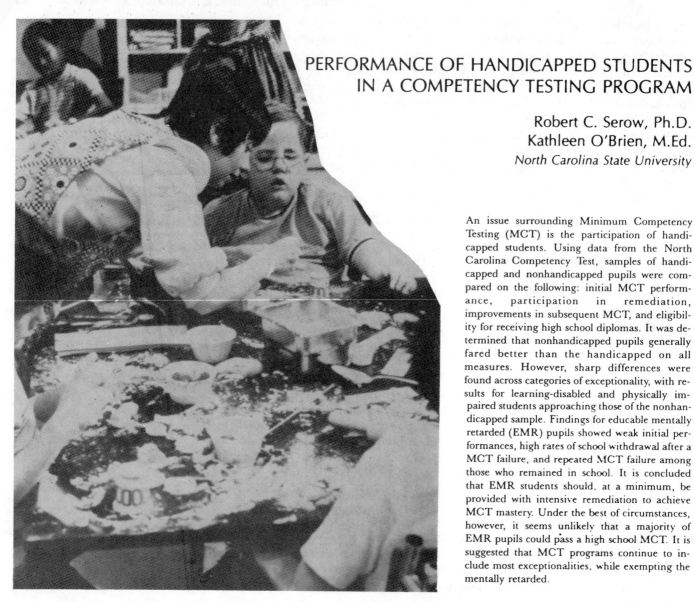

An issue surrounding Minimum Competency Testing (MCT) is the participation of handicapped students. Using data from the North Carolina Competency Test, samples of handicapped and nonhandicapped pupils were compared on the following: initial MCT performance, participation in remediation, improvements in subsequent MCT, and eligibility for receiving high school diplomas. It was determined that nonhandicapped pupils generally fared better than the handicapped on all measures. However, sharp differences were found across categories of exceptionality, with results for learning-disabled and physically impaired students approaching those of the nonhandicapped sample. Findings for educable mentally retarded (EMR) pupils showed weak initial performances, high rates of school withdrawal after a MCT failure, and repeated MCT failure among those who remained in school. It is concluded that EMR students should, at a minimum, be provided with intensive remediation to achieve MCT mastery. Under the best of circumstances, however, it seems unlikely that a majority of EMR pupils could pass a high school MCT. It is suggested that MCT programs continue to include most exceptionalities, while exempting the mentally retarded.

The implementation of Minimum Competency Testing (MCT) in a majority of states has raised questions about the participation of handicapped children. Among the issues involved are the nature and extent of accommodations afforded to exceptional students (Morrissey, 1980), the inclusion of MCT requirements within individual educational plans (Danielson, 1980; Fenton, 1980), and, more generally, the difficulty that schools will have in assuring that pupils attain a given level of performance while also providing for the special needs of the handicapped (Ross & Weintraub, 1980). Perhaps the most fundamental concern centers on the impact that MCT programs will have on the long-term educational and economic prospects of handicapped individuals. As suggested by Ewing and Smith (1981), the requirement of some states that high school diplomas be denied to MCT failers is likely to have a stronger adverse effect on exceptional children than on their nonhandicapped peers. To date, little evidence on this issue has been reported. Initial concern over the consequences of high failure rates among handicapped students in Florida may be unwarranted, as Grise (1980) has noted, since most handicapped students are exempted from participation in that state's MCT. On the whole, therefore, it is uncertain whether MCT will have the negative consequences for handicapped students that have been forecast.

The purpose of the present paper is to report findings on the participation of exceptional students in one statewide MCT program that does carry a diploma-

"Performance of Handicapped Students In A Competency Testing Program," Robert C. Serow, Kathlenn O'Brien, *The Journal of Special Education*, Vol. 17, No. 2, Summer 1983. Copyright 1983 by the Buttonwood Farms, Inc.

denial provision and that exempts only a small proportion of the handicapped population. Specifically, we will compare both the processes and outcomes of the North Carolina MCT for samples of handicapped and nonhandicapped students, in order to show what is being done for both groups and what the consequences of MCT participation may be.

THE NORTH CAROLINA COMPETENCY TEST

The major goal of the North Carolina MCT is "to assure that all high school graduates possess those minimum skills and that knowledge thought to be necessary to function as a member of society" (N.C. House Bill 204, Chapter 522, 1977). As is true in most MCT programs, North Carolina assesses proficiency in language and computation skills among high school students. The tests used are TOPICS (math) and SHARP (reading), both published by CTB/McGraw-Hill. Each exam consists of 120 items, with cutoff scores of 87 and 77 correct answers in reading and math, respectively. Students are initially tested in the fall semester of 11th grade, and if unsuccessful, receive remediation and as many as three additional opportunities to demonstrate the specified level of mastery prior to graduation. Students who are unable to pass both sections receive a certificate of attendance in lieu of a diploma. After high school, individuals may take the test as many as six times, until their 21st birthday.

In contrast to some other states, North Carolina requires the participation of the majority of its handicapped pupils. For instance, while Florida exempts the mentally retarded, emotionally handicapped, learning disabled, and hearing impaired, (Grise, 1980), only the trainably and severely retarded are exempted from the North Carolina MCT. In the cases of handicapped children whose parents request an exemption, students receive only the certificate of attendance upon graduation. Test adaptations for the handicapped include provision of audiocassettes, large print, extended test periods, and other physical modifications, rather than adjustments in performance standards. On the whole, the adaptations appear to be equivalent to those used in other states (Amos, 1980).

PROCEDURES

The data reported here were collected during the first three semesters of the North Carolina MCT (fall 1978 to fall 1979). In order to attain a sample reasonably representative of the statewide test-taking population, school districts in various types of communities throughout North Carolina were invited to participate. Five systems agreed to do so. However, data from one district were not of sufficient quality to be included in this report. The final sample, totaling 1,760 students, consisted of the entire class of 1980 in one metropolitan high school and in each of three rural districts. When compared with statewide enrollments, handicapped, minority, and rural students are somewhat overrepresented in the present sample. Overall, however, MCT performances for this sample generally approached the statewide results.

Data were gathered from two sources. During each semester, participating schools provided information on the average weekly amount of remediation received in reading and/or math by each pupil who had failed one or both sections of the previous MCT, and on the type of instructional format (individualized, small group, large group, combination, other, or none) used. In addition, data on students' background characteristics (including exceptionality) and MCT results were provided by the North Carolina Department of Public Instruction.

ANALYSES AND RESULTS

The MCT experiences which will be compared for handicapped and nonhandicapped pupils include initial performance, participation in remediation, results of subsequent testing, and eligibility for receiving a high school diploma. Table 1 shows that while the participation of most nonhandicapped pupils began and ended with their successful performance on the first exam, a majority of the handicapped failed on their first attempt. However, results differed sharply among categories of exceptionality, with passing rates among the learning disabled (LD) and "other handicapped" (OH) (mainly physically impaired) students greatly exceeding those of the educable mentally retarded (EMR). Thus, the sample of handicapped MCT-failers considered in the next several analyses consists overwhelmingly of EMR pupils.

Upon failing the MCT, students are entitled to receive remediation in the subject area(s) in which they have demonstrated deficiency. While funding and broad guidelines for remediation are provided by North Carolina, the amounts and type of instruction actually received vary according to school resources and individual interests and needs. On the whole however, we would expect that relatively intensive programs of remediation would be offered to pupils who fared especially badly on the initial MCT, including a majority of the present sample of handicapped students. Table 2 breaks down remedial participation in spring 1979 (the period after the first MCT, in which the greatest number of students were remediated) according to pupil classification. To facilitate comparisons, the handicapped and nonhandicapped samples are subdivided into high-, medium-, and low-failing, according to the margins by which a pupil failed the reading and/or math sections of the initial exam. Results indicate that exceptional students in the high- and medium-fail categories received more intensive reading remediation than did their nonhandicapped counterparts, while differences among low-failers were minimal. However, the low-failing group (in which most of the handicapped sample was located) averaged less than 2 hours of reading instruction per week, a figure well

TABLE 1
PASSING RATE ON FIRST MCT, BY EXCEPTIONALITY

Classification	N	% Passing
Nonhandicapped	1652	80.5
Handicapped	108	27.7
EMR	56	3.5
LD	37	51.3
OH (other)	15	60.0
Total	1760	77.3

below that of the high- and medium-failers. Analyses of variance indicated significant effects for handicap status, level of performance, and interaction of these two variables. In math, roughly equal amounts of remediation were offered to both classifications and to all three performance levels. No significant main or interactive effects were found. Separate analyses (not presented here) were also conducted on the types of remedial formats (individualized, small group, large group, combination, other, and none) used for each subsample. Handicapped and normal students were found to be remediated in about the same ways, with two minor exceptions: The latter were somewhat more likely to receive no remediation at all, while the former were more frequently offered instruction in groups rather than individually.

A third issue is the change in students' academic skills that occurs during the course of MCT. As has been noted elsewhere, the primary goal of MCT programs is the improvement of language and computational skills among marginal pupils to at least a minimally acceptable level (Haney & Madaus, 1978). In the present instance, interest centers on the degree of improvement shown by handicapped students, relative to that of their normal peers. The data presented in Table 3 show raw-score gains (increases in the number of correct answers) from the first to the third tests. As can be seen, improvements were registered by both groups. In the case of reading, the gains were virtually identical, while the average math improvement of the nonhandicapped slightly exceeded that of the exceptional students. Overall, these data indicate that both groups improved their initial scores in each subject area by about 20%. However, the similarity in raw-score gains does not

TABLE 2
AVERAGE WEEKLY HOURS OF READING AND MATH REMEDIATION (SPRING 1979),
BY FIRST MCT AND EXCEPTIONALITY

Group	Remedial hours (N)	
	Reading	Math
Handicapped		
High-fail	3.7 (6)	2.0 (6)
Medium-fail	3.9 (13)	3.1 (9)
Low-fail	1.8 (35)	2.7 (44)
Total	2.5 (54)	2.7 (59)
Nonhandicapped		
High-fail	2.3 (59)	2.9 (77)
Medium-fail	2.3 (65)	3.2 (102)
Low-fail	1.9 (27)	3.0 (67)
Total	2.2 (151)	3.1 (246)
	F	
	Reading	Math
Exceptionality	5.4*	1.0
Performance	3.3*	1.1
Exceptionality × performance	3.4*	0.3

*$p < .05$.

mean that similar proportions of each group were approaching the requisite level of competence. While the mean scores of the normal students were within 10 points of passing on each section of MCT 3, the handicapped sample was still answering only about half of all items correctly, and so remained far behind.

These disparities are further evidenced in the outcomes of the MCT program summarized in Table 4. As of the conclusion of the third testing, most of the non-handicapped, LD, and OH were eligible for a high school diploma. This was not true of the EMR students, who had for the most part either failed all three exams or dropped out of school after a previous MCT failure. Although we are not able to report the results of the final exam that took place immediately prior to graduation, it can be assumed that some pupils passed on their fourth attempt. However, it is also probable that the number who actually did so was very small, inasmuch as failure rates have been found to increase sharply with each successive exam (Serow, Davies, & Parramore, in press). Therefore, we surmise that the majority of students listed here as failing were denied a high school diploma at graduation.

TABLE 3
MEAN SCORES, MCT 1 AND MCT 3, BY EXCEPTIONALITY

Classification (N)	MCT 1	MCT 3	Change
		Reading	
Handicapped (35)	52.0	63.6	+ 11.6
Nonhandicapped (55)	68.3	79.8	+ 11.5
		Math	
Handicapped (39)	45.7	55.4	+ 9.7
Nonhandicapped (60)	54.2	67.3	+ 13.1

Note. Passing scores are 87 for reading and 77 for math; Each section consists of 120 items.

CONCLUSION

While the experiences of one small sample of students in the North Carolina MCT are not necessarily representative of performances and outcomes of students elsewhere, the results reinforce concerns about the participation of exceptional students in MCT programs. To reiterate the major findings, it was determined that handicapped pupils in general, and the EMR in particular, fared less well than did nonhandicapped students. More precisely, handicapped students scored lower on the initial exam, more frequently withdrew from school after an MCT failure, and were less likely to attain the requisite level of academic mastery prior to graduation. Thus, the negative consequences seemed to fall disproportionately on the handicapped, and most heavily of all on the EMR. This is true not only of the present sample but of the statewide population as well, as figures from the North Carolina Department of Public Instruction have indicated that of all attendance certificates awarded in lieu of high school diplomas in 1980, 62% were received by pupils classified as EMR. In light of this evidence, it is reasonable to ask whether EMR students benefit in any meaningful way from their MCT participation. Several answers to this question may be possible. On the positive side, previous analyses of this data set have found that handicapped pupils were most likely to attain a passing score on a retest when they received intensive remediation, on the order of 5 or more hours per week (Serow, O'Neal, & Barnes, 1981). However, there is also reason to believe that exceptional students do not always receive such concentrated remediation. Recall, for example, that most of the handicapped sample placed in the very lowest sector of the MCT score distribution, and that this low-scoring group received the least remedial assistance in reading during the spring 1979 semester (Table 2). It would seem obvious that if exceptional pupils are to be included in MCT programs, they must be provided with the instructional resources needed to boost them to the level required for receipt of the diploma. On

TABLE 4
MCT OUTCOMES (AS OF JANUARY 1980), BY EXCEPTIONALITY

Classification	Passing		Failing (3 MCTs)		Failed/ withdrew		Total
	N	%	N	%	N	%	
Nonhandicapped	1515	91.70	56	3.39	81	4.90	1652
Handicapped	46	42.59	36	33.33	26	24.07	108
EMR	6	10.71	29	51.79	21	37.50	56
LD	29	78.38	4	10.81	4	10.81	37
OH (other)	11	73.33	3	20.00	1	6.66	15
Total	1561	88.70	92	5.20	107	6.00	1760

the other hand, there remains the larger question of whether MCT is an appropriate vehicle for identifying and remediating those academic deficiencies associated with certain types of exceptionality. In the case of students whose handicap does not entail a basic inability to perform at or near grade level, MCT may be useful. Thus, sample members classified as LD or OH (again, mainly physically impaired) performed nearly as well as did their nonhandicapped counterparts. However, mental retardation seems quite a different matter, as it is a classification applied only to students who have significant permanent deficiencies in academic and certain other skills. In view of findings for the present sample and for the statewide North Carolina population (N.C. Department of Public Instruction, 1981), it seems reasonable to conclude that most EMR pupils are not able to attain the requisite level of competence even when using maximum remedial and testing opportunities prior to graduation. If this is true, then the forced participation of EMR students in MCT programs may be not only pointless from an academic standpoint, but even harmful to their social and psychological development. Previous research has found that while demonstration of academic competence by retarded students can build self-acceptance and acceptance by peers, demonstrations of academic deficiency may reinforce stigma and set exceptional students apart from their classmates (Gottlieb, Semmel, & Veldman, 1978).

Various alternatives to comprehensive MCT of the handicapped have been suggested elsewhere and include separate (and lower) test standards for exceptional pupils and determination of competency on the basis of successful completion of the individual educational plan (Ross & Weintraub, 1980). Another option would be the exemption of nearly all categories of exceptionality, as is currently the practice in Florida. However, in light of the findings of successful performance by most members of this sample who are LD or whose primary impairment is physical, such sweeping exemptions may not be necessary if there are appropriate modifications in testing environments and formats. Instead, perhaps the fairest and most realistic policy would be to exempt only those students classified as mentally retarded. Unless states come to acknowledge the disadvantages of including EMR students within MCT programs, it can be anticipated that the negative consequences of such programs will continue to fall disproportionately on the retarded.

References

Amos, K. Competency testing: Will the LD student be included? *Exceptional Children,* 1980, *47,* 194–197.

Danielson, L. Educational goals and competency testing for the handicapped. In R. Jaeger & C. Tittle (Eds.), *Minimum competency achievement testing.* Berkeley: McCutchan, 1980.

Ewing, N., & Smith, J. Minimum competency testing and the handicapped. *Exceptional Children,* 1981, *47,* 523–524.

Fenton, K. Competency testing and the handicapped. Some legal concerns for school administrators. In R. Jaeger & C. Tittle (Eds.), *Minimum competency achievement testing.* Berkeley: McCutchan, 1980.

Gottlieb, J., Semmel, M., & Veldman, D. Correlates of social status among mainstreamed mentally retarded children. *Journal of Educational Psychology,* 1978, *70,* 396–405.

Grise, P. Florida's minimum competency testing program for handicapped students. *Exceptional Children,* 1980, *47,* 186–191.

Haney, W., & Madaus, G. Making sense of the competency testing movement. *Harvard Educational Review,* 1978, *48,* 462–484.

Morrissey, P. Adaptive testing: How and when should handicapped students be accommodated in competency testing programs? In R. Jaeger & C. Tittle (Eds.), *Minimum competency achievement testing.* Berkeley: McCutchan, 1980.

North Carolina Department of Public Instruction. *Report of student performance: Class of 1980 and class of 1981.* Raleigh, N.C.: Author, 1981.

Ross, J., & Weintraub, F. Policy approaches regarding the impact of graduation requirements on handicapped students. *Exceptional Children,* 1980, *47,* 200–203.

Serow, R., Davies, J., & Parramore, B. Performance gains in a competency testing program. *Educational Evaluation and Policy Analysis,* in press.

Serow, R., O'Neal, C., & Barnes, N. *Competency testing in North Carolina: Remediation and subsequent test performances.* ERIC Clearinghouse on Teacher Education, February, 1981. (ERIC Document Reproduction Service No. ED 194 458).

Programs for the Mentally Handicapped

The limitations of EMR individuals must be recognized if the children are to progress. EMR children are not capable of learning at the same rate as normal children. Their abstract reasoning abilities are curtailed, as are their abilities to understand complicated game rules. This disability causes the EMR child to have difficulty reacting in group play. Recognition of limitations, however, must also contain recognition of possibilities for growth. The EMR can learn many things; they can learn to read, write, do simple arithmetic problems, and learn to socially "fit" into a classroom and the surrounding community.

Trainable mentally handicapped/retarded (TMR) individuals are capable of self-care, adjustment to the home or neighborhood, and economic usefulness in the home, a sheltered workshop of an institution. TMR individuals will never achieve academic success, but with proper programming and education, they can become useful citizens. The programming that works best for the TMR population is life-skill instruction and vocational education.

The purpose of a trainable program is to provide an environment in which the TMR individual can be evaluated and trained for employment in a sheltered workshop or private industry. The objectives of such a program are, first to determine the potential for occupational training, then to develop those skills necessary for employment i.e., punctu-ality, regular attendance, following directions, and completing assigned tasks. The program tries to teach "getting along" with co-workers and finding employment situations for the student. Positive programming should help TMR individuals to make the most of their abilities; to help them make a transition to the real world of work and community and to benefit society and themselves. Since severely and profoundly retarded are for the most part unable to care for themselves, they must receive constant care at home or in an institution. Their programming involves training in the most basic aspects of self-help tasks. In the past, the profoundly retarded were hidden away in institutions, with nothing provided but the basics required to sustain life. The present situation is greatly improved. Children with measureable I.Q.'s in the 0 to 30 range are capable of learning. Constant and loving care must be provided and the tasks must be broken down into their smallest steps. When the proper environment is provided, many of the severely retarded are able to learn basic communication skills, and basic self-care skills. The training must be constant, and the trainer must be a person who truly loves the work. Many of the causes of mental retardation are still unknown, and even when the cause has been determined, there is usually no way to correct the defect. Only with the introduction of better programs and the continued efforts of talented teachers will the lives and futures of handicapped individuals continue to improve.

MATH STRATEGY FOR MH CHILDREN

A simple technique requiring few materials is effective in teaching simple addition to mildly handicapped children.

Walter N. Creekmore
Nancy N. Creekmore

Walter N. Creekmore, PhD, is on the faculty of the Department of Special Education, 230 Strauss Hall, Northeast Lousiana University, Monroe, LA 71209. Nancy N. Creekmore, PhD, is on the staff of the G.B. Cooley Hospital for Retarded Citizens, West Monroe, LA 71291.

"The math workbooks just don't work with my kids!"

"I can teach them anything unless it's math—then forget it!"

"I know I'm supposed to be teaching my students how to add, but I just don't seem to be getting through to them."

These statements are not unique to just one school. They seem to be echoed far and wide. Out of the protracted concern over the dismal results experienced by many teacher of the learning disabled when they attempted to teach math to their students, we created, with the help of a public school education teacher, a simple aid for the mildly handicapped. The results, reported in *Academic Therapy's* March 1981 issue, were gratifying. Because of the interest shown in this approach by more than 200 professionals in the field, we decided to conduct additional research into the effectiveness of the aid with other handcapping conditions.

The literature is replete with material that attempts to compare and contrast the learning characteristics of the mildly handicapped. This classification has included the mildly mentally retarded, the mildly learning disabled, and the mildly emotionally disturbed. It has been suggested that these three categories of students possess many more common than unique learning and behavioral characteristics. If, for the sake of argument, this is true, then the possibility exists that strategies and aids created to remediate learning difficulties with one population might prove equally effective with another similar population. This possibility prompted us to research the effectiveness of the "Add Card Math Strategy" with mildly mentally retarded children.

This article deals with one area of arithmetic instruction – specifically, simple addition – used with mildly mentally retarded children. As is the case with all children, and especially with the mildly retarded, arithmetic instruction is given to develop well defined, dependable methods for solving number-related problems. (Payne, Palloway, Smith and Payne 1981).

Developmental Considerations and Problems

In many cases, mildly retarded students show difficulty in learning functional addition. Research by Rudolph Wagner (1981) finds this true with other mildly handicapped groups as well. Piaget has suggested that in order for any child to master addition, he must understand the concept of reversibility of thought (ex: from whole to parts to whole again) (Creekmore 1981).

It is known and accepted that mentally retarded learners possess functional difficulties with short term memory, manipulation of abstraction, and generalization of concept abilities. For that reason, we applied the math strategy developed for learning disabled students to mildly mentally retarded elementary-level students.

With a randomly selected heterogeneous group of mildly retarded elementary level children chosen from four school districts, the "Add Card Math Strategy" was introduced to 90 students. To determine if difference existed between numbers of correct math answers derived by the sample, total mean responses for the population were compared between solutions attempted without the use of the "Add Card" and with the use of the aid. Mean correct responses for the unaided attempt was 3.60 with a standard deviation of 1.21. A one-tailed correlated t-test was computed. The results of the t-test revealed statistically significant differences between the means ($t_d(19) = 6.672$; 9 .001). (The intent of the simple analysis was to support the effectiveness of the strategy rather than to suggest that this is a research article.) In an attempt to establish some measure of reliability of performance using the device, repetitive sessions have been conducted which replicate the accuracy performance of the mentally retarded children over time. The strategy appears to aid the mildly mentally retarded child in simple addition functions as much as it did with the mildly learning disabled students evaluated previously.

In addition to simple increases noticed in the study, it was apparent that the children were demonstrating more assertive behaviors as they related to math. Documentation included incidents of children asking for their "Add Cards" as they entered the room first thing in the morning and carrying them on their person throughout the day. They also asked their teacher to aid them in the construction of a "take-home" copy of the aid, which was done. Utilization of the aid was facilitated by the teacher's sizing all addition related activities so that the aid could easily be used by the child if so desired. This contributed greatly to the generalization of the skill.

Because of the major learning problem associated with difficulties in short-term memory in the mentally retarded, many aided strategies have fallen short of their marks. Early data suggest that, because of the simplicity of this operation along with the concrete manipulation aspects that is built in, the child is more likely to be able to reduce the vital information into a critical nucleus and disregard that which is unnecessary. This being so, the child uses a smaller chain of critical information and can process it and retrieve it more efficiently. This should aid in long term retention of newly acquired material until it can be accommodated into the child's body of usable knowledge.

Antecedents to the "Add-Card" Addition Strategy

- Enough concrete objects available for addition work to be done—located on the work table
- "Add-Card" available for use (laminated if possible)
- Page of addition problems arranged to fit the "Add-Card" accurately
- Pencil available for recording the concluded sum

Basic number facts must be taught prior to the use of this aid.

FIGURE 1

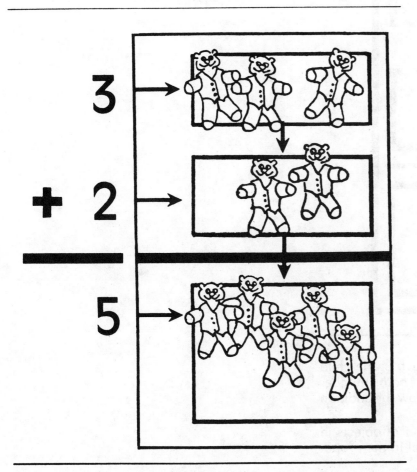

Use of the "Add-Card"

The "Add-Card" (see Figure 1) can be placed on a small index card and arranged size-wise to match the physical size of the addition problems used by individual teachers. It is important that the arrows on the "Add-Card" be aligned with the appropriate addends and sum space in the problem.

1. The child places the "Add-Card" next to and in line with the addition problem on his worksheet. Next, the child places the available counting objects within easy reach and in clear sight

2. The child then calls the name of the "top" addend, selects the proper number of counting objects to represent that numeral, and places them in the number block (see Figure 2).

3. Step two is repeated by the child for the second addend, placing the collected number of objects in the middle number block.

FIGURE 2

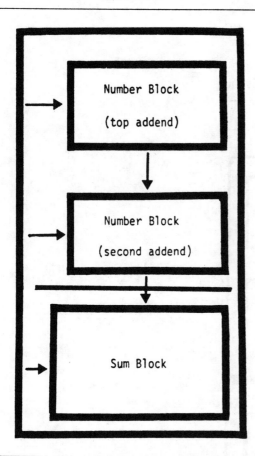

---

4. After completion of steps 1 through 3, the child moves all counting objects in *both* number blocks down to the *sum block* below the addition line.

5. The child now counts the number of objects in the sum block and writes his total in the proper location on the work sheet.

6. The child may wish to recheck answers audibly for accuracy. This may be done by counting the objects aloud and checking the counted number against the written answer.

7. Finally, the child removes all counting objects from the "Add-Card" and positions the "Add-Card" appropriately beside the next problem. The procedure is repeated.

Tips for the Teacher

In our dealings with this strategy and its application to the mildly handicapped, we have found it useful to consider the following:

—Have the "Add-Card" drawn on a card which is the favorite color of the student who will "own" it.

—Laminate the card so that it will last longer.

—For those students who are visually impaired, outline the *blocks* with automobile penstriping tape that will stand away from the card and give tactile clues. This tape comes in various colors and is easy to work with.

—Encourage the students to use the strategy at home for practical exercises as well as "maintenance" exercises.

—Consider the possibility of supplying a home copy of the "Add-Card" equipped with a lariet for hanging.

The "Add-Card" addition strategy can eventually be abbreviated, allowing the child to use counting objects only in the first number block and to write the actual numeral in the second number block. The sum block will be completed with the correct numeral only. Finally, this method can be enhanced, especially with the mentally retarded, with a data jamming strategy known as cognitive behavior modification. Other variations on the basic "Add-Card" theme will make this teaching aid more functional for use with the mentally retarded and other mildly handicapped students.

It appears that the strategy has some usefulness when used with learning disabled and mildly mentally handicapped children at the elementary school level. The flexibility and concrete nature of the aid allow for modifications that can be adapted by the classroom teacher to make it more functional.

References

Berdine, W.H. & Cagelaka, P.T. 1980. *Teaching the trainable retarded.* Columbus, OH: Charles E. Merrill.

Copeland, R.W. 1972. *How children learn mathematics:* Teaching implications of Piaget's research. New York: MacMillan.

Creekmore, W.N. 1981. Add Card: Math strategy for L.D. children: *Academic Therapy,* 17:2, pp 141-145.

Creekmore, W.N. The relationship between development of visual preference and selected affective responses in normal infants (Doctoral dissertation, University of North Carolina at Chapel Hill, 1979). Dissertation Abstracts International, 1980, 40, 4523A. (University Microfilms No. 80-05, 027).

Lloyd, J. 1980. Academic instruction and cognitive behavior modification: The need for attack strategy training. *Exceptional Education Quarterly,* 1.

Meichelbaum, D. 1980. Cognitive behavior modification with exceptional children: A promise yet unfilled. *Exceptional Education Quarterly,* 1.

Wagner, R.F. 1981. Remediating common math errors. *Academic Therapy,* 16:4, pp 449-453.

SEX EDUCATION FOR MENTALLY RETARDED PERSONS

R. E. C. PENNY   **J. E. CHATAWAY**
Department of Psychology
University of Adelaide

This paper is a report of an evaluation of a sex education programme conducted by the Family Planning Association of South Australia at some South Australian workshops and training centres for mentally retarded persons. Sex knowledge was pre-tested and post-tested, before and after the educational programme, using a sex vocabulary test especially designed for this evaluation. Subjects were post-tested twice, at less than a week and at about two months after the conclusion of the programme. The results support the conclusion that the programme was efficacious but methodological problems prevent us from concluding that the educational programme, as such, was solely responsible for the increases in sex knowledge. It is suggested that, in addition, the small group teaching situation may have facilitated the sharing of sex information among group members. This seems likely as sex knowledge continued to increase for some time after the completion of the educational programme.

"Normalization", when used with reference to mentally retarded persons, is the point of view which emphasizes that attempts should be made, through treatment and the provision of services, to make the lives of the mentally retarded as much as possible like those of non-retarded persons. The development of these ideas began in Denmark 20 years ago (Attwell and Jamison, 1977) and appeared in Sweden in legislation as recently as 1969. It has been observed (Attwell and Jamison, 1977) that normalization is hindered by the fears of the parents of mentally retarded persons and of others responsible for their well-being concerning their sexual activities.

In recent years, the sexuality of mentally retarded people has become a subject of increased attention, both among persons in the helping professions who work with mentally retarded persons and among the general public. This increased interest coincides with the widespread realization that the needs of mentally retarded persons to express themselves as fully as possible in most aspects of living are similar to those of non-retarded persons. Gordon (1973) has emphasized that all human beings have sexual needs whether or not they are mentally retarded. These sexual needs exist in children and continue into old age. The changes which take place in the body at puberty in response to hormonal changes and the associated increase in awareness of erotic feelings and fantasies provide major sources of sexual information for mentally retarded people, just as they do for other human beings. Most children pick up information about sex within the home, from peers, and in the classroom (Sengstock, cited by Vockell and Mattick, 1972). However, while retarded persons, like the non-retarded, are confronted with a variety of sexual stimuli and experiences (Gordon, 1975; Cameron, 1976) their sources of information may be somewhat different from those of non-retarded persons, especially if they live within an institution. Thus, results of a study (Gebhardt, 1973) concerned with the sources of information of 84 white male residents of institutions for retarded persons (including prisons) revealed that most residents named their institutionalized peers as their sources of information. Only five named a parent and none named a teacher or clincian.

In a sense, a mentally retarded youth should be better informed about sexual matters than the average young person, so that "he or she will not be caught off guard, made fun of, or considered (at best) naive" (Gordon, 1975, p. 103). It has also been noted (Wagner, 1974; Gordon, 1975) that, in addition to being fully informed about the emotional and reproductive parts of sex, it is essential, that young people generally also understand the language of the street. If they are not so informed they may continue to be ignorant or "hear half truths, myths or distortions that can cause great suffering" (Wagner, cited by Cameron, 1976, p. 149). There would seem to be no reason why this proposition should not be extended to include mentally retarded young people. However, sex education for mentally retarded persons requires special consideration since, as emphasized by Sengstock (cited by Vockell and Mattick, 1972), with the retarded person even more than with the non-retarded, what is learnt in childhood is likely to persist, unlearning or inhibition is hard to induce, and that therefore proper early training is of great importance. Furthermore, according to Robinson and Robinson (1965), mentally retarded children do not readily generalize from one situation to another. Thus, special help will be necessary to help them transfer what they know to new situations. In the absence of appropriate early training it is possible that major problems will develop.

Possible deficiencies in the social adjustment of retarded persons may also pose special problems for the sex education of such people. Thus, Meyers, Walden, Moran, Gardner, Showalter, Levi and Phillips (1971) have noted that differences in adjustment which exist between young people of normal intelligence and those who are mentally retarded introduce a particular difficulty experienced by the mentally retarded young person who meets with repeated failure in the school. A retarded person may turn to sexual activities which may be perceived as a more likely source of social success. Rosen (1972) has observed that another complicating problem lies in the probability that many retarded persons spend much of their lives in isolation from others. As a result, retarded persons tend to be unaware of the effect they have on others, indicating their difficulty in generalizing from experience with the opposite sex so that a wide range of socializing behaviours and resulting self-assurance are absent. Results of a review of 250 individual cases of retarded persons who had returned from institutional to independent living (Rosen, Floor, and Baxter, 1971) revealed five personality and behavioural characteristics showing poor adjustment to the new circumstances: low self-esteem; helpless, dependent behaviour and inability to cope with emergency situations; overly compliant or acquiescent behaviour; socially inappropriate or bizarre behaviour; and deficits in heterosexual functioning.

A number of studies of existing sex knowledge and attitudes of retarded persons (independent of any training programme) are of interest. The results from a sex knowledge questionnaire presented to 66 non-institutionalized retarded adolescents and 105 institutionalized retarded adolescents (Hall and Morris, 1976) showed that while both groups could identify what masturbation, menstruation, sexual intercourse, and pregnancy were, less than half of the subjects in both groups could identify what venereal disease, family planning, and birth control were. Only a very small percentage knew about the purposes or procedures of sterilization.

Fischer and Krajicek (1974) interviewed 16 trainable retarded children (aged 10 to 17) with IQs ranging from 33 to 57. Parents of the children watched the questioning of their children's awareness of sex through a one-way vision screen. The purpose was to ascertain the children's general level of interest and knowledge about sexual identification, bodily parts and functions, emotional functioning, and pregnancy. Fischer and Krajicek found that the children's range of awareness and level of functioning were considerable. They also found the children were interested in learning more, including unfamiliar terms and concepts; and that parents had not suspected the high level of knowledge and interest demonstrated by their retarded children.

Hall, Morris, and Barker (1973) assessed 61 non-institutionalized retarded adolescent subjects using a structured multiple choice questionnaire (knowledge) and true/false attitude statements (sex and self concept) while the parents were asked to answer the same questions as if their children were answering. Results of this procedure showed that whereas parents could predict accurately their child's total number of responses on knowledge and self concept, they could not predict their child's sexual attitude: they judged their children to be significantly more "puritanical" with regard to sexual behaviour than they actually were.

Some authorities on sex education (Fischer and Krajicek, 1974) feel there has been insufficient emphasis on *eliciting* responses from retarded persons. A sex education guide has been developed by Fischer and Krajicek for use with mildly and moderately retarded persons. (The use of the terms "mildly retarded" and "moderately retarded", with IQ ranges 50/55 to 75/80 and 25/35 to 50/55, respectively, has been advocated by the American Association for Mental Deficiency, see Robinson and Robinson, 1976.) The guide involves a series of sexually oriented pictures about which the individual is asked various prescribed questions. Using similar techniques, Edmondson and Wish (1975) have shown that although their sample of institutionalized retarded males gained some understanding of human anatomy and sexual activity, the concepts were "rife with error and misinformation". It was also shown that the outcomes of tests of body terminology do not necessarily indicate comprehension of sexual activity.

Few evaluations of sex education programmes for mentally retarded persons have been carried out. It has been pointed out (Hall, 1974) that there is a need, not for more evidence of the need for sex education for retarded persons, but for the development of teaching methodologies and for sex education assessment methods.

The aim of the present study was to evaluate the effectiveness of a programme of sex education for mentally retarded persons, conducted by the Family Planning Association of South Australia.

Method

Subjects

The 49 subjects in this study were drawn from three South Australian institutions (workshops and training centres) for mentally retarded persons. Forty-four of the subjects were mildly retarded and five moderately retarded. There were 21 female subjects (age $\overline{X} = 22$, SD = 4.6) and 28 males (age $\overline{X} = 22$, SD = 6.6). It should be noted that the subjects were selected by the institutions' supervisors from among those who were considered capable of taking part in and benefitting from a sex education programme.

For the teaching sessions (see below), subjects were divided into eight small groups of from five to eight members. All groups contained both sexes. It should also be noted that group composition was determined by the institutional staff and that no consideration had been given to the selection of control groups.

The sex education programme

Each group received six teaching sessions, one each week, each session lasting from one and a half to two hours. Throughout the programme, strong emphasis was placed on the human relationship context of sex activity. Each of the six sessions focused on a particular topic, as follows:
(1) the body, with emphasis on adolescent development and the noticeable anatomical differences between the sexes;
(2) human reproduction and foetal development;
(3) personal relationships and sexual responsiblity;
(4) male and female roles, particularly in the home;
(5) planning for parenthood, and contraception;
(6) venereal disease.
Group discussion was encouraged and a large part of the instruction was provided on a one-to-one basis between the teacher and particular individuals within the group whenever this need arose, the remaining group members learning through listening and observation. The teachers were careful to involve other members in the discussion wherever possible and questions were encouraged. Diagrams and lifesized models were used to illustrate anatomical parts and large sheets of paper and crayons were used freely by group members to convey their understanding of what was being taught. A major aim at all times was to promote a relaxed and enjoyable atmosphere.

The Sex Vocabulary Test

The primary data collection technique used in this study was an especially constructed sex vocabulary test (SVT). Copies of this test are available from the authors. A pilot study based on a questionnaire devised by Kempton and Forman (1976) using a true/false forced choice procedure suggested that questions of this type did not provide maximum opportunity for subjects to supply information and proved, at times, to be confusing to them. The following is an example which demonstrates difficulties encountered in the forced choice situation. The question: "Semen and sperm are words used for the same substance (True or False?)" may have been "incorrectly" answered as true yet the subject may have possessed some useful knowledge concerning sperm or semen. For example, the subject may have been aware that sperm were produced by the male testes or that both were emitted during sexual intercourse or masturbation.

It also became apparent during the pilot study that mentally retarded persons usually gave very brief, two or three word replies and that without prompting the reply was not extended. Through prompting it often emerged that subjects possessed more knowledge than had at first appeared. For example, if the subject were asked: "Will you tell me what you know about the penis?" a likely reply was of the form: "The man has it". With prompting, further relevant information was likely to be forthcoming.

The 30 words included in the SVT were contained in material actually taught in the programme. They were:

1. Fertilization	16. Penis
2. Clitoris	17. Vagina
3. Menstruation	18. Sexual intercourse
4. Condom	19. Uterus
5. Ovary	20. Wet dreams
6. Ovum	21. Masturbation
7. Sperm	22. Homosexual
8. Semen	23. Lesbian
9. The pill	24. Contraceptive
10. V.D.	25. Safe period
11. Vasectomy	26. Orgasm
12. Tubal ligation	27. Puberty
13. Erection	28. Menopause
14. Ejaculation	29. Testicles
15. Breasts	30. Scrotum

The presentation of the 30 words in the SVT was the same for all subjects. (All testing was done by J. E. Chataway.) Each word was read aloud and immediately followed by the first question. The following example illustrates this: "Uterus. Who has a uterus?" Where this question was answered correctly, e.g. "The woman has it", a probing question was then asked: "What is the uterus?" All the further probing questions were then asked whether or not the first probing question was correctly answered. The remaining probing questions for this word were as follows: "Where is the uterus?" "What is it for?" "Tell me anything you know about the uterus". The first question ("Who has a . . .?") was always presented except when it was inappropriate, for example, for words which described a process (e.g. fertilization) or an activity (e.g. masturbation). If an incorrect answer was given to the "Who has a . . .?" question, it was assumed that the subject possessed no knowledge of the word in question and, after a pause, the tester moved on to the next word on the list.

When presenitng each word, alternative colloquialisms and synonyms were presented only if the correct technical term appeared unfamiliar to the subject. Use of alternative terms maximised the subject's opportunity to provide information. The responses were written down verbatim. No indication was given as to whether the answer was correct or incorrect but praise and encouragement were given in a general way. Remarks such as "you're going well" and "that was a hard one, wasn't it?" encouraged the subject to continue. When the subject showed signs of fatigue or discouragement the test was briefly interrupted and a topic of known interest discussed, or the subject was asked how he/she felt about being asked all these questions. After this brief break, the subject was encouraged to proceed.

The SVT was used on three occasions: first, as a pre-test (in fact, immediately after the introductory teaching session); second, as a post-test (Post-test 1) at the end of the six-week teaching programme; and third, as another post-test (Post-test 2) approximately two months after Post-test 1. On each occasion, the SVT administration procedure was the same.

Concerning the scoring of the SVT, information gained during pilot study sessions indicated that subjects seldom provided more than four pieces of information in relation to any one word presented; nor were any subjects able to demonstrate an advanced level of understanding (for example, concerning hormonal effects on the reproductive system). Thus, it was decided to score the responses on a five point scale from zero to four. For each word, one point was awarded for each acceptable piece of information up to the maximum score of four. Thus, if all 30 words produced the maximum item score, the maximum possible total score was 120. No reduction in score was imposed for an incorrect answer.

A test of sex vocabulary would seem to be a justifiable evaluation method for a sex education programme such as the present one although, obviously, being able to define a word is no guarantee that its meaning is understood; but, given the methods used during the teaching and the emphasis placed on understanding the functions of sex organs and processes, a vocabulary test of this kind, with its probing enquiries and with its acceptance of colloquialisms and street language, would seem to be an appropriate evaluation method. In addition, it would seem, from results to be discussed later, that *getting to know the words* enhanced the sex communication skills of the subjects. Being able to talk to one another after the teaching course was over seems to have facilitated discussion and the sharing of sex knowledge among those who participated in the course.

Results

As already mentioned, subjects received their teaching in small groups. Three of these (Groups A, B, and C), were from one training institution, three (Groups D, E, and F) from another, and one (Group G) from another. These seven groups comprised mildly retarded persons. Another group (Group H) came from a fourth institution and comprised five moderately retarded persons. For some of the data analyses, the groups are treated separately and for some others the data are combined intra-institutionally in order to increase statistical reliability.

The main data analyses concern:
1. Sex differences;
2. Pre-test/Post-test 1 comparisons;
3. Post-test 1/Post-test 2 comparisons.

Sex differences

Table 1, with the groups combined intra-institutionally, shows the extent of the sex differences in the Pre-test, Post-test 1, and Post-test 2.

It can be seen that although the female means are lower than the male means in all instances, only one comparison (Groups A, B, and C, Post-test 1) reaches statistical significance (.05 level).

In addition to the sex differences data, Table 1, at this stage of the analysis, already shows the main effects of the teaching programme. Figure 1 shows these effects, which are treated statistically in the next section, quite clearly. For the data pooled in this way, all groups, both males and females, show steep increases in mean scores going from the Pre-test and Post-test 1 and quite noticeable increases going from Post-test 1

Table 1. *Group means of SVT scores from pooled groups showing sex differences.*

		Males		Females			
	Groups	N	X̄	N	X	t*	p
Pre-test	ABC	13	25.46	7	15.00	1.85	0.081
	DEF	8	14.00	8	8.75	1.32	0.206
	G	4	23.75	4	19.25	1.48	0.648
	H	3	7.67	2	4.50	1.20	0.317
Post-test 1	ABC	12	43.75	7	26.86	2.28	0.036
	DEF	8	27.00	8	21.63	0.90	0.385
	G	4	40.50	4	29.25	1.26	0.254
	H	3	13.00	2	6.50	1.77	0.175
Post-test 2	ABC	13	49.62	7	33.86	1.98	0.063
	DEF	7	32.71	8	27.63	0.74	0.470
	G	4	42.50	4	38.75	0.34	0.748
	H	No	Post-test 2				

* Unrelated samples test, 2-tail.

to Post-test 2 which, it will be recalled, was administered about two months after Post-test 1, with no teaching in between those two post-tests.

The effects of the teaching programme as shown by the Post-test 1 scores compared with the Pre-test scores

Table 2, below, shows the mean scores and the statistical significance of the score differences between the Pre-test and Post-test 1. For this analysis the groups were treated separately.

All groups show an increase in mean score at Post-test 1 compared with the Pre-test and, with the exception of two groups (B and E), these increases are statistically significant (.05 level). Using the chi square test for combined probabilities (Guilford, 1965), the overall significance of the increase gives a p value of less than .005.

It is worth noting that the sizes of the mean differences are not significantly related to the Pre-test averages (Spearman Rho = 0.19).

Post-test 2 results compared with those of Post-test 1

In experimental terms, the "treatment" that intervened between the Pre-test and Post-test 1 was, of course, the teaching. No specifically identifiable treatment existed between Post-test 1 and Post-test 2 except the passage of time (about two months). Usually, after learning, some forgetting takes place. That this was not the case in the present instance has already been mentioned. Table 3 below shows, in greater detail, the increases in mean scores at Post-test 2 compared with those of Post-test 1. For all groups (except Group H which did not do Post-test 2), the Post-test 2 means

are higher than those for Post-test 1. However, for only two groups (C and F) were these differences statistically significant (.05 level) although the difference for Group G is very close to being significant. Overall, however, the combined probability (x^2 = 37.07, df = 14) is significant at the .005 level.

Individual data

The data from individual subjects needs to be interpreted within the context of the overall results. As mentioned previously, the maximum SVT score was 120. The distribution of individual scores for each of the three tests is shown in Figure 2.

The maximum SVT score of 89 (one subject on Post-test 2) together with the positive skewness of the Pre-test and Post-test 1 distributions suggest that the level of difficulty of the test was somewhat too high.

At the level of individual subjects rather

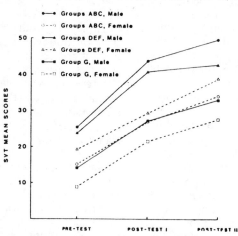

Figure 1: Group means of SVT scores.

Table 2. *Group means of SVT scores for the Pre-test and Post-test 1 and significance levels of the $\overline{X}$ differences.*

Group	N	Pre-test $\overline{X}$	Post-test 1 $\overline{X}$	Diff. $\overline{X}$	t*	p
A	8	17.75	38.50	20.75	6.27	0.001
B	5	24.50	35.00	10.50	2.82	0.064
C	8	26.43	37.85	11.43	3.65	0.011
D	5	9.80	25.80	16.00	5.59	0.005
E	5	12.40	21.60	9.20	2.03	0.112
F	6	13.67	25.33	11.67	6.76	0.001
G	8	21.50	34.88	13.38	4.31	0.004
H	5	6.40	10.40	4.00	3.81	0.019

* related samples test, 2-tail.

than groups, 96% of them showed an increase in score at Post-test 1 over their Pre-test scores and 76% showed an increase at Post-test 2 over their Post-test 1 scores. An analysis of the responses made by that 76% showed that, in about one-third of the instances, correct information was supplied at Post-test 2 which was not supplied at Post-test 1. This seemingly paradoxical improvement is referred to in the Discussion.

Discussion

The aim of this study was the evaluation of the effectiveness of a sex education programme and, as already mentioned, the SVT was devised for this purpose. It should be understood that the test is specific to this study and was not designed to be of more general use. At the same time, the apparent effectiveness of the test, especially with its use of colloquialisms and its form of probing enquiry, suggests that the use of similar devices in such situations may be worthwhile. At least, one can say that knowing the words for sexual parts and processes is obviously basic to the development of sex communication skills.

In our opinion, the results of the present study have shown that mentally retarded young people (both mildly and moderately retarded) have the ability to learn and to retain knowledge about human sexuality and relationships from teaching situations of the kind used in this study. Whilst the effect of *small group* teaching cannot be isolated (there being no control group in the present study), this form of teaching did facilitate discussion among group members during the course and it seems very likely that such discussion led to a sharing of information during the two month interval between Post-test 1 and Post-test 2. In this connection, supervisors at the institutions reported several instances of friendships formed among group members during and after the course.

Although it seems reasonable to attribute

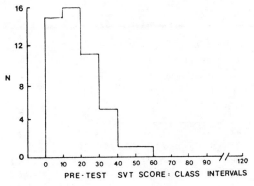

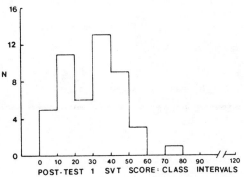

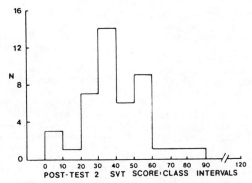

Figure 2: Distributions of individual scores for pre-test and post-tests.

the Post-test 2 improvement primarily to the conditions facilitated by the small group teaching situation, there are other factors which should be noted. Not the least of these is a kind of "experimenter effect" (Rosenthal, 1966). The de-sensitizing effect of repeated testing sessions with the same person could well have increased the subjects' confidence and trust. Thus, lack of confidence or embarrassment may have been responsible for deflating Pre-test and Post-test 1 scores compared with Post-test 2 scores. In the case of two of the groups which showed marked Post-test 2 improvement, a community nurse employed by the institution gave information on contraception from time to time. In the case of another group, a supervisor sat in on the course. Members of that group said that, as a consequence of this, they felt free to discuss course issues with that person. The extent of the contribution of these factors, and perhaps others, to the Post-test 2 improvement cannot be assessed.

Clearly, there is great scope for further research into course content, teaching methods, and evaluation in the area of the present study; and probably these will need to be specifically designed or adapted for particular situations. The present study adds to the relatively small accumulation of experience in this area.

Acknowledgements

The co-operation of the institutions which participated in this study is gratefully acknowledged as is the work of the Family Planning Association of South Australia, particularly that of Mrs. Jan Tottman.

Table 3. *Group means of SVT scores for Post-test 1 and Post-test 2 and significance levels of the mean differences.*

Group	N	Post-test 1 $\overline{X}$	Post-test 2 $\overline{X}$	Diff. $\overline{X}$	t*	p
A	8	38.50	43.38	4.88	1.81	0.113
B	4	35.00	42.25	7.25	2.02	0.137
C	7	37.85	46.71	8.86	4.91	0.003
D	5	25.80	27.20	1.40	0.62	0.567
E	5	21.60	26.80	5.20	1.40	0.235
F	5†	28.20	36.20	8.00	3.51	0.025
G	8	34.88	40.63	5.75	2.25	0.058
H	5	No Post-test 2				

* related samples test, 2-tail.
† one subject from Group F was absent for Post-test 2.

References

ATTWELL, A. A. and JAMISON, C. B. *The Mentally Retarded: Answers to Questions About Sex.* Los Angeles, Western Psychological Services, 1977.

CAMERON, H. C. Psychosexual Problems and the Life Cycle. In S. Crown *Psychosexual Problems: Psychotherapy, Counselling and Behavioural Modification.* London: Academic Press, 1976.

EDMONDSON, B. and WISH, J. Sex knowledge and attitudes of moderately retarded males. *American Journal of Mental Deficiency,* 1975, 80, 172-179.

FISCHER, H. L. and KRAJICEK, M. J. Sexual development of the moderately retarded child: Level of information and parental attitudes. *Mental Retardation,* 1974, 12, 28-30.

GERHARDT, P. H. Sexual behaviour of the retarded. In F. F. Cruz, and G. D. La Veck (Eds.), *Human Sexuality and the Mentally Retarded.* New York: Brunner/Mazel, 1973.

GORDON, Sol. *The Sexual Adolescent.* Belmont, California: Div. of Wadsworth Publ. Co. Inc., 1973.

GORDON, Sol. *Living Fully.* New York: The John Day Co., 1975.

GUILFORD, J. P. *Fundamental Statistics in Psychology and Education,* 4th edition, McGraw-Hill, 1965.

HALL, J. E., MORRIS, H. L. and BARKER, H. R. Sexual knowledge and attitudes of mentally retarded adolescents, *American Journal of Mental Deficiency,* 1973, 77, 706-709.

HALL, J. E. and MORRIS, H. L. Sexual knowledge and attitudes of institutionalized and non-institutionalized retarded adolescents. *American Journal of Mental Deficiency,* 1976, 80, 382-387.

KEMPTON, W. and FORMAN, R. *Guidelines for training in sexuality in the mentally handicapped.* Philadelphia: Planned Parenthood Association of S.A. Pennsylvania, 1976.

MEYERS, R., WALDEN, S., MORAN, S., GARDNER, S., SHOWALTER, R., LEVI, K. and PHILLIPS, D. In E. Vockell and P. Mattick. Sex education for the mentally retarded: An analysis of problems, programmes, and research. *Education and Training of Mentally*

Retarded, 1972, 7, 129-134.

MITCHELL, L., BUTLER, D. C. and DOCTOR, R. M. Attitudes of caretakers toward the sexual behaviour of mentally retarded persons. *American Journal of Mental Deficiency,* 1978, 83, 289-296.

MORGENSTERN, M. Community attitudes towards sexuality of the retarded. In F. F. de la Cruz, and G. D. La Veck, (Eds.), *Human Sexuality and the Mentally Retarded.* New York: Brunner/Mazel, 1973.

ROBINSON, H. B. and ROBINSON, N. M. *The Exceptional Individual.* New Jersey: Prentice-Hall, 1965.

ROSEN, M., FLOOR, L. and BAXTER, D. In M. Rosen and Kivits, M. Beyond normalization: psychological adjustment. *British Journal of Mental Subnormality,* 1973, 19, 64-70.

ROSENTHAL, R. *Experimenter Effects in Behavioral Research,* New York: Appleton-Century-Crofts, 1966.

VOCKELL, E. and MATTICK, P. Sex education for the mentally retarded: An analysis of problems, programmes, and research. *Education and Training of Mentally Retarded,* 1972, 7, 129-134.

"The Music Came from Deep Inside"

A new report: handicapped children respond to the arts

Charles B. Fowler

 A new book called *The Music Came from Deep Inside* (published by McGraw-Hill, 1982) presents a very personal and moving account of how artists and the arts can make an impact on severely and profoundly handicapped children and youth. It is actually a documentary report on the first year of a project administered by the National Committee/Arts for the Handicapped, but it is much more. It tells in very compelling words (by Junius Eddy) and photographs (by Roger Vaughan) the special nature of these special children and their teachers.

"The pain you feel . . ."

The reader "lives" with Eddy through his first encounter with these children: "It's a shock to be confronted suddenly with so little comprehension in their faces, such complete neglect of the ordinary niceties, such intense and dedicated a response to invisible impulses—the children fill many of these rooms with human noises, but little human speech. And finally it's the pain you feel for them, because the damage inflicted on their minds and bodies has left them so helpless, so vulnerable."

We feel, too, for their teachers, through firsthand accounts that show us in poignant terms how progress with these children is measured in the smallest increments: Speaking of "Little Mario," Kathy Saylor, a teacher, tells us, "most of the time he just lies on one of the green beds with his head flopped down. He can't sit upright alone at all. But we've worked with him for a year now and if I sit behind him and prop his head up, he can now sit

Even the paint tastes good at Walton Developmental Center

Musical activities at the Texas Special Care School

alone for *one full second*. To us, that's a great deal of progress."

Invading this world, how can the arts assert any positive affects upon such damaged youth? Two intertwined project goals were proposed at the outset: to use the art forms of puppetry, music, the visual arts, dance, and drama (1) to improve the quality of life, and (2) to improve the functional skills of these children. Teams of artist-teachers were set up in each of three institutions. The Great Oaks Center, north of Silver Spring, Maryland, is a state operated residential facility with a

Photos by Roger Vaughan

Music in full swing at Great Oaks Center

school for about one hundred severely and profoundly retarded children and adolescents. The Special Care School, located on three and a half acres in Dallas County, Texas, is a private, nonprofit day school for children three to twenty-one years of age who are mentally retarded, brain damaged, or are physically and emotionally handicapped. The Roger Walton Development Center, administered by the Stockton (California) Unified School District, serves students suffering from delayed development or mental retardation.

Vivid detail

The bulk of this book, Chapter 4—"An Infusion of Artists," (pages 48-118)—describes in vivid detail the trial-and-error process used by the various artists in these different schools as well as with their regular teachers, to evoke desired responses from these children.

Drama is used to engage kids in make-believe to pretend they can walk, talk, or lick the world. A severely retarded child who doesn't respond to anything puts on a king's robe and crown and suddenly there is a "real radiance of personal energy."

Music is used to stimulate the children to produce sounds. Rhythm instruments give children a reason to practice gross motor actions in response to a cue. The broad applications of music for these children are spelled out: "Obviously there is a deep measure of sheer enjoyment that can be generated among the higher functioning children whenever familiar tunes are played or sung. . . . But music lends itself to work with the more seriously involved children as well—when it can cue a specific physical or verbal response, emphasize a body part or an action, and provide teachers with fresh ways to bring about a response or to work on a specific objective."

Dance & puppetry

Dance is used as a way to move ambulatory and nonambulatory children. Teachers learn to scoop up nonambulatory children and dance with them. The idea is to get these children to respond, to "attend," for this is the basis for establishing any productive relationship with the world.

Visual arts prove more difficult because many of these children do not have the fine motor control required to manipulate artists' materials. Activities such as body tracing, finger painting with foodstuffs, and making sculptures by gluing wooden blocks together have to be invented. But the children begin to respond.

Puppetry is used to make basics, like jumping up and down, absorbing to the children. The puppet gives the lesson a playful feeling. First the frog puppet jumps and then the "frog's friend" jumps. The arts serve as a way through. They engage the children, hold their attention, and provide a delightful kind of motivation.

So it goes with all the arts. Seventeen individual artists worked in the three locations, and much detail is provided about the activities they invented for these children, their own responses to the children and teachers, and their thoughts about themselves and the arts.

Benefits

The outcomes? They are difficult to assess. It seems clear that, in general, the regular teachers benefitted from the creative approaches of these artists. Stephanie Mance, a Great Oaks teacher, is quoted: "Lack of inhibition is what is most effective in getting a response from the kids—doing whatever you have to do to get a reaction. And the artists really supported that idea through their uninhibited behavior and presentations in the classroom." And other teachers give similar testimony.

But how does one measure whether the artists and the arts improved the quality of life or the functional skills of these youngsters—the twin goals of the project? The book raises serious questions about measuring improvement in such students: "What behaviors will be measured? In how many children—all of them, or just a representative sample? Will it be 'improvement' if *any change at all* is noted? How long must a noted improvement persist to be valid?" Indeed, how can we know for certain that the artist's intervention should be credited for a particular improvement?

Improvements

In spite of the many difficulties assessing these youngsters, Dr. Hugh McBride, the educational psychologist who served as the project's evaluator and data analyst, was able to discern from tests and other data he collected that the arts did help to improve skills. But perhaps the most positive note is sounded in the area of quality of life. It seems clear that the arts had their strongest effect on socialization.

As one teacher says, "The kids have learned to be more attentive in group activities, and they've learned to play together. Because, even if they never got any real dance concepts out of dancing (which they do), they're dancing *together*—doing a lot of things together. They're caring more about their classmates and their own friends, too."

It seems evident from the dozen case studies that complete this volume, as well as the many teachers, artists, volunteers, and parents who are quoted throughout, that the arts are necessary for simply making the lives of these young people more joyous and pleasurable. For many of these children, so often regarded as unlovable, the arts offer a reason to exist. They turn on the spirit of life. That, I think, is the inspired story of this project and of this book.

Teaching Severely Handicapped Adolescents to Follow Instructions Conveyed by Means of Three-Dimensional Stimulus Configurations

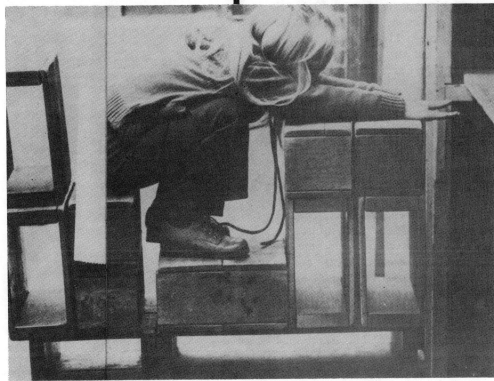

Giulio E. Lancioni

University of Nijmegen, Holland

Paul M. Smeets

University of Leiden, Holland

Doretta S. Oliva

Lega F. D'Oro Research Center, Italy

The present study investigated the feasibility of teaching three low-functioning (one sighted and two blind) adolescents a large repertoire of instruction-following responses. Three-dimensional cues, that is, dolls and small copies of objects, were used to convey the instructions. Training was structured in a stepwise fashion. Initially, the subjects were taught to take full-size objects in response to the experimenter presenting small copies of such objects. Then, they were trained to assume body positions represented through dolls. Subsequently, they were trained to assume body positions in relation with objects (represented through dolls and small copies of objects). Finally, they were trained to perform activities each of which was represented through two dolls in relation with small copies of objects. All subjects learned successfully. Generalization responding was observed at each stage of the program.

In recent years, numerous studies have been aimed at teaching severely handicapped individuals non-speech communication (receptive and/or expressive) skills. The strategies most frequently used have consisted of *manual signs* (e.g., Benaroya, Wesley, Ogilvie, Klein, & Meaney, 1977; Bonvillian, Nelson, & Rhyne, 1981; Carr, Binkoff, Kologinski, & Eddy, 1978; Konstantareas, Hunter, & Sloman, 1982; Reich, 1978), *Carrier symbols* (e.g., Arick & Krug, 1978; Carrier, 1974; Deich & Hodges, 1982; Porter & Schroeder, 1980), *Bliss symbols* (e.g., Song, 1979; Vanderheiden, Brown, MacKenzie, Reinen, & Scheibel, 1975), and *pictorial representations* (e.g., Hurlbut, Iwata, & Green, 1982; Murphy, Steele, Gilligan, Yeow, & Spare, 1977; Reid & Hurlbut, 1977; Robinson-Wilson, 1977; Spellman, DeBriere, Jarboe, Campbell, & Harris, 1978).

Professionals involved in the use of signs have often maintained that the acquisition of signs may be largely facilitated by their structural similarity or guessable relationship with the referents, that is, by their transparency (Hoffmeister & Farmer, 1972; Konstantareas, Oxman, & Webster, 1978; Brown, Note 1; Mandel, Note 2; Robbins, Note 3). Linguistic research, however, has indicated that most signs are not so transparent as to be easily acquired by a naive observer (Bellugi & Klima, 1976; Hoemann, 1975). The findings of this research seem indirectly validated by the fact that only a few studies have reported the establishment of a large repertoire of signs in low-functioning subjects (Benaroya et al., 1977; Brookner & Murphy, 1975; Fulwiler & Fouts, 1976; Konstantareas, Webster, & Oxman, 1979; Linville, 1977).

The Carrier system is carefully designed and highly structured. Yet, its application does not seem economical or successful with a number of severely mentally retarded individuals (Arick & Krug, 1978; Carrier, 1973, 1974; Deich & Hodges, 1982; McLean & McLean, 1974). The symbols are concrete and permanent, but generally have no transparency. Lack of transparency also characterizes the Bliss symbols. Their use has mostly been accompanied by modest results (Song, 1979; Vanderheiden et al., 1975). Finally, pictorial representations (which are admittedly transparent) have been comparatively easy to establish (Hurlbut et al., 1982; Murphy et al., 1977).

In view of the above, it may be suggested that cue transparency is a condition to take into account while teaching severely mentally retarded subjects non-verbal communication skills (Griffith & Robinson, 1980; Hurlbut et al., 1982). Although pictorial means seem appropriate for a variety of training situations, their degree of transparency may prove insufficient for some low-functioning individuals (Dixon, 1981). Moreover, pictorial means are not suitable for subjects who suffer from visual handicaps. In all these cases, the use of transparent three-dimensional configurations (e.g., small copies of real objects) could be considered an effective alternative. In fact, these configurations (more than the pictures) present structural similarity with the referents. Additionally, three-dimensional configurations can be discriminated through tactile inspection.

This study was an effort to assess the feasibility of teaching severely handicapped adolescents to follow instructions conveyed through three-dimensional cues, that is, dolls and small copies of familiar objects. Given the exploratory purpose of the study, training and probing items were selected to satisfy procedural conditions rather than standards of social relevance.

METHOD

Subjects

Two girls and one boy of 16.8, 15.0 and 14.1 years of age, respectively, served as subjects. The two girls were blind from birth. The younger one also suffered from severe hearing loss. The boy was affected by nystagmus which interfered with his visual focusing. Moreover, he presented restlessness, limited attention to environmental events and tantrums. All subjects had been living in a residential institute for at least seven years. Their mental ages (MAs) had been estimated (through non-standard assessment procedures) to be around the 24-month level. None of the subjects possessed verbal skills or comprehension of verbal instructions (except for a few commands understood by the boy and the girl with normal hearing). Previous prolonged training aimed at establishing basic gestures had resulted in the subjects' acquisition of 20, 41 and 34 of such gestures. At the start of the study, however, the subjects' responding to these gestures was not very reliable. Furthermore, only one girl could demonstrate them. All subjects were able to match identical objects, could orient themselves in their living environment, and were toilet trained. Their Vineland SQs were 16, 18 and 20, respectively.

PROCEDURE

With a few exceptions, the study was carried out six days a week for about four hours (divided in several sessions) a day. Four experimenters implemented all procedural conditions and collected the data. Every subject was exposed to training and probing (baseline and post-training probes) on four target instruction-following behaviors: a) Matching Objects (i.e., matching small copies of familiar objects with the corresponding full-size objects); b) Performing Body Positions (represented through dolls); c) Performing Body Positions in Relation with Objects (represented through dolls and small copies of objects); and d) Performing Activities (represented through dolls and small copies of objects). Each of these behaviors was considered prerequisite for the subsequent one. Training and probing took place in two quiet rooms.

Training

A summary of the training sequence on the different target behaviors is presented in Table 1.

Matching objects. Most of the small copies measured 4-11 cm on their larger side. The two largest ones (i.e., a board and a mattress) reached 65 cm. These dimensions made them suitable for use with the dolls (on the last two target

TABLE 1
Training Sequence

Target Behaviors	Training Phases	Stimuli	Training Procedures
Matching Objects	I	7 objects	Stimulus fading
	II	73 objects	Successive and Random Sequence Trials
Performing Body Positions	I	10 arm positions	Stimulus shaping + Successive and Random Sequence Trials
	II	62 arm-leg positions	" "
Performing Body Positions in Relation with Objects	I	40 representations of positions on top of objects	Successive and Random Sequence Trials
	II	35 representations of positions with an object in front	" "
	III	45 representations of positions on top of an object with another object in front	" "
	IV	60 representations of positions with one or two objects in the hand(s)	" "
	V	50 representations of positions on top of an object, with a 2nd object in front and a 3rd one in the hand(s)	" "
Performing Activities	I	18 representations of arm movements	" "
	II	160 representations of activities requiring the use of arms	" "
	III	25 representations of movement from one place to another	" "
	IV	75 representations of activities requiring movement from one place to another and use of arms	" "

behaviors). Training was divided into two phases. In the *first phase*, the subjects were introduced to the task gradually, so as to minimize the number of errors. Initially, the experimenter presented seven full-size objects (one at the time). While holding the object presented, the subjects had to take an identical object from a table in front of them. The object on the table was always displayed with three other objects (which belonged to the group of seven and served as distractors). When the subjects had given three consecutive correct responses on each object, a stimulus-fading procedure (Etzel & LeBlanc, 1979) began. That is, while the objects displayed on the table remained full-size, the objects presented to the subjects were gradually smaller, until reaching the dimensions set for the small copies. The fading procedure involved eight steps. At each step, the subjects were requested 4–5 consecutive correct responses on every object.

During the *second phase* of training, the subjects were taught to match 73 new copies with the corresponding full-size objects. No stimulus fading took place. The training of each copy was carried out through successive and random sequence trials (Striefel, Bryan, & Aikins, 1974). That is, at first the experimenter presented the copy and guided the subjects to take the full-size object (two successive trials). Then, he/she continued to present the copy (the corresponding full-size object was on display with one or two distractors) and the subjects had to respond independently. After three successive correct responses, this new copy was interspersed with a copy already trained (i.e., in the same or previous phase). During the presentations of these copies, the two corresponding full-size objects and a distractor were on display. An average of five successive correct responses was requested, in total. Finally, the presentation of the new copy was interspersed with that of five copies already trained (7–11 full-size objects were on display). An average of 14 successive correct responses was requested, in total.

During the training of the first 18 copies (but not afterwards), the subjects were allowed to hold the copy while searching for the corresponding full-size object.

Performing body positions. The subjects were trained to perform body positions in response to the presentation of dolls showing such positions. The dolls (which were of plaster and rough plastic) were made for this study and measured about 50 cm in height. Training was divided into two phases. During the *first phase,* the subjects were taught ten arm positions (e.g., arms up, arms forward, one arm on chest one open on the side). The first doll introduced showed 'arms up'. From hips down, it had the form of a truncated pyramid (as all dolls used in this phase). The experimenter guided the subjects (a) to inspect the doll tactually or tactually and visually, and (b) to assume the position. When the subjects had given four successive correct responses independently, a stimulus-shaping procedure (Etzel & LeBlanc, 1979) was used to introduce the second arm position. This procedure was designed to facilitate discrimination of the relevant aspects of the stimuli. Initially, the doll with 'arms up' was interspersed with a doll having an irregular cylindrical form sticking out of its chest, that is, in place of its arms. At the presentation of this doll (S-Delta doll), the subjects were not to respond, but to keep their hands on the table. Correct performance on six successive trials (involving three presentations of each doll) led to the replacement of the S-Delta doll with a second one, which had the cylindrical form slightly shaped toward the final arm position. The shaping of the cylindrical form continued over eight additional dolls, the last of which showed "arms forward." When the subjects had refrained from responding also to this doll, the experimenter presented it in successive trials. From now onward, the 'arms forward' position was treated as a discriminative stimulus, that is, the subjects had to perform it at the presentation of the doll. After they had given four successive correct responses independently, the presentation of this doll was interspersed with that of the doll showing "arms up." Ten successive correct responses were requested, in total.

The procedure followed for introducing and training the subsequent five arm positions was similar to that used for "arms forward." For the last three arm positions, however, no stimulus shaping took place. The training of each position was carried out through successive trials (until the subjects had given four successive correct responses independently), and through random sequence trials. For the latter trials (during which the position in training was interspersed with those already trained), 20 successive correct responses were requested, in total.

During the *second phase,* training involved 62 arm-leg positions. The first 54 consisted of six different leg positions combined with the previously trained arm positions. Training started with the random presentation of two dolls having different arm positions but the same leg position (i.e., on knees). When the subjects had given eight successive correct responses independently, the presentation of these dolls was interspersed with that of two other dolls. The latter dolls showed the same arm positions as the former ones, but had legs unshaped (i.e., from hips down, they were formed as a truncated pyramid). To respond to the latter dolls, the subjects had to perform the arm positions, while maintaining a neutral leg position (one leg straight one bent with the foot on a brick), which they had at the presentation of all dolls. After the achievement of 16 successive correct responses, the procedure was repeated. That is, training involved two new dolls on knees (their arm positions were different from those shown by the previous dolls) and then two other dolls with legs unshaped. Finally, the four dolls with legs unshaped were substituted with dolls in which the truncated pyramid was gradually changed into "legs wide apart" (stimulus shaping). This leg position was then treated as a discriminative stimulus. Training was carried out through successive and random sequence trials.

Training continued with dolls showing the combination of "on knees" and "legs wide apart" with the remaining six arm positions. No stimulus shaping was used.

Procedures similar to those described above were applied (a) for shaping "legs forward in a seated posture" in combination with two arm positions, and for training this leg position in combination with all ten arm positions; (b) for shaping "legs crossed under the body" in combination with two arm positions, and for training this leg position in combination with all ten arm positions; (c) for shaping "legs bent in a squatting position" in combination with two arm positions, and for training this leg position with all ten arm positions; and (d) for training the remaining 12 arm-leg positions for none of which stimulus shaping was used.

Performing body positions in relation with objects. The subjects were trained to assume arm-leg positions in relation with objects. If the experimenter presented a doll squatting on a mat with a vase just in front and a stick in its hands, the subjects had to take a stick, get onto the mat and assume the arm-leg position in touch with the vase (which stood next to the mat). Objects to be used in relation with the arms were displayed on a table. The other objects were positioned on the floor. Distracting objects were always present. Objects and arm-leg positions were those used for the previous target behaviors. Training was divided into five phases none of which involved stimulus shaping. The training of each representation was carried out through successive trials (until the subjects had given an average of three successive correct responses independently) and through random sequence trials. For the latter trials (during which the representation in training was interspersed with 1-8 representations already trained), an average of 15 successive correct responses was requested, in total. Physical guidance from the experimenter was available to ensure (a) appropriate inspection of the representations, and (b) appropriate responding to new representations (i.e., as training started on them).

The *first phase* of training involved 40 representations of body positions on top of objects (e.g., doll standing with legs straight, one arm forward one down, on top of a block). The *second phase* involved 35 representations of body positions with an object in front (e.g., doll on knees and arms on chest, with a container touching its knees). The *third phase* involved 45 representations of body positions on top of an object, with another object in front (e.g., doll seated on a cushion with arms down and a wheelbarrow at its feet). The *fourth phase* involved 60 representations. Of these, the first 30 showed body positions with an object in the hands or in the hand (e.g., doll with legs wide apart and arms forward, holding a sack with both hands); the last 30 showed body positions with an object in each hand. The *fifth phase* involved 50 representations of body positions on top of an object, with a second object in front and a third one in the hand(s).

Performing activities. The subjects were trained to perform activities which were represented through two dolls in relation with small copies of objects. For example, in the representation of "dropping a purse into a container while on knees," the first doll was on knees with a container touching its knees and a purse in its hands. The second doll (placed beside the first one, at a distance of 25-30 cm) was on knees and arms open with the purse in the container. To respond to such representation, the subjects had to (a) take a purse from a table, (b) assume the appropriate body position in relation with the container displayed on the floor, and (c) drop the purse into the container. Training was divided into four phases which implied procedural conditions similar to those used for the previous target behavior.

The *first phase* served to introduce the subjects to representations involving two dolls. The initial eight representations included no objects. In each representation, the two dolls had the same leg position but a different arm position, thus portraying a specific arm movement (i.e., a movement starting from the position of the first doll and ending at the position of the second doll). Subsequently, training involved ten representations which differed from the previous ones in that the dolls were in relation with two or three small copies of objects.

During the *second phase,* the subjects were trained to respond to 160 representations of 55 activities. These activities required only the use of the arms for their execution (e.g., dropping or throwing an object, brushing an object, putting an object inside another or taking it out, piling or aligning objects, taking apart objects glued together, sorting out objects, watering two of three adjacent objects). For each activity, there were two or three representations involving dolls in different leg positions and/or with different objects (e.g., dropping a brush into a bucket while on knees, dropping a brush into a box while squatting, dropping a sponge into a vase while on knees). Figure 1 shows the representation of "placing plastic rings on a chair."

During the *third phase,* the subjects were trained to respond to 25 representations of movement from one place to another (e.g., on knees, on buttocks, with legs apart, on hands and knees). The movement was portrayed on or alongside objects. Figure 2 shows the representation of "moving on knees from the first to the third target object displayed on a mattress."

During the *fourth phase,* the subjects were taught to respond to 75 representations of movement conditions (similar or identical to those of the third phase) combined with activities of the second phase (e.g., moving on buttocks alongside a row of blocks and matching the second object displayed on the row with the object carried during the movement; walking on a board and watering the first and third object displayed on the board; moving on knees alongside a row of chairs, taking the object displayed on the last chair and putting it into the container carried during the movement; walking on a mattress with legs apart until reaching a box, and sliding the content of a bucket into the box). Figure 3 shows the representation of "moving on buttocks from the first to the second target object displayed alongside a wooden board, and covering the second target with a cloth."

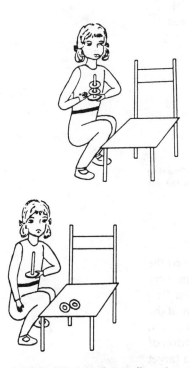

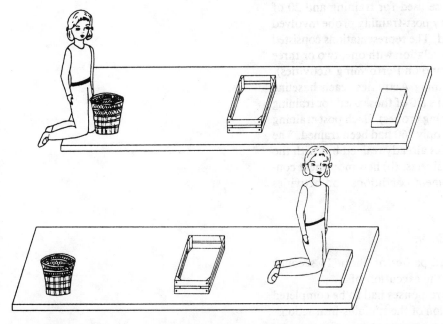

FIGURE 1. Pictorial reproduction of the stimulus configurations used to represent "placing plastic rings on a chair."

FIGURE 2. Pictorial reproduction of the stimulus configurations used to represent "moving on knees from a container to a block displayed on a mattress."

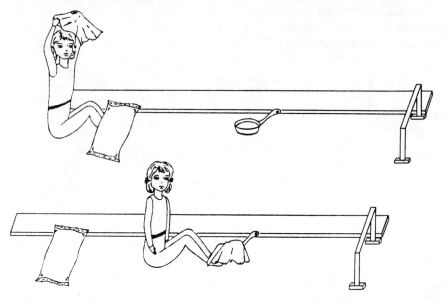

FIGURE 3. Pictorial reproduction of the stimulus configurations used to represent "moving on buttocks from a pillow to a pot displayed alongside a wooden board, and covering the pot with a cloth."

Baseline and Post-Training Probes

Each baseline and post-training probe on Matching Objects involved the presentation of 110 copies of as many full-size objects (80 of them were trained). At each trial, about ten full-size objects were on display. On Performing Body Positions, each baseline and post-training probe involved the presentation of 68 arm-leg positions (i.e., the 62 trained and six new ones). Physical guidance was available but only to ensure appropriate inspection of the stimulus-instructions (the same also applied on the following two target behaviors).

On Performing Body Positions in Relation with Objects, each baseline probe involved 40 representations (20 of those used for training and 20 of those used for the post-training probes). Every post-training probe involved 528 representations which had not been trained. The representations consisted of the aforementioned 68 arm-leg positions in relation with one, two or three objects. During the probes on this behavior (and on Performing Activities), distracting objects were present. On Performing Activities, each baseline probe was carried out through 40 representations (20 of those used for training and 20 of those used only during the post-training probes). Each post-training probe involved 1010 representations of which only 260 had been trained. The other 750 representations involved (a) activities already trained but with the dolls in different positions and with different objects; (b) new movement conditions; and (c) new combinations of movement conditions and activities requiring the use of the arms.

Responding Conditions and Correction of Errors

During baseline, the subjects were allowed pauses of about 15 seconds before starting a response as well as during the execution of it.

During training on Matching Objects, the responses had to be completed within 10 or 15–20 seconds from the presentation of the stimulus-instructions. The larger time limit applied during the random sequence trials of the second phase (when a larger number of objects was on display). Failure to respond within the limits was considered an error.

During subsequent training, no pauses longer than about 5 seconds were allowed before or during a response. While on the initial presentation(s) of a new stimulus-instruction (before the first independent response had occurred) such pauses would be prevented through guidance, on other trials they would be scored as errors. The only exception concerned the first or the first two pauses within every 100 random sequence trials. That is, they would not be scored as errors, but would be followed by a repetition of the trial.

During the post-training probes, the conditions for responding were as in the last part of training, that is, in the random sequence trials.

During baseline, errors were not corrected. By contrast, during training every error was immediately followed by correction trials. That is, the experimenter kept presenting the stimulus-instruction (at first, guided the response) until the subjects had given two successive correct responses independently. During post-training probes, correction trials were available, but only at the end of each probe. At that point, every stimulus-instruction on which an error had occurred was presented until the subjects had given 4–6 consecutive correct responses independently.

Reinforcement Conditions

During baseline probing, social reinforcement (praise and caressing) and tangible reinforcement (edibles or vibrotactile and kinesthetic stimulation) followed each correct response, or every block of 6–10 trials in which no correct responding had occurred. At the beginning of training on Matching Objects, social and tangible reinforcement were continuous. During all other training, social reinforcement was continuous, while tangible reinforcement was intermittent. That is, it was available on variable ratios 1:2 to 1:8 and only for correct responses the subjects performed independently. During the post-training probes, social reinforcement was continuous, tangible reinforcement was on a variable ratio 1:8.

Experimental Design

A modified version of the multiple-probe technique (Horner & Baer, 1978) was used for each subject. The initial baseline probing on all target behaviors was followed by training and five post-training probes on Matching Objects. The completion of the fifth probe on this behavior led to new baseline probing, training and five post-training probes on Performing Body Positions. These post-training probes were interspersed with a sixth probe on Matching Objects. The study continued with new baseline probing, training and two post-training probes on Performing Body Positions in Relation with Objects and on Performing Activities, respectively.

Reliability

Each experimenter was joined by one of two observers over a total of 60 reliability sessions. During baseline, a reliability session encompassed the presentation of 25 stimulus-instructions. During training and post-training probes, a reliability session lasted until the subjects had completed 25 responses. The observer was always behind a one-way window. Except during baseline, he/she did not see the stimulus-instructions presented and recorded the responses (including possible pauses) descriptively. Agreement on a response scored as correct by the experimenter implied that the observer described it as (a) matching the stimulus-instruction presented, and (b) occurring within the time limits allowed.

RESULTS

The mean percentage of agreement between experimenters and observers ranged from 92 to 100 ($\bar{X} = 99.6$). All subjects completed the program successfully. From the start of training on Matching Objects to the end of the post-training probes on Performing Activities, they required 98 days (boy), 110 days (blind girl) and 119 days (deaf-blind girl). Table 2 reports their individual performance during training (i.e., the total number of training trials and errors on each target behavior). Figure 4 reports their mean percentage of correct responding during baseline and post-training probes (these data were averaged across subjects since individual differences were minimal).

On Matching Objects, baseline correct responding for the three subjects averaged 6% (first probe) and 7% (second probe). Training involved 2156 to 2261 trials during which 20–28 errors occurred. Post-training correct responding averaged 99.1% (a total of three errors) in the first probe, 99.7% (one error) in the second and sixth probe, and 100% in all other probes.

On Performing Body Positions, baseline correct responding was zero. Training involved 3270 to 3562 trials during which 49–76 errors occurred.

TABLE 2
Total Number of Training Trials and Errors for Each Target Behavior

Target Behaviors	BOY		BLIND GIRL		DEAF-BLIND GIRL	
	Trials	Errors	Trials	Errors	Trials	Errors
Matching Objects	2156	20	2261	28	2207	25
Performing Body Positions	3474	68	3562	76	3270	49
Performing Body Positions in Relation with Objects	5032	79	5175	92	5235	101
Performing Activities	7953	142	9014	261	8062	156

Post-training correct responding averaged 99.0% (two errors) in the first probe, and 100% in the remaining probes.

On Performing Body Positions in Relation with Objects, baseline correct responding was zero. Training involved 5032 to 5235 trials during which 79-101 errors occurred. Post-training correct responding averaged 99.1% (15 errors) in the first probe, and 99.5% (eight errors) in the second probe.

Finally, on Performing Activities, baseline correct responding was zero. Training involved 7953 to 9014 trials during which 142–261 errors occurred. Post-training correct responding averaged 98.7% (38 errors) in the first probe, and 99.3% (22 errors) in the second probe.

During the post-training probes on the last two target behaviors, the subjects never failed on stimulus-instructions used also during baseline probing.

DISCUSSION

The results of this study show that severely handicapped subjects were able to acquire a large repertoire of instruction-following responses. Given numerous differences in training conditions, it is difficult to compare these findings with those reported by previous investigators (e.g., Carr et al., 1978; Deich & Hodges, 1982). Yet, several events seem to indicate that the present program was highly effective. First, the discrimination and association of a vast number of stimulus-instructions were established through a relatively limited amount of training, that is, the subjects received 18615 to 20012 training trials for 660 stimulus-instructions. Moreover, the error rates during training were quite low. Second, the subjects were able to acquire responding to complex stimulus-instructions such as the representations of activities. Third, they showed high generalization learning (particularly significant was their achievement on the last two target behaviors).

With regard to the subjects' performance during training, one may argue that the employment of transparent three-dimensional means was critical. In fact, these means, more than others, appear directly related with their refer-

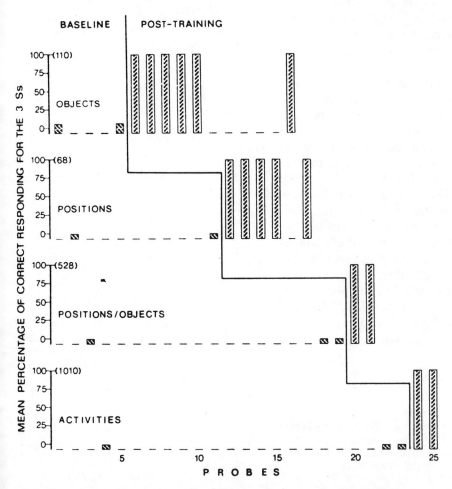

FIGURE 4. Each bar represents the mean percentage of correct responding provided by the three subjects during a probe. Within parentheses, there is indicated the number of stimulus-instructions presented at each baseline and post-training probe (Matching Objects and Performing Body Positions), or at each post-training probe (Performing Body Positions in Relation with Objects and Performing Activities).

ents. This relationship could have facilitated their acquisition and retention. Nevertheless, specific training procedures may also have had a decisive effect on the results. For example, the stimulus-fading procedure adopted at the beginning of training on Matching Objects may have been responsible for the virtually errorless learning recorded at that stage of the program (i.e., when errors were very likely to occur). Likewise, the stimulus-shaping procedure adopted for introducing arm and leg positions, and the different steps adopted for introducing arm-leg combinations may have ensured that the subjects (a) focused their attention on the relevant aspects of the stimuli, and thus (b) learned with a few errors. Finally, the different steps used for training Body Positions in Relation with Objects and Activities allowed the introduction of one new element at the time. This strategy, which structured the training in a chaining-like fashion, may have been crucial for preventing stimulus overselectivity (Lovaas, Koegel, & Schreibman, 1979) and bringing the subjects to respond to complex instructions.

The generalization learning observed within each target behavior probably depended on two conditions: extensivity of training and similarity between stimulus-instructions used for training and stimulus-instructions used for testing generalization (Baer, Peterson, & Sherman, 1967; Stokes & Baer, 1977). The lack of generalization across behaviors, on the other hand, may be explained by the fact that the conditions mentioned above did not apply in this case. For example, although the training of the first two target behaviors had enabled the subjects to discriminate the cues used for representing Body Positions in Relation with Objects, the combination of these cues in single representations was new and implied responses quite different from those trained.

In general, it may be suggested that the results obtained in the present study provide new perspectives for the training of low-functioning individuals. The practicality of the three-dimensional system may appear limited, particularly for the presentation of complex instructions. With regard to this issue, several considerations can be made. First, low-functioning subjects are unlikely to acquire responding to complex instructions when these are presented through strings of signs or of other non-transparent cues (Deich & Hodges, 1982; Murphy et al., 1977; Poulton & Algozzine, 1980). Second, systems based on signs, Carrier symbols or Bliss symbols are not free from restrictions. Their effective use by teachers, caretakers and parents requires considerable effort and preparation. Third, for some sighted subjects, the acquisition of the three-dimensional system may be the basis for learning less transparent strategies (e.g., pictorial representations, or combinations of gestures and smaller-size three-dimensional means). Similarly, for some visually handicapped subjects, the reduction in the size of the three-dimensional means as well as the integration of these means with basic gestures could be considered.

Acknowledgement — The execution of the present study was supported by funds from the Lega F. D'Oro Research Center (Italy).

REFERENCE NOTES

1. Brown, R. *Why are signed languages easier to learn than spoken languages?* Keynote address, National Symposium on Sign Language Research and Teaching, Chicago, 1977.
2. Mandel, M. *Iconicity of signs and their learnability by non-signers.* Paper presented at the National Symposium on Sign Language Research and Teaching, Chicago, 1977.
3. Robbins, N. *Selecting sign systems for the multihandicapped students.* Paper presented at the annual meeting of the American Speech and Hearing Association, Houston, 1976.

REFERENCES

Arick, J. R., & Krug, D. A. Autistic children: A study of learning characteristics and programming needs. *American Journal of Mental Deficiency,* 1978, **83,** 200–202.

Baer, D. M., Peterson, R. F., & Sherman, J. A. The development of imitation by reinforcing behavioral similarity to a model. *Journal of the Experimental Analysis of Behavior,* 1967, **10,** 405–416.

Bellugi, U., & Klima, E. S. Two faces of sign: Iconic and abstract. In S. Harnard, D. Horst, & J. Lancaster (Eds.), *Origins and evolution of language and speech.* New York: Annals of the New York Academy of Science, 1976.

Benaroya, S., Wesley, S., Ogilvie, H., Klein, L. S., & Meaney, M. Sign language and multisensory input training of children with communication and related developmental disorders. *Journal of Autism and Childhood Schizophrenia,* 1977, **7,** 23–31.

Bonvillian, J. D., Nelson, K. E., & Rhyne, J. M. Sign language and autism. *Journal of Autism and Developmental Disorders,* 1981, **11,** 125–137.

Brookner, S. P., & Murphy, N. O. The use of a total communication approach with a nondeaf child: A case study. *Language, Speech, and Hearing Services in Schools,* 1975, **6,** 131–139.

Carr, E. D., Binkoff, J. A., Kologinski, E., & Eddy, M. Acquisition of sign language by autistic children. I: Expressive labeling. *Journal of Applied Behavior Analysis,* 1978, **11,** 489–501.

Carrier, J. K. *Application of functional analysis and a nonspeech response mode to teaching language.* Parsons Research Center Report No. 7, Parsons State Hospital and Training Center, 1973.

Carrier, J. K. Nonspeech noun usage training with severely and profoundly retarded children. *Journal of Speech and Hearing Research,* 1974, **17,** 510–517.

Deich, R. F., & Hodges, P. M. Teaching nonvocal communications to nonverbal retarded children. *Behavior Modification,* 1982, **6,** 200–228.

Dixon, L. S. A functional analysis of photo-object matching skills of severely retarded adolescents. *Journal of Applied Behavior Analysis,* 1981, **14,** 465–478.

Etzel, B. C., & LeBlanc, J. M. The simplest treatment alternative: The law of parsimony applied to choosing appropriate instructional control and errorless-learning procedures for the difficult-to-teach child. *Journal of Autism and Developmental Disorders,* 1979, **9**, 361–382.

Fulwiler, R. L., & Fouts, R. S. Acquisition of American Sign Language by a noncommunicating autistic boy. *Journal of Autism and Childhood Schizophrenia,* 1976, **6**, 43–51.

Griffith, P. L., & Robinson, J. H. Influence of iconicity and phonological similarity on sign learning by mentally retarded children. *American Journal of Mental Deficiency,* 1980, **85**, 291–298.

Hoemann, H. W. The transparency of meaning of sign language gestures. *Sign Language Studies,* 1975, **7**, 151–161.

Hoffmeister, R. J., & Farmer, A. The development of manual sign language in mentally retarded deaf individuals. *Journal of Rehabilitation for the Deaf,* 1972, **6**, 19–26.

Horner, R. D., & Baer, D. M. A multiple-probe technique: A variation of the multiple baseline. *Journal of Applied Behavior Analysis,* 1978, **11**, 189–196.

Hurlbut, B. I., Iwata, B. A., & Green, J. D. Nonvocal language acquisition in adolescents with severe physical disabilities: Blissymbol versus iconic stimulus formats. *Journal of Applied Behavior Analysis,* 1982, **15**, 241–258.

Konstantareas, M. M., Hunter, D., & Sloman, L. Training a blind autistic child to communicate through signs. *Journal of Autism and Developmental Disorders,* 1982, **12**, 1–11.

Konstantareas, M. M., Oxman, J., & Webster, C. D. Iconicity: Effects on the acquisition of sign language by autistic and other severely dysfunctional children. In P. Siple (Ed.), *Understanding language through sign language research,* New York: Academic Press, 1978.

Konstantareas, M. M., Webster, C. D., & Oxman, J. Manual language acquisition and its influence on other areas of functioning in four autistic and autistic-like children. *Journal of Child Psychology and Psychiatry,* 1979, **20**, 337–350.

Linville, S. E. Signed English: A language teaching technique with totally nonverbal, severely mentally retarded adolescents. *Language, Speech, and Hearing Services in Schools,* 1977, **8**, 170–175.

Lovaas, O. I., Koegel, R. L., & Schreibman, L. Stimulus overselectivity in autism: A review of research. *Psychological Bulletin,* 1979, **86**, 1236–1254.

McLean, L., & McLean, J. M. Language training program for non-verbal autistic children. *Journal of Speech and Hearing Research,* 1974, **35**, 186–193.

Murphy, G. H., Steele, K., Gilligan, T., Yeow, J., & Spare, D. Teaching a picture language to a non-speaking retarded boy. *Behaviour Research and Therapy,* 1977, **15**, 198–201.

Porter, P. B., & Schroeder, S. R. Generalization and maintenance of skills acquired in non-speech language initiation program training. *Applied Research in Mental Retardation,* 1980, **1**, 71–84.

Poulton, K. T., & Algozzine, B. Manual communication and mental retardation: A review of research and implications. *American Journal of Mental Deficiency,* 1980, **85**, 145–152.

Reich, G. Gestural facilitation and expressive language in moderately/severely retarded preschoolers. *Mental Retardation,* 1978, **16**, 113–117.

Reid, D. H., & Hurlbut, B. Teaching nonvocal communication skills to multihandicapped retarded adults. *Journal of Applied Behavior Analysis,* 1977, **10**, 591–603.

Robinson-Wilson, M. A. Picture recipe cards as an approach to teaching severely and profoundly retarded adults to cook. *Education and Training of the Mentally Retarded,* 1977, **12**, 69–72.

Song, A. Acquisition and use of Blissymbols by severely mentally retarded adolescents. *Mental Retardation,* 1979, **17**, 253–255.

Spellman, C. R., DeBriere, T., Jarboe, D., Campbell, S., & Harris, C. Pictorial instruction: Training daily living skills. In M. E. Snell (Ed.), *Systematic instruction of the moderately and severely handicapped.* Columbus, Ohio: Merrill, 1978.

Stokes, T. F., & Baer, D. M. An implicit technology of generalization. *Journal of Applied Behavior Analysis,* 1977, **10**, 349–367.

Striefel, S., Bryan, K. S., & Aikins, D. A. Transfer of stimulus control from motor to verbal stimuli. *Journal of Applied Behavior Analysis,* 1974, **7**, 123–135.

Vanderheiden, D. H., Brown, W. P., MacKenzie, P., Reinen, S., & Scheibel, C. Symbol communication for the mentally handicapped. *Mental Retardation,* 1975, **13**, 34–37.

Microcomputers and Severely Handicapped Students: Are We Overbidding Our Hand?

Karen Hughes
Dan Smith

DAN SMITH is Coordinator for Development with the Instructional Media Production Project for Severely Handicapped Students. He has served as Information Specialist with the National Media Materials Center for Severely Handicapped Persons and has an M.S. in psychology and education.

KAREN HUGHES is the Coordinator for Public Information with the Instructional Media Production Project for Severely Handicapped Students. She has served as the Coordinator for Development with the National Media Materials Center for Severely Handicapped Persons and has served on the Handicapped Advisory Board for the Tennessee State Museum. Ms. Hughes' background is in media production and communications.

TECHNOLOGY: AN HISTORICAL PERSPECTIVE

Let us look at technology, especially educational technology, as a room full of tools. We are always making additions to the collection. In the corner of the room is the first sharp stick used to write in the sand, and next to it is a pot of pigment and a roll of papyrus. In another corner we see the first graphite pencil, and close by, and old slate and some chalk. We also spot, in the distance, a slide rule and a bulky table-model calculator. Closer to us sits a compact, hand-held calculator with memory functions. Finally, we come to the newest addition in the collection: a dual disk drive microcomputer with output modes for video display and videodisc. It is in our nature to reach for the newest and best, so we reach for the microcomputer. But have we reached too fast?

If we have not taken a close look at the student and at the material to be taught, we have reached too fast. Severely handicapped students make up a very small segment of the total

Microcomputers are the wave of the future and will revolutionize educational technology as they revolutionize almost every other aspect of our lives. But are they always the most effective and efficient learning tool for severely handicapped students? Perhaps not. At least, they are not the best tool for all severely handicapped learners. There are less complex, less expensive, easier-to-produce, and easier-to-use media that can do an outstanding job of teaching specific skills. We need to be imaginative enough to realize that microcomputers may not always be the best answer, and we need to be realistic enough to look for simple or "low tech" methods when "high tech" is literally beyond the grasp of our learners. If we are truly committed to creating student-use materials, we need to learn from our severely handicapped students. They can tell us which medium and which method is best for them as individual learners. This paper will describe some of the media and methods now being investigated by the Instructional Media Production Project for Severely Handicapped Students as it develops student-use materials.

"Microcomputers and Severely Handicapped Students: Are We Overbidding Our Hand?" Karen Hughes, Dan Smith, *American Annals of the Deaf*, Vol. 127, No. 5, September 1982. Copyright 1982 by the American Annals of the Deaf.

student population, but within that small segment we find students with a wide range of abilities and disabilities. The situation is described by Liberty (1982): "Severely handicapped" may be one of the most heterogeneous classifications ever formed. Individuals differ so much from one another that researchers must be very specific and individualistic in describing subjects—unlike homogeneous groups, who may be described by their chronological age and/or grade level.

A student, for example, who is blind and severely physically disabled may well be able to use a microcomputer with basic adaptations such as a head wand and an Optacon reader. A student who is hearing impaired and learning disabled may be able to use a microcomputer programmed to remediate the specific learning disability. But a student who is severely or profoundly retarded or severely behaviorally disordered (other than autistic), even if he or she has no serious physical disability, is going to have trouble using the microcomputer without extensive teacher/trainer assistance.

There are ways to program the computer to present vivid visual displays in response to a single "hit" on an adapted switch. These are used in creating "match" or "recognition" tasks. But what we have done is to create an expensive "high tech" set of flash cards, and this is certainly not the best use of the technology, the teacher/trainer's time, or the students' time.

Aeschleman & Tawney (1978) described an interesting example of an innovative, "high tech," computer-based telecommunications system for educating severely handicapped preschoolers in their homes. By using a NOVA 1200 minicomputer, a mainframe consisting of a prewired card file for accommodating up to eight stations, master-power supplies, a system clock, a probability generator, an interconnecting cable, two ASR-33 model teletypewriters with paper-tape punch, a high speed paper-tape reader, and an Automated Contingency Translator (ACT) language, a system was devised to deliver two basic types of instructional programs.

The programs developed served to strengthen or increase the rate of motor response in the severely handicapped learners and to teach several visual discriminations. During the 3-year project, 18 families were served by the system. Eighteen severely handicapped, preschool children from rural or isolated areas received instruction they may never have gotten without the marvelous system. But can we look at this intricate, expensive, and somewhat esoteric model as a realistic means of education? Probably someday, because of advances in technology, it will become practical. But what about today? And what about your community?

Let us not be so eager to explore the newest technology that we overlook some of the ways in which older technology can be used. Educational technology is advancing at such a rapid rate that it has not been possible for materials developers to fully explore potential uses for all media. So it is not "backtracking" if we take some time to investigate new ways of using "older" media with handicapped learners. It is really a step forward. Bork (1982) puts it this way:

> When a new education medium develops, understanding its use can be a long and painful process. For example, many computer based learning materials treat the page of the screen as if it were the page of a book; yet even a cursory consideration shows that the capabilities of these two media are entirely different. (p.36)

THE BEGINNING OF STUDENT-USE MEDIA

The Instructional Media Production Project for Severely Handicapped Students (IMPPSHS) is now in the second year of its second contract. The project began as the National Media Materials Center for Severely Handicapped Persons and as such produced many mediated materials now commercially available. Some of these materials were directed at a broad audience; some were directed at teachers, trainers, and parents and presented new teaching methods on a broad scope. Some materials were developed to teach specific training techniques. But it was not until this past year that the workscope included student-use media. It was a case of perfect timing.

In all honesty, if we had been asked to produce student-use media without an extensive background in instructional media production, we might have been stymied. But, as it was, many of the products and their corresponding development processes provided clues as to how to begin conceptualizing student-use, instructional media (Hughes, 1981). We had, for example, some idea of the elements found in commercial films that would attract and hold the interest of severely retarded learners. We also had investigated the television-viewing habits of severely behaviorally disordered learners and severely or profoundly retarded students and what elements in the programs (or commercials) seemed to attract them.

The first student-use material produced by our first contract was an "adaptation" product (i.e., a product based on an already existing idea or material). The product was a new soundtrack for 16mm commercially available sex education film FERTILIZATION AND BIRTH. We coined the term "verbal captioning" for the process that we used with this film which involved removing the original soundtrack and replacing it with a soundtrack designed for severely retarded learners. This effort was made in 1980, and although it has not been a huge commercial success, the study that went into developing the technique and selecting the particular film which was to undergo this process has assisted us greatly in the work of our current contract.

The first student-use material developed as an original product by the project was completed in 1981. It is a videotape and an accompanying teacher/trainer manual of activities. The tape BASIC SOCIAL SKILLS: GREETING PEOPLE is designed along the same general lines as regular broadcast television commercials. It includes short segments of high interest involving simple interactions among a small group of individuals—each of whom was selected because he or she could be easily recognized by our student audience. We included several handicapped students, and for our adult figure, we were fortunate to have Betty Aberlin who plays

phisticated, professional editing of the tape. We used special effects to move from one scene to the next, and the quality of production is totally professional. Because our goal was to produce a set of "commercials" that teach, we had to use as many professional techniques as possible in order to encourage viewers to attend to the screen. In the past few years, we have realized that our severely handicapped students are "media wise" and that they have been exposed, especially through regular broadcast television, to every special effect imaginable. Therefore, it would be unrealistic of us to expect learners to be impressed with anything less than an imaginative production. (This is something to be remembered in any instructional media production planning.)

Apple Computer is advancing computer literacy among children by donating nearly 10,000 Apple //e personal computer systems to California schools.

Lady Aberlin on the "Mister Rogers" television show. The characters are depicted in many situations where a greeting is or is not appropriate, and the cues for behavior are repeated for the viewer. The characters also interact and invite interaction with the viewer by addressing him or her through the camera. The tape can be stopped for any of the 17 segments that the teacher selects. Activities suggested in the manual can be used to reinforce the learning method.

Although the use of videotape is not always a "high tech" production method, in the case of BASIC SOCIAL SKILLS: GREETING PEOPLE it became "high tech" because of the so-

The success of BASIC SOCIAL SKILLS was really above our expectations. Although our contract does not fund extensive field testing, we took every opportunity to share the tape with severely handicapped students in a variety of settings including a product showing on the Peabody Campus. During that product showing, one of the students who had played roles in two of our other productions saw BASIC SOCIAL SKILLS for the first time. When BASIC SOCIAL SKILLS began, he interacted well with the characters on the screen, and he greeted and said "good-bye" to Lady Aberlin in a loud, clear voice in spite of his mother's stern look and nudges. You could identify project staff members by their mile-wide grins.

The technique used in producing BASIC SOCIAL SKILLS is obviously a good model for interactive videotape program production. It is cost-efficient; it attracts and holds the attention of most severely handicapped students; it promotes the desired interaction; and, in a very important way, it affords the teacher/trainer real opportunities to plan and carry out activities appropriate for the student or student group. We realize that although this is only one of the many possible formats that professionals can use in producing student-use media successfully, it is a strong beginning because with this format additional programs can be developed. We hope to produce several new tapes during our third contract year using the BASIC SOCIAL SKILLS' format to teach other social skills, such as taking directions or accepting criticism.

CURRENT STUDENT-USE MEDIA DEVELOPMENT

Because videotape is such a practical medium to use, the current student-use product being developed by the project takes advantage of videotape. The new product ME, MY SELF, AND EYE is, however, very different from BASIC SOCIAL SKILLS: GREETING PEOPLE. ME, MY SELF, AND EYE is actually a model or plan designed so that teachers (with or without the assistance of a media specialist) can produce tapes for classroom use wherein the individual instructional needs of severely handicapped students are met. The primary focus of our first tapes has been to develop coordinated, visual-motor tracking skills. We hope to expand this focus to include, perhaps, left/right discrimination, sequencing, and other tasks that can be presented well on a video screen.

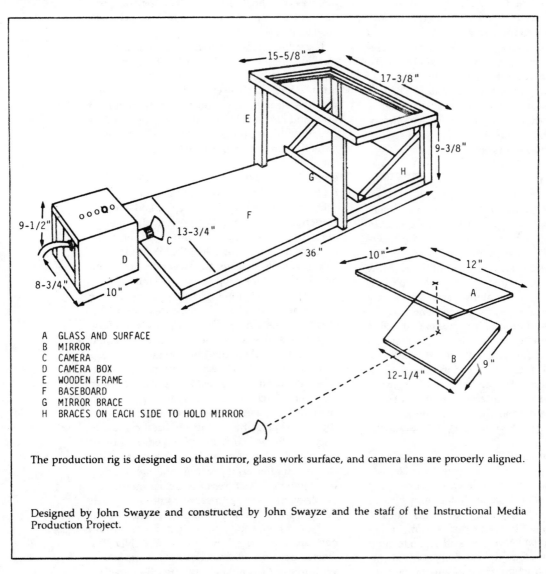

A   GLASS AND SURFACE
B   MIRROR
C   CAMERA
D   CAMERA BOX
E   WOODEN FRAME
F   BASEBOARD
G   MIRROR BRACE
H   BRACES ON EACH SIDE TO HOLD MIRROR

The production rig is designed so that mirror, glass work surface, and camera lens are properly aligned.

Designed by John Swayze and constructed by John Swayze and the staff of the Instructional Media Production Project.

Figure 1.   Production rig.

The ME, MY SELF, AND EYE video programs allow for direct interaction between the severely handicapped student and the highly personalized instructional content displayed on the television screen. How can material presented on the television be personal, and how can the student interact with it? Last year the project was fortunate to work with two consultants: Dr. John Swayze, a psychologist with a penchant for invention, and Joan Forsdale, a freelance media design consultant.

The great variety of instructional innovation developed jointly by these two consultants over the years is applicable to these questions. We held an inhouse workshop in which John Swayze showed us how to build an ingenious rig similar to one he developed years ago for "Super 8" film equipment. The rig, consisting of no more than a plate glass work surface, a mirror mounted beneath it, and a video camera aimed at the mirror, allowed us to lay materials out on the glass surface, to draw on those materials, and to move them around to create animated forms (Figure 1). The effect as it appears on the television screen is somewhat magical. Lines appear and take various shapes. Objects appear and disappear. A dot becomes a line. The line becomes a letter of the alphabet. The letter is followed by other letters. A student's name appears stroke by stroke on the television screen, as if written by an invisible hand.

In this same workshop, Joan Forsdale demonstrated a number of the practically infinite instructional possibilities available to the teacher and student because of this relatively inexpensive and easy-to-use production process. During the remainder of the workshop, we brainstormed and experimented with instructional applications for our target audience. How can material presented on television be personal? By designing materials specifically for a student's needs and by including elements such as the child's photograph or a scene showing his or her "totem" or favorite object, a teacher can tailor the content to both the student's capabilities and interest and can include the personal recognition factor. How can a severely handicapped student interact with the material? Joan Forsdale demonstrated that the mode of interaction is dependent upon each student's capabilities.

In some cases, the student may make a simple gesture and point at the screen to indicate a choice of or the answer to a visually presented problem. In other cases, a student may be able to use "wipe-off" dry markers to track lines or forms directly on the television screen. Excitement among members of our staff began to build as we envisioned all the capabilities of this inexpensive production process—one that would enable teachers to make materials for students and would allow students, in turn, to interact with those materials.

Subsequent to the inhouse workshop, the project staff has been involved in laying out not only instructional content but also an entire do-it-yourself process so teachers can develop their own production rigs. The ME, MY SELF, AND EYE process enables teachers to design highly specific mediated materials for their own students.

At our recent national symposium, the ME, MY SELF, AND EYE concept was demonstrated for a great variety of teachers and special educators. Our staff presented the program in a workshop session where we explained the construction of the production rig, the basic equipment required, and the description of the process used in creating video materials for a student or an entire class with a minimal investment of time and money. We demonstrated ME, MY SELF, AND EYE using a number of handicapped students. Each student worked through a series of exercises in which he or she drew directly on the screen with the wipe-off markers.

The exercises, which focused on visual-motor tracking, required each student to attempt to follow a dot as it moved across the screen to form a line. Each exercise increased in complexity—straight lines came first, then curved lines and circles followed. Each set of exercises ended with the student writing his or her own name. Polaroid pictures of students flashed on the screen as reinforcements following each exercise. The students were delighted. They were motivated by this approach to learning.

During the time in which we worked with the students prior to our symposium demonstration, we noticed a marked improvement in the learners' tracking skills. The ME, MY SELF, AND EYE materials that we demonstrated reflected much work by the project staff. We refined both the instructional content as it appeared on the screen and the production process itself numerous times. The end result is now a carefully designed and easy-to-use production method that can be implemented by teachers. Key elements designed to make any content idea workable have been anticipated and provided for in the model. Such elements include a "pen ready" cue which appears on the screen instructing the student to place his or her pen down prior to tracking; "wipe" cues are displayed, and these are models showing the learner how to clean the screen after each exercise; and we use personal totems or pictures of objects from the student's surroundings to serve as links between the instructional content and the student's world.

The response by our national symposium participants to the ME, MY SELF, AND EYE workshop was overwhelmingly supportive. Within less than a week, two teachers had returned to their school systems and were building rigs. Like many teachers, they found that their school system already had most of the equipment they needed—a television, a video-cassette recorder, and a camera. The only materials that had to be bought were a mirror, the plate glass work surface, and the wooden frame to hold everything together properly. Many others left the symposium with similar plans of getting started, and the project staff aims to keep in close touch with as many participants as possible so that it can follow their progress and incorporate their discoveries into the overall product design.

One of the final products of ME, MY SELF, AND EYE will be a production guidebook that will instruct teachers on how to build the rig and how to create materials with an overview of instructional content ideas. We say "one of the final products," because we hope that in year three of our contract we will be able to further develop instructional content and perhaps produce sample tapes of more complicated tasks with descriptions of the types of students this product will benefit.

Although our project has been most involved with using videotape, we are also aware of several other efficient and effective plans for developing student-use media on an "as needed" basis. While a doctoral candidate at the University of Georgia, Sharpton (1981) developed an interesting plan for teaching his severely retarded, junior-high school students transportation skills. He developed both a videotape and a slide sequence to teach students the specific cues they needed to learn to cross streets safely, to locate a pay phone, and to give the signal to the bus driver as he/she approaches their stops. The slides and videotapes were made of the actual locations where students need to use the skills.

Mike Dixon at the Bureau of Child Research in Parsons, Kansas, has done work using Polaroid pictures of both people and locations around that facility in which he tries to develop recognition skills in severely retarded learners. The goal for part of this program is to develop students' confidence in walking or moving alone from one location to another.

Both of these ideas are admittedly "low tech" uses of media, but both are cost-effective and have a built-in reward for students—the learners can see their own environments in a mediated format! Also, almost any special education teacher—even those who have some resistance to using new technology—can use both of these ideas.

CONCLUSION

Because the population of severely handicapped students is so varied and complex, we must use caution when applying the label "severely handicapped" to statements of our goals relating to developing instructional software for microcomputers. We would be wrong to say that all severely handicapped students can ultimately be taught to use computers; but we would be just as wrong to say that no severely handicapped students can use them. We must examine each student's capabilities and do so optimistically!

There is a case study of a young student with cerebral palsy and severe communication problems in the resource guide "Personal Computers for the Physically Disabled" produced by Apple Computer, Inc. This case study about John Glicksman was written by his parents Hal and Mary Ann (n.d.). They describe their success in adapting the "joy stick" and the "Breakout" game pattern and speed to their son who began to play games using the Apple II. They were later able to adapt a head wand and now use the computer as a communication device rather than investing in several single-purpose communication devices (Glicksman & Glicksman, n.d.).

Other case studies show that autistic students can use microcomputers as both communication and creative outlets where no other equipment or methods have been effective in making contact with them (Swezey, 1982). Dr. Sylvia Weir, in the March 1982 fifth annual Symposium of the Instructional Media Production Project for Severely Handicapped Students, described several success stories where some severely physically handicapped and autistic students were able to use the LOGO computer language system (developed at the Massachusetts Institute of Technology and now commercially available) to write programs, communicate, and find creative outlets.

We cannot say that these students are "exceptional" within our given population because that implies that there are only a few for whom microcomputer programs or materials are effective learning devices. We do not know at this point; indeed, it may be several years before we know how the infinitely varied student group now labeled "severely handicapped" breaks down statistically into possible computer users and nonusers. The students about whom we have real reservations in their ultimate use of microcomputers are the severely or profoundly retarded and the severely behaviorally disordered groups (other than autistic). Microcomputers are an instructional medium that make real demands on the attention span of the learner. The efficient use of microcomputers requires some ability to generalize and to remember. When dealing with students for whom these things are very difficult, perhaps we cannot realistically employ microcomputers. To use the practical and descriptive phrase created by Brown (1976), perhaps it is not within their "criterion of ultimate functioning."

But let us look at these ideas in a positive light. If a student cannot benefit from interaction with computers, what other media are appropriate? Which medium is practical for the student and the teacher? Which medium is the most cost-efficient in teaching a particular skill? And after we have selected a medium, what format or instructional design works best with that student?

These are questions we ask at the Instructional Media Production Project as we explore student-use media development. We have had very encouraging results with videotape in both a professionally produced package that allows for teacher intervention and interaction and in the ME, MY SELF, AND EYE model where teachers create their own tapes to meet specific students' needs. But we know we are just be-

ginning to find the answers. We are not at all frustrated by the fact that some of our target learners cannot use computers, because computers are just one of the many categories of instructional media with which we can work.

Even though it looks as if we are placing the burden of choice on the teacher/trainer or parent, ultimately, the student chooses. We must learn from our students whether or not the microcomputer is a realistic mode of instruction, and if it is not, we must decide which medium can best meet the need. When we find the most preferable medium, then it is time to create materials with all of the imagination and technical sophistication we can muster.

REFERENCES

Aeschleman, S. R., & Tawney, J. W. Interacting: A computer-based telecommunications system for educating severely handicapped preschoolers in their homes. *Educational Technology*, October 1978, pp. 30–35.

Bork, A. Reasonable uses of computers. *Instructional Innovator*, February 1982, pp. 27, 36.

Brown, L., Nietupski, J., & Hamre-Nietupski, S. The criterion of ultimate functioning. In M. A. Thomas (Ed.), *Hey, don't forget about me!* Reston, Va.: The Council for Exceptional Children, 1976.

Glicksman, H., & Glicksman, M. The difference a personal computer can make. *Personal computers for the physically disabled: A resource guide.* Cupertino, Ca.: Apple Computer, Inc., n.d.

Hughes, K. Exploring "direct-use" media for severely handicapped students. *Media Management Journal*, 1981, *1*, 6–16.

Liberty, K. Instructional technology—where is it? *The Association for the Severely Handicapped Newsletter*, March 1982, pp. 1–3.

Sharpton, W. Adapting media and materials for community skills instruction. *The Journal of Special Education Technology*, Spring 1981, *4*, 20–23.

Swezey, S. How did that computer get into the bedroom? *The Directive Teacher*, Winter/Spring 1982, pp. 14–30.

BIBLIOGRAPHY

Beck, J. J. The microcomputer bandwagon: Is it playing your tune? *The Directive Teacher*, Winter/Spring 1982, pp. 12–27.

Computers are objects to think with: interview with Seymour Papert. *Instructor and Teacher*, March 1982, pp. 86–89.

Thomas, L. *Lives of a cell: Notes of a biology water.* New York: Penguin Books, 1978.

MICROS IN THE SPECIAL ED CLASSROOM

PROFILE: *One Student's Success Story*

—*Dina Loebl and Ilene Kantrov*

Dina Loebl, a program developer and consultant on computers in special education, conducted the research described here. Ilene Kantrov is an Associate of the Center for Learning Technology of Education Development Center, Newton, MA.

SEAN HAS CEREBRAL palsy. He can walk, but he cannot talk—he communicates mainly with sounds, and some sign language.

Sean is nine years old, but his performance on tests and in school shows that he has the mental capacity of a child of three. He knows the numbers 1 and 2, recognizes eight colors, and is able to identify a circle, triangle, and square. Sean rarely spends more than two or three minutes on an assigned classroom task, but he watches his favorite TV shows for 45 minutes or more.

Not long ago, Sean participated in a study, conducted at several Boston area institutions for special education, that used a microcomputer-based system to teach perceptual discrimination skills (matching and distinguishing colors and shapes) to developmentally impaired children with multiple handicaps. The analysis of the educational barriers that such

children encounter, and the design and testing of a system created to overcome those barriers, provide an instructive case study for the use of microcomputers in special education.

The Challenge

A developmentally impaired child who cannot speak, cannot manipulate a pencil, and cannot concentrate on a workbook or even a set of blocks for more than several minutes presents a particularly difficult challenge to a teacher. The challenge is twofold: on the one hand, to determine what the child knows and is capable of learning; and on the other hand, to teach the child what he or she needs to learn in order to function as independently as possible.

Conventional methods and materials used in special education often compound these problems. Consider the materials commonly used to teach colors in special education classrooms.

A child, like Sean, has to pick up a colored peg and place it in a matching slot—a task that requires several capacities. Sean must be able to follow instructions, must remember what to do and how to do it, must have sufficient fine motor coordination to pick up the peg and insert it into the slot, and must pay atten-

tion and be motivated long enough to carry out the task.

If Sean cannot complete the task, the teacher may decide he is incapable of learning, when in fact he may simply be unable to hold onto the peg. And, if he does get the peg into the right slot and is rewarded in some way, he may not realize that the reward is for matching the colors, rather than for holding the peg or staying at the table where the materials are set up.

Most conventional instructional materials used to teach developmentally impaired children have similar limitations. They do not permit the targeting of specific skills; they do not intrinsically motivate the handicapped child; and they do not provide feedback directly tied to the learning goal. Children like Sean can seldom be induced to spend more than a few minutes at a time using such materials.

The Software

The programs written for the research study in which Sean participated were specially prepared. They were based on a thorough analysis of what children like Sean can do and what they like to do, as well as what they need to learn.

Because these children's senses of sight and hearing are neurologically mature, the programs rely heavily on the computer's graphics and audio capabilities. Sean is typical in that he will sit and watch TV for long periods of time, so it was expected that programs incorporating pictures, action, and sound would significantly increase his attention span.

The interactive potential of the computer was also tapped. Children like Sean need continual and immediate feedback if they are to remain motivated to learn, and they delight in any opportunity to exert control over their environment—a control, unfortunately, that their physical disabilities usually deny them.

Finally, for Sean to be able to use the programs, an easily operable input device—such as a game paddle—was required as well. Unlike conventional computer keyboards, the specially-designed game paddles used in the study can be manipulated by users with minimal fine motor coordination.

The two programs developed—Colors and Shapes—operate in much the same way. The color program, for example, presents one color at a time on the monitor. Each of four paddles is marked with one of the colors, and to answer correctly a child must press the appropriate paddle when a color appears on the screen.

A correct response produces music with a strong march beat, and animated graphics that were carefully designed to incorporate familiar objects and situations (and to avoid the potential hazard of flashing visuals that might produce seizures in children who suffer from epilepsy and related disorders). No sound is produced for an incorrect response.

Both programs can be used with from one to four paddles at a time, and the order of the colors or shapes can be controlled. The program records the number and sequence of correct and incorrect responses.

The Results

The results of the tests were dramatic in terms of increased attention span, and promising (though mixed) in mastery of the skills being taught. Out of the ten children tested, nearly all showed improvement in response time and number of correct responses.

During his first 35-minute session at the computer, Sean learned quickly that he had to press the appropriate paddles and wait for the animation. He was elated when he realized he could control what came on the screen, and he wanted to be sure he gave the right answers.

The three sessions conducted with Sean suggested that at least some of his previous difficulty in learning shapes and colors derived from his short attention span with the conventional materials used to teach those skills. Interaction with the computer increased the length of time he would focus on a task from 3 to 35 minutes, and he demonstrated his ability to learn new skills rapidly.

In Sean's case, moreover, the diagnosis that he suffered from severe mental retardation had to be revised. Using the computer, he was able to learn in one half-hour session what might have taken months for him to learn with traditional methods.

Basic Support for Curriculum: Teacher Preparation and Community Involvement

The decade of the seventies was characterized by parent involvement with special education. The involvement was so intense as to be pervasive. The questions now being asked concern how much parent involvement is necessary, and whether more or less involvement make a difference in the education for the handicapped child. The prevailing view in the seventies was that, because handicapped children are in need of extra or special education, they must also be in need of extra support for the curriculum that is designed for them. Differing points of view are still being espoused as to how much or how little extra support the school and the child need.

The degree to which parents are expected to be involved in educational decisions concerning their children was outlined in the Federal Register (1981): "The IEP meeting serves as a communication vehicle between parents and school personnel, and enables them as equal participants to jointly decide what the child's needs are, what services will be provided to meet those needs, and what the anticipated outcomes will be" (p. 5462). The word "equal" in the foregoing statement means that parents are expected to take an active role in deciding what curriculum will be used to educate their child. There are even some school systems that have attempted to force either the parents, or a parent substitute, to take a course of study designed to familiarize them with the special education for their child. Many parents object to this idea, because they lack either the interest or the time. The school and the professionals are expected to provide what is necessary for the needs of the special child.

Support for curriculum includes elements, other than parent involvement that provide help for both the teacher and the student. In any given community there is an attitude of acceptance or one of rejection toward the mentally handicapped. Either attitude can have a profound impact on the progress of these individuals. A community that provides places in private industry for the retarded helps the programs that are set up to train them. If it desires, private industry can provide tremendous amounts of support. There are fund raising drives and contributions that are enhanced when they are backed by concerned executives. Money for sheltered workshops, much of which can come from the community, can provide places for the trainably retarded to go each day where they can be productive and contribute to the economy of the community. Trainable mentally retarded individuals, who are capable of living in a group home, should be given the opportunity. Group home living allows the retarded individual to experience life as others in the community do — in "the least restrictive environment." Each group home needs at least one counselor to help the residents to cope with day to day living chores; doing the wash, paying the bills, cleaning their rooms. The residents feel, and are, more self-sufficient than they would be in an institution, or at home with their parents.

One of the most important aspects of curriculum support involves special teacher training. In order for any program to work to its optimum, the teachers involved must be correctly trained. Teacher training can be accomplished by extra course work and workshops. All teachers who will be involved with special children must understand their special needs. The teachers must also have the correct attitude toward special students. A regular classroom teacher cannot feel that the handicapped child, mainstreamed in the class, is a burden that the teacher and class must endure. Each child must be viewed as an individual with individual interests, strengths and weaknesses, feelings. Each individual is a challenge to the ability, creativity and sensitivity of the teacher. With the correct attitude, teachers can greatly enhance the future of each handicapped child.

Integrated Counseling Services for Exceptional Children: A Functional, Noncategorical Model

Greg H. Frith
Reba M. Clark
Susanne H. Miller

Greg H. Frith is chairman of the Special Education Department, Jacksonville State University. Reba M. Clark is director of Instruction and Guidance, Vestavia Hills Schools, Vestavia Hills, Alabama. Susanne H. Miller is special education coordinator for Vestavia Hills Schools.

Since the adoption of Public Law 94-142, counseling services for exceptional children have been widely described in the professional literature (Boyer, 1979; Carey, 1977; Humes, 1978). More specifically, the literature has focused on elementary programs (Prescott & Iseline, 1978; Rudolph, 1978), secondary programs (ASCA Governing Board, 1977; Lambie, 1976), parent strategies (Connoly, 1978; Morris, 1976; Wandler, 1978), training programs (Baker, 1976; Sweeney, 1979), mainstreaming concerns (Cochrane & Marini, 1977), and a variety of exceptionalities (Monacco, 1978; Morris, 1976; Owsley, 1978; Rudolph, 1978; Vargo, 1978). Each of these reviews has contributed to the theoretical constructs included in comprehensive counseling for exceptional children. What the literature has lacked is a description of an actual system-wide counseling program in which all of these theoretical constructs are integrated into a functional unit.

This article describes such a program, administered by the Vestavia Hills Public Schools, Vestavia Hills, Alabama. Special emphasis is placed on three major support systems that facilitate interaction between regular and special education. These support systems are staffing considerations, school and community resources, and peer participation. Several subcomponents within each of these support systems are also discussed.

REGULAR–SPECIAL EDUCATION INTEGRATION

To strengthen the integration between regular and special education programs, teachers (regular and special) and counselors work with students from all exceptionalities. Also, labeling is minimized, as children who are eligible for special education services attend the "Learning Lab," rather than "special education classes."

The placement process is facilitated by stressing four strategies in addition to traditional considerations. These strategies are: (a) the inclusion of a counselor from referral through IEP implementation (referrals are first made to the counselor); (b) a documented history of intervention techniques that are attempted before referrals are initiated with the counselor; (c) the option of eligible students to attend the "Learning Lab"; and (d) complete integration of handicapped and nonhandicapped students during the home room period.

The time required for a counselor to be this actively involved in the provision of services to exceptional students is significant. However, since 18% of the school system's student population has been diagnosed as exceptional, the time commitment is certainly proportional to the total number of students being served. In addition, the counselor's active participation in the referral/placement process serves to minimize communication problems that might occur later—that is, counselors do not usually learn of problems "after the fact." By being informed early, they often function in a preventative role.

COUNSELING SUPPORT SYSTEMS FOR EXCEPTIONAL STUDENTS

Staffing Considerations

The Vestavia Hills school system consists of two elementary schools, a middle school, and a high school. One counselor is assigned to each elementary school, two to the middle school, and four to the high school. In addition to these eight counselors in grades

K–12, each school is equipped with a counselor aide (paraprofessional) to assist with clerical functions. Total student enrollment is 3,186, of which 18% are exceptional.

Each of the four high school counselors is primarily assigned to a particular grade. Eash counselor rotates upward on an annual basis with the same students to promote counselor–student familiarity. Evaluative feedback indicates that this supporting process is particularly useful for exceptional students and for others who have limited coping skills.

All counseling staff, including the aides, work for a month prior to the beginning of each school year to facilitate planning and evaluation and to assist with faculty and student orientation sessions. During this time, the counseling staff participates in a 3- to 5-day workshop to coordinate counseling activities for the year and to identify needs of incoming students. To facilitate this effort, teachers of exceptional students provide the counseling staff with information relating to their respective pupils. This information is helpful in fostering interaction between special and regular education students. It also promotes communication among the professional staff.

School and Community Resources

The three basic resources that support the integration of regular and special education are: (a) an affective counseling curriculum guide; (b) parents and volunteers; and (c) the physical plant. The Vestavia Hills counseling program is based on an affective curriculum guide, which was developed by the professional staff. In designing this guide, the staff considered the competencies of currently employed personnel, fiscal resources, community support, recommendations in the professional literature, and priorities of the students. Counseling activities involving exceptional students are described throughout the guide. An example of such an activity follows.

CATEGORY: Students in Fifth and Sixth Grades, Students New to School

GOAL: Educational Development

OBJECTIVE: Fifth and sixth grade students will be presented with an orientation about the nature and needs of children who function at the moderate level of intellectual development. Students will be told why these children attend this school, what can be expected of them, and how they, as nonhandicapped students, can assist these children.

ACTIVITIES: 1. Counselors and teachers of the moderately retarded children will meet with fifth and sixth grade students to discuss this special program.
2. Counseling personnel will provide information to students who wish to serve as volunteer tutors (helpers) to assist moderately retarded children.

EVALUATION: 1. Following the presentations in the orientation sessions, counselors will administer an informal questionnaire questionnaire that includes the following:

   a. why moderately retarded children attend Pizitz Middle School;
   b. what can be expected of these children;
   c. how nonhandicapped students can help.

2. Counselors will carefully observe mutual adjustment among regular and moderately retarded students, with input from teachers being given particular attention.
3. Participation by nonhandicapped students in volunteer programs working with moderately retarded peers.

The counseling guide contains well-defined activities in three major developmental areas: personal/social, educational, and career. Activities in each of these developmental areas are grade specific, beginning with kindergarden and proceeding through the 12th grade. Implications that pertain exclusively to exceptional students are clearly identified.

Parents and volunteers from the community are a second major resource that supports the integrated counseling program. These individuals serve as a "resource bank" and are particularly useful for counseling. People from a wide variety of professions, many of which are appropriate for exceptional adults, are invited into the schools to share pertinent career information. Career counseling includes vocational awareness at the elementary level, exploration in the middle school, and preparation for eventual employment in the high school.

Community involvement is fostered through a quarterly newsletter published by the counseling staff. Information concerning exceptional students is featured regularly in the newsletter. In addition, ideas and topics for inclusion in the newsletter are frequently generated by the students.

Another important resource for the counseling program is the physical plant. The counseling facilities in each school are situated away from the administrative offices. Ample space is provided for individual and group counseling, the counselor's aide, a career information room, and parent conferences. (Group counseling is done primarily at the middle and high school levels.)

Peer Participation

Evaluative feedback from the counseling staff indicated that student participation was a major factor in determining whether regular and special education programs could be successfully integrated. Student participation meant more than merely coexisting or getting along with each other. It also referred to active cooperation and the desire to provide supportive assistance when it was needed. The counseling staff believed that achieving this type of integration would require more than rules established by authority figures. Students needed to become personally involved, thus identifying with the effort. The idea of a student tutoring program was therefore conceived.

To participate in the peer tutoring program, nonhandicapped students must file a formal application with the counseling staff. Students who are selected to work as tutors are carefully matched with handicapped peers in terms of age, interests, schedules, or other factors that the staff considers important. Being selected as a tutor is viewed as an honor by the students, a position that is reinforced by parents, teachers, and counselors.

Another example of student participation is counseling services provided to moderately retarded pupils. (Refer to the example taken from the counseling curriculum guide.) These particular handicapped students spend an average of 3 hours per day interacting with nonhandicapped peers in such classes as adapted physical education, home economics, homeroom, lunch, and middle school exploratory programs. To facilitate the cooperation of nonhandicapped students, a training session for them is provided at the beginning of each school year by the counselor and the appropriate "Learning Lab"" teacher who has primary responsibility for moderately retarded students. For example, a teacher might say, "Carolyn will hug you a lot" or "Michael needs a lot of encouragement to get involved."

A third approach for encouraging peer participation includes two orientation sessions conducted during the last month of the fifth and eighth grades. The fifth grade session is exclusively for exceptional students. Both exceptional and nonexceptional student participate in the second session. The purpose of these orientation programs is to prepare students for middle and high school. Students are told what behaviors are expected of them, as well as what they can expect from their teachers and counselors and from each other. In addition, information is provided about facilities, schedules, extracurricular events, homework, and the tutoring program. The counseling staff contends that this extra support is needed to facilitate a smooth transition between educational levels.

VESTAVIA'S EFFECTIVE COUNSELING PROGRAM

The counseling program in the Vestavia Hills School System is a noncategorical, functional model that incorporates the best tenets of the professional literature into a viable unit.

Emphasis is placed on integrating regular and special education programs by conducting activities that foster interaction between exceptional and nonexceptional students. Support systems within the counseling program include staffing considerations, school and community resources, and peer participation.

The comprehensive counseling program is involved in a continuous evaluation process. The entire staff is included, especially those individuals who work with exceptional students. Each objective of the program is evaluated by the staff in terms of its affect on students. This formative evaluation is done fairly, as specific activities are implemented.

A summative evaluation of the entire program is conducted once a year, at the end of the school term in May. This evaluation is based on input compiled from formal questionnaires completed by parents, students, teachers, and administrators. In addition to program evaluation, the performance of each counselor is also reviewed on an annual basis. The director of instruction and guidance and the respective building principal are responsible for this evaluation.

Replication of the Vestavia Hills model could be facilitated through using the affective curriculum guide developed by the counseling staff. The various components of the Vestavia Hills program that are described here could be adapted, or specific elements could be added, depending on the needs and resources of a particular school system and the community in which it functions. Replication costs would be nominal, and preparation of personnel could be conducted along with regular staff development activities.

REFERENCES

ASCA Governing Board. The role of the secondary school counselor. *The School Counselor*, 1977, *24*, 228–234.

Baker, L.D. Preparing school counselors to work with exceptional students. "*School Guidance Worker*, 1976, *32*, 27–30.

Boyer, E.L. P.L. 94-142: A promising start. *Educational Leadership*, 1979, *26*, 298–301.

Carey, R. Trends in counseling and student services. *NASSP Bulletin*, 1977, *61*, 3–10.

Cochrane, P.V., & Marini, B. Mainstreaming exceptional children: The counselor's role. *The School Counselor*, 1977, *25*, 17–22.

Connoly, C. Counseling parents of school aged children with special needs. *Journal of School Health*, 1978, *48*, 115–117.

Humes, C.W. School counselora and P.L. 94-142. *The School Counselor*, 1978, *25*, 192–195.

Lambie, W.J. Special education and counseling services for secondary schools. *School Guidance Worker*, 1976, *32*, 27–30.

Monacco, J.C. Helping the learning disabled student: What counselors can do. *Journal of Counseling Services*, 1978, *2*, 21–24.

Morris, J. The counselor, the parents, and the mildly retarded student. *School Guidance Worker*, 1976, *32*, 39–43.

Prescott, M.R., & Iseline, K.L. Counseling parents of a disabled child. *Elementary School Guidance and Counseling*, 1978, *12*, 170–177.

Owsley, P.J. Parent counseling/guidance for the hearing handicapped child. *School Guidance Worker*, 1978, *33*, 40–42.

Rudolph, L.B. The counselor's role with the learning disabled child. *Elementary School Guidance and Counseling*, 1978, *12*, 162–169.

Sweeney, T.J. Trends that will influence counselor preparation in the 1980's. *Counselor Education and Supervision*, 1978, *18*, 181–189.

Vargo, J.W. On counseling the physically handicapped. *Canadian Counselor*, 1978, *13*, 14–17.

Wandler, J. Interpreting test results with the parents of problem children. *School Guidance Worker*, 1978, *33*, 33–38.

Counselor Trainees' Attitudes Toward Mainstreaming the Handicapped

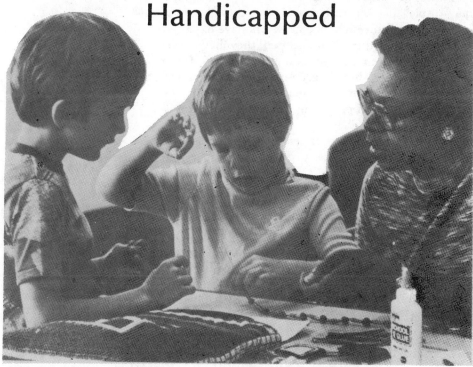

PEGGY SOMMERS FILER

Peggy Sommers Filer is an assistant professor in the Behavioral Studies Department at the University of Missouri-St. Louis.

This study reports the results of a questionnaire on attitudes toward mainstreaming handicapped students administered to graduate counseling students at a Midwestern university. Implications for counselor education programs are suggested.

Mainstreaming, the integration of handicapped children into the regular classroom, has produced significant changes in the schools. These changes, in turn, are modifying the traditional role of school counselors. In response, counselor educators have assessed the functions of school counselors in providing services to these children (Cristiani & Sommers, 1978; Hosie, 1979; McDowell, Coven, & Eash, 1979). As counselor education programs identify how counseling methodologies can be modified to provide effective guidance and counseling programs in mainstreaming settings, consideration must be given to the attitudes of counseling students toward the integration of the handicapped into the mainstream, and toward counseling handicapped children.

Various investigators studying the relationship between attitudes and behaviors have noted that positive or negative attitudes affect helping professionals' treatment of persons with whom they are working (Brophy & Good, 1970; Kester & Letchworth, 1972; Rosenthal & Jacobson, 1968; Silberman, 1969). These studies suggest that teachers holding more positive attitudes toward particular students demonstrate in their behavior greater acceptance and more positive interactions with those particular individuals. Conversely, negative attitudes and low expectations are demonstrated by less accepting behavior and negative or infrequent interactions.

Tyler (1969) identifies one component of acceptance as a "willingness to allow individuals to differ from one another in all sorts of ways" (p. 34). Working with handicapped children may strain acceptance, since the handicapped may display marked differences intellectually, emotionally, and physically. Unless future school counselors have explored and dealt with their attitudes toward the handicapped, they may not be able to give handicapped children the acceptance necessary for a productive counseling relationship. Therefore, counselor educators may need to assist future counselors in examining their attitudes toward the concept of mainstreaming and toward providing guidance and counseling services to the handicapped.

In order to identify counselor training experiences that might be valuable for future counselors who will be providing guidance and counseling services to the handicapped in mainstreaming schools, a survey was conducted using self-report inventory. The purpose of this survey was to examine attitudes of counseling students in one graduate counselor education program toward the practice of mainstreaming handicapped children into regular classrooms and offering counseling services. The self-report inventory in total examined attitudes toward the acceptance of mainstreaming. Specific clusters of items within the inventory focused on (a) the respondents' perception of counseling services for the handicapped, (b) changes in the school necessitated by mainstreaming, (c) the effects of mainstreaming on nonhandicapped students, and (d) the effects of mainstreaming on handicapped students.

PROCEDURE

Graduate level students at one university were asked to respond to a self-report inventory composed of 29 items derived from a 40–item composite scale. The scale was adapted from the Attitude Toward Disabled Persons Scale and Baker's Mainstreaming Inventory (May & Furst, 1977). Items omitted from the 40–item scale were those judged to be primarily noneducational, such as "handicapped persons should not have to compete with nonhandicapped for jobs." Wording on several of the original items was altered where appropriate, substituting counselor for teacher, counseling for teaching.

Item response was 1 (strongly disagree) to 5 (strongly agree). Twelve items were scored inversely because of the wording of those items.

The inventory was administered to 52 graduate level counseling students, 9 male and 43 female. The respondents were enrolled in graduate counseling courses and the data were collected during class meetings. Of the respondents, 83% reported work experiences as classroom teachers.

RESULTS AND DISCUSSION

For each item of the survey inventory, a frequency of response and a mean score was calculated. Table 1 presents a summary of the data, with

TABLE 1
Survey Inventory Results

Item	Agree	Disagree	No Opinion	Mean
1. A handicapped child will respond to your best counseling efforts[a]	96%	4%	0%	4.46
2. Having to work with handicapped pupils does not place an unfair burden on counselors[a]	87%	3%	4%	4.06
3. Average children will profit from their contact with handicapped students	85%	14%	2%	3.94
4. Integration of handicapped students will				

TABLE 1 (continued)

Item	Agree	Disagree	No Opinion	Mean
require changes in the physical arrangement and management of classrooms	82%	12%	6%	3.87
5. Integration of handicapped students represents an opportunity for the counselor to grow both personally and professionally	81%	15%	4%	3.85
6. Integration of handicapped students will require most counselors to learn and use new techniques and materials	81%	17%	2%	3.92
7. Average students need the experience of being in contact with handicapped students in a school setting	80%	12%	8%	3.90
8. A handicapped child will likely form positive social relationships with other children in the regular classroom	79%	12%	10%	3.77
9. Integration of handicapped students into the regular class will not harm the educational achievement of average students[a]	73%	21%	6%	3.73
10. As a counselor, I have confidence in my ability to control whether students make scapegoats out of handicapped students[a]	72%	23%	6%	3.52
11. The experience of being in a regular class will increase the chances of a handicapped student attaining a more productive and independent place in society	67%	19%	15%	3.62
12. Integration of handicapped students will require most counselors to use time differently and perhaps more efficiently than is now the case	67%	22%	12%	3.59
13. Placing a handicapped child in a typical classroom would not damage the student's self-concept[a]	66%	27%	7%	3.46
14. A handicapped student will not be disruptive in a regular classroom[a]	64%	19%	16%	3.52
15. Placement of a handicapped student in a regular classroom will not likely result in the student becoming socially withdrawn[a]	62%	25%	13%	3.40
16. With a handicapped student in a regular classroom, there will be an increase in the number of behavior problems in the other children[a]	62%	29%	10%	3.38
17. I am confident that I will be able to make handicapped students feel comfortable in a regular school setting	56%	27%	17%	3.27
18. Full-time special education class is not the best placement for handicapped students[a]	55%	37%	8%	3.25
19. I generally look forward to the challenge of working with handicapped children	54%	23%	23%	3.46
20. Mainstreaming will benefit the counselor as well as all children	54%	25%	21%	3.42
21. There is enough time in a counselor's day to deal satisfactorily with the different needs of both average and handicapped pupils[a]	52%	40%	8%	3.06
22. If I were the parent of a child who had a learning problem, I would want him or her to be in a regular classroom for most of the whole day	50%	31%	19%	3.21
23. A handicapped child will be motivated to learn in a regular classroom	46%	21%	33%	3.27
24. A handicapped child will develop a more positive self-concept as a result of being placed in a regular classroom	46%	27%	27%	3.27
25. If I were the parent of a child who had an emotional problem, I would want him or her to be in a regular classroom for most of the school day	46%	39%	15%	3.06
26. Average students are not uncomfortable when they are with children who have obvious physical deformities[a]	44%	50%	6%	2.92
27. Assignment of a handicapped child to a regular classroom is a wise administrative decision	41%	37%	23%	3.10

28. The presence of a handicapped student in a regular classroom will not be a cause for complaints from the parents of the other children[a]	39%	42%	19%	2.98
29. As a result of placement in a regular classroom, a handicapped child will develop a more positive attitude toward school	33%	37%	31%	3.02

Note. Because percentage figures were rounded off, some items have a total exceeding 100%.
[a]Reworded to reflect the reverse made in scoring.

items ranked from highest to lowest in terms of combined percentage of agree and strongly agree responses. The starred items, the 12 originally negatively worded statements, have been reworded to reflect the reverse made in scoring those items.

The mean for all 29 items was 3.48 on a scale from 1 to 5. This overall mean reflected a slightly favorable attitude toward mainstreaming.

On the cluster of items related to counseling services for the handicapped (items 1, 10, 17, 19, & 21), the mean score was 3.56. Of the counseling students, 96% agreed that "handicapped children would respond to your best counseling efforts." Over 70% of the future counselors expressed confidence in their "ability to control whether students make scapegoats out of mainstreamed handicapped students." Fewer counseling students, 56% and 54% respectively, declared confidence in assisting a handicapped student to feel comfortable in a regular school setting and looked forward to "the challenge of working with handicapped students." Moreover, the lowest average responses in the cluster of items were to item 21, "there is enough time in a counselor's day to deal satisfactorily with the different needs of both nonhandicapped and handicapped pupils." Of the counseling students, 52% agreed and 48% had no opinions or disagreed with this statement. The students in this study generally supported the value of counseling for handicapped children, yet a sizable minority believed that they did not look forward to working with the handicapped. Furthermore, the counseling students did not believe that there was sufficient time to deal with this additional responsibility. These concerns may suggest that the students feel unprepared to cope with the handicapped, a perception supported by Lombana (1980), who in a recent survey found that school counselors believed themselves unprepared to provide counseling and guidance services to the handicapped.

On the cluster of items concerning changes necessitated by mainstreaming, the respondents tended to agree that adjustments were needed to accomodate the handicapped in the regular classroom and within the counseling services (e.g., different techniques, materials, and different use of time). Four items in the inventory (4, 5, 6, & 12) related to this topic. The mean for this cluster of items was 3.81. The responses to these items indicate that a strong majority of counseling students were aware that reorganization in the schools brought about by mainstreaming will be reflected in changes in counselors' roles and working conditions.

The counseling students held a moderately positive view of the effects that mainstreaming would have on nonhandicapped students. Six items dealt with the issue, items 3, 7, 9, 14, 16, and 26. The mean response for this cluster was 3.57. Of the students, 85% agreed that nonhandicapped students would "profit from contact with handicapped students" and 80% agreed that nonhandicapped students "need the experience of being in contact with handicapped students." Furthermore, over 60% of the counseling students did not see the integration of the handicapped as detrimental to the academic achievement of nonhandicapped students, disruptive in regular classrooms, or causative of increased behavior problems in other children. On the lowest ranked item in this cluster (item 26), however, 50% of the respondents thought nonhandicapped students were uncomfortable with children who had obvious physical deformities. The responses on this cluster of items would suggest that the majority of the students believed that mainstreaming was beneficial or at least not detrimental to nonhandicapped children.

Counseling students were somewhat less assured of the effects of mainstreaming on handicapped children. On the cluster of 7 items (8, 11, 13, 15, 23, 24, & 29) dealing with the effects of mainstreaming on handicapped students, the mean score was 3.40. Of the respondents, 79% indicated that handicapped children will likely "form positive social relationships with other children" (item 8). More than 65% of the students believed that mainstreaming would "promote the productivity and independence of the handicapped in society" and would not "damage the handicapped's self-concept." Nevertheless, the majority of counseling students did not view mainstreaming as beneficial to handicapped children in terms of motivation to learn, development of a better self-concept, or development of more positive attitudes toward school. This seems to suggest that counselor trainees had reservations about the benefits of mainstreaming for the handicapped.

In summary, the results of this survey suggest that for this group of counseling students certain training issues could be addressed that may facilitate more positive attitudes toward mainstreaming the handicapped.

In a survey of this type, certain limitations must be recognized. First, only tabular data were reported. Second, the inventory used has not been documented for validity or reliability, although some investigation of the psychometric properties of the original 40–item inventory has been conducted by May and Furst (1977). Third, a paper and pencil measure of attitudes has inherent restrictions. The respondents were asked to make abstract judgments out of context about handicapped children as a group, which tends to elicit generalized and oversimplified responses. The forced choice of responses does not allow for qualifications. Also, a response to an item may not be indicative of how a person would behave in a life situation. Therefore, caution is necessary in interpreting the results of this survey.

Although the findings of this survey should not be generalized to all students training to be counselors, the results might provide an index against which the attitudes of students in other counseling programs can be compared. The 29–item inventory can also be used as a vehicle for counseling students to examine their thoughts and feelings about mainstreaming issues. In addition, counselor educators may wish to use this inventory to take their own survey in determining counseling students' needs specific to their own programs.

SUGGESTIONS FOR TRAINING

To assist counseling students in clarifying and perhaps modifying their attitudes toward mainstreaming as well as broadening their counseling and guidance competence in mainstreaming schools, counselor educators may wish to provide specific instruction and experiences related to mainstreaming. The issues of concern identified with this group of counseling trainees might be addressed through the following activities.

The first activity would involve experiences to increase interest in providing counseling services to handicapped children, and would include:

1. Structured interactions with handicapped persons who have successfully adjusted to their handicaps. Personal encounters with handicapped persons who do not behave in stereotyped ways may reduce the avoidance behaviors of counselors. Live presentations and open discussion provide opportunities for counseling students to look at, question, and share concerns with a handicapped person.

2. Videotapes and films about the handicapped as part of instruction, which may furnish a basis for identifying potential counseling and guidance needs of the handicapped.

3. Disability simulations, which are instrumental in developing empathy in both the role players and observers, particularly if there is an opportunity to observe the reactions of strangers. Simulations in which the role player appears handicapped (such as in a wheelchair) or wearing nonvisible ear plugs are more successful than simulations in which the participants are obviously pretending to be disabled, perhaps wearing a blindfold. Glazzard (1979) presents a step-by-step procedure for such simulations.

4. Observations of counselors successfully working with the handicapped. These may provide counseling students with positive role models. Observations of counseling sessions with handicapped individuals, groups of all handicapped children, or mixes of both handicapped and nonhandicapped may be valuable.

The second activity would concern training in techniques, materials, and time arrangements for working with the handicapped, including:

1. Demonstrations of counseling strategies with handicapped students, including the use of basic counseling strategies as well as approaches for modifying guidance and counseling strategies for the handicapped (Lombana, 1980, pp. 273–274).

2. Review of affective materials that can be used by the counselor or supplied by the counselor to classroom teachers for psychological education.

3. A focus on the consultive role of the school counselor in assisting other school personnel in providing humanistic school environments for the handicapped (Westling & Joiner, 1979).

4. Instruction on methods of participating in developing Individual Education Programs (IEP) that address the psychological needs of the handicapped in addition to academic and vocational needs (Filer, 1981).

The third activity would focus on skills in helping nonhandicapped students feel more comfortable with handicapped students with obvious differences. The following would be included:

1. Experiences in initiating and facilitating interventions that stress the importance of individual differences, provide information, and confront physical and behavioral differences in students. Children observe diversity in others as well as in themselves, and appear to profit from open discussion (Gottlieb, 1980; Thurman & Lewis; 1979).

2. Demonstration of strategies for improving the status of handicapped children, such as buddy systems, peer tutoring, cooperative work projects, values education, and reading books about the handicapped. Weishahn and Baker's (1980) *BUDY: Better Understanding Disabled Youth* is one example of affective materials that may be used.

The final activity involves training in procedures to assist handicapped students in obtaining maximum personal and academic benefit from mainstreaming, and includes the following:

1. Experiences in observing and assessing social–emotional needs of the handicapped in order to provide optimal counseling and guidance intervention.

2. Practice of counseling strategies that address feelings of self-worth, expectations of achievement, and ability to cope with success and failure so that handicapped students are able to contain the effects of their disability.

3. Presentations on teaching handicapped children more proficient social interaction skills using activities such as role-playing, games, and cooperative work projects (Downing, 1977).

4. Techniques in assisting teachers to structure the psychological environment so that handicapped students can have successful learning experiences (Moracco, 1981).

5. Strategies in providing vocational counseling to the handicapped, including referral of secondary handicapped students to vocational rehabilitation counselors. Such counseling may provide greater impetus for the handicapped student to participate in school classes and activities that will lead to a vocational goal (Brolin & D'Alonzo, 1979).

In conclusion, the school counselor's attitudes toward mainstreaming handicapped children may be a decisive factor in whether optimum services are provided to these children. To expect that school counselors, with the current demands on their time, will spontaneously welcome the responsibility of serving handicapped children is not reasonable. Therefore, counselor educators might be advised to provide experiences for future counselors to explore, clarify, and, if appropriate, modify their attitudes about the handicapped and mainstreaming.

REFERENCES

Brophy, J.E., & Good, T.L. Teacher's communications of differential expectations for children's classroom performances. *Journal of Educational Psychology*, 1970, 61, 365–374.

Brolin, D., & D'Alonzo, B. Critical issues in career education for handicapped students. *Exceptional Children*, 1979, 45, 246–253.

Cristiani, T., & Sommers, P. The counselor's role in mainstreaming the handicapped. *Viewpoints in Teaching and Learning*, 1978, 54, 20–28.

Downing, P. Teaching children behavior change techniques. *Elementary School Guidance and Counseling*, 1977, 11, 277–283.

Filer, P.S. Preparing for IEP conferences. *School Counselor*, 1981, 29, 46–50.

Glazzard, P. Simulation of handicaps as a teaching strategy for preservice and inservice training. *Teaching Exceptional Children*, 1979, 11, 101–104.

Gottlieb, J. Improving attitudes toward retarded children by using group discussion. *Exceptional Children*, 1980, 47, 106–111.

Hosie, T. Preparing counselors to meet the needs of the handicapped. *Personnel and Guidance Journal*, 1979, 58, 271–275.

Kester, S.W., & Letchworth, G.P. Communications for teacher expectations and their effects on achievement and attitude in secondary school students. *Journal of Educational Research*, 1972, 66, 51–55.

Lombana, J.H. Guidance of handicapped students: Counselor in-serivce needs. *Counselor Education and Supervision*, 1980, 19, 269–275.

May, B.J., & Furst, E.J. Evaluation and revision of an inventory for measuring attitudes toward mainstreaming. Unpublished manuscript, University of Arkansas, 1977.

McDowell, W.; Coven, A.; & Eash, V. The handicapped: Special needs and strategies for counseling. *Personnel and Guidance Journal*, 1979, 58, 228–232.

Moracco, J. A comprehensive approach to human relations training for teachers. *Counselor Education and Supervision*, 1981, 21, 119–135.

Rosenthal, R., & Jacobson, L. *Pygmalion in the classroom: Teacher expectations and pupils' intellectual development*. New York: Holt, Rinehart, & Winston, 1968.

Silberman, M.L. Behavioral expressions of teacher attitudes toward elementary school students. *Journal of Educational Psychology*, 1969, 60, 402–407.

Thurman, S.K., & Lewis, M. Children's responses to differences: Some possible implications for mainstreaming. *Exceptional Children*, 1979, 45, 468–470.

Tyler, L.E. *The work of the counselor* (3rd ed.). New York: Appleton-Century-Crofts, 1969.

Weishahn, M., & Baker, C. *BUDY: Better Understanding Disabled Youth*. Oak Lawn, Ill.: Ideal School Supply, 1979.

Westling, D., & Joiner, M.D. Consulting with teachers of handicapped children in the mainstream. *Elementary School Guidance and Counseling*, 1979, 13, 207–213.

Enhancing Social Support for Parents of Developmentally Disabled Children: Training in Interpersonal Problem Solving Skills

James Intagliata and Nancy Doyle

Abstract: This paper is a description of the rationale for and implementation of Interpersonal Problem-Solving Skills Training with parents of developmentally disabled children. It reviews the multiple stresses which confront these parents and indicates the important role that social support networks can play in helping them cope more effectively. A training program for enhancing parents' support networks by improving their interpersonal problem-solving skills is described. Overall, the training seemed to be effective and provided a much needed supplement to the package of helpful services now made available to parents of the developmentally disabled.

Authors: **JAMES INTAGLIATA, Ph.D.,** Research Associate Professor and Director of Research, University Affiliated Facility for Developmental Disabilities, University of Missouri-Kansas City, 2220 Holmes, Kansas City, Mo. 64108. **NANCY DOYLE, M.S.W.,** West Seneca Developmental Disabilities Service Office, Amherst, N.Y. 14150.

Families with developmentally disabled children have been the focus of a considerable amount of research over the past 30 years. In general, this work has demonstrated that these families experience a greater level of stress when compared to similar families with normal children. The specific types of stresses documented for families of the developmentally disabled are myriad and include periodic grief and chronic sorrow, strain resulting from the constant unrelieved burden of caretaking, shifts in the role expectations for individual family members, marital conflict, social isolation, sibling adjustment problems, and financial burden (Boggs, 1979; Davidson & Dosser, 1982; Farber, 1959; 1968; Holt, 1958; Menolascino, 1977; Mercer, 1966; Wikler, 1981; Willer, Intagliata, & Atkinson, 1979).

These stresses are a matter of concern for several reasons. They may, for example, endanger the physical health, mental health, and overall life quality of individual family members. They also place great strain on the marital bond and, when not managed effectively, may contribute to separation and/or divorce. Finally, these stresses often detract from the capability of the family to provide quality care to their developmentally disabled child and, in many cases, are the reason why parents request out-of-home placement for their child.

In response to the obvious needs of families of the developmentally disabled, service providers and parents' groups have developed and offered a wide range of supportive services and interventions for families. These include (a) information and referral services that are designed to increase parents' knowledge about developmental disabilities and their awareness of available services (Matheny & Vernick, 1969; Wolfensberger, 1967); (b) self-help parent groups which reduce parents' sense of isolation and uniqueness and provide them with much needed support by offering them the opportunity to share their feelings and experiences with other persons facing similar stress (Davidson & Dosser, 1982; Porter, 1978; Weber & Parker, 1980); (c) individual and/or family therapy to help family members to better understand and cope with their stress and negative emotions related to their developmentally disabled child (Cummings & Stock, 1962; Mandelbaum, 1967; Solnit & Stark, 1961); (d) training programs in behavior modification techniques to assist parents in teaching skills and managing behavior problems (Bricker & Bricker, 1971; Roos, 1972); and (5) respite care to relieve parents from the physical exhaustion and continued psychological burden of caring (Wikler, Hanusa & Stoychef, 1982).

The common thread that ties most of these intervention strategies together is that their focus is usually either directly or indirectly on the developmentally disabled child. For example, in therapy or skills training settings, rather than taking into account the needs and problems of family members that may be unrelated to the developmentally disabled child, many counselors and trainers focus their attention on helping parents to deal with their feelings regarding having a disabled child or on advising them how to manage their child's behavior more effectively (Hill, Raley & Snyder, 1982). Even respite care, which seems to be a service directed to meet parents' own needs, is typically portrayed as helpful to parents primarily because it relieves the stress "caused by their child." Thus, not unlike families of developmentally disabled children who have been described as making their disabled children the "scapegoat" by directing an inordinate amount of activity to them (Ro-Trock, Kostoryz, Corrales & Smith, 1981), many of those who work with these families have also placed their primary focus on the child or on relieving the stress created by the child.

This observation is in no way meant to suggest that the supportive interventions discussed above are not helpful to parents and families. However, while they help families to meet some of their needs, they neglect to address the fact that a considerable amount of the stress that parents report results from the difficulties they have in managing many normal life demands unrelated to their child. These demands are those that most parents face daily regardless of whether they have a developmentally disabled child and relate to the challenges of maintaining a healthy marriage, developing and nurturing satisfactory relationships with extended family members and friends, and dealing with occupational stress. While the added demands of parenting a handicapped child may exacerbate the difficulties of coping successfully with other real-life problems, the use of intervention strategies that focus primarily on the child may not be sufficient for helping parents of the developmentally disabled

to alleviate their reported stress. A good illustration of this point is provided by Fotheringham, Skelton, & Hoddinott (1972) who found that the out-of-home placement of a mentally retarded child, who presumably was the cause of reported marital stress, did not result in improvement or resolution of the marital difficulties.

Social Support and Stress

In recent years increasing attention has been given to the importance of social support in contributing to physical and psychological health (Cassel, 1974; Cobb, 1976; Caplan, 1974). According to O'Connor (1983), social support is made up of the emotional, informational, and material support provided by persons with whom one has an ongoing relationship and to whom one can turn in times of need or crisis. The availability and provision of such support can be crucial for enabling both individuals and families to remain healthy and intact when confronted with stressful life events (Drabek & Boggs, 1968; Hill, 1949; Imig, 1981; Polansky, Chalmers, Buttenweiser, & Williams, 1979).

As part of the ongoing development of the theory and research surrounding social support, a number of researchers have begun to highlight the need for individuals to have different types of assistance available from their support networks. Weiss (1974), for example, suggested a typology which identified six distinct types of "social provisions" that support networks can offer, all of which individuals may need in order to maintain their personal well-being over time. These provisions include a sense of attachment, a feeling of social integration, the opportunity for nurturance, the reassurance of self-worth, a sense of ongoing reliable alliance, and the opportunity to receive guidance or advice. Other typologies that have been offered identify such distinct types of aid as instrumental support, emotional/social support, and referral/information (Cobb, 1976; Dean & Lin, 1977; Unger & Powell, 1980).

The development of such typologies of social support implies that in order for an individual or family to be able to receive the variety of support that they need to cope effectively with stress, their social network must be comprised of a variety of individuals, each of whom may provide a somewhat unique but needed resource. The different types of relationships required to provide such varied resources might include marriage, friendship, parenting, membership in a club, ties to extended family, and professional or work-related relationships. While an individual or family may not require all of these supportive relationships at any given point in time, it is unlikely that their ongoing or periodic needs for social support can all be met through a single person or type of relationship.

Because parents of developmentally disabled

people are under a great deal of stress they could be expected to need and benefit significantly from well-developed social support networks. However, the strains upon and the deficiencies that have been identified in the support networks of families of the developmentally disabled are multiple and significant. They include (1) stress and tension in the marital relationship itself which often diminishes the amount of support the parents can provide each other and may endanger the stability of the marital relationship itself (Frederickson, 1977; Waisbren, 1980); (2) strained or broken relationships with extended family members who could potentially provide the parents with assistance in the care of the child as well as much needed personal emotional support; and (3) breaks in relationships with or isolation from friends and neighbors, also a potential source of important social support (Wikler, 1981).

Of the various family intervention alternatives discussed earlier, the only one that is responsive to parents' needs to increase their available social support is the self-help parent group. Perhaps as a reflection of the pressing need these groups meet, they have been extremely popular among parents of developmentally disabled individuals (Davidson & Dosser, 1982; McCubbin, 1979). One reason why they are so popular is that they offer parents a chance to spend time with a very special group of others all of whom share the same types of stress and burden as they do. However, despite the fact that such specialized support groups may help to reduce the social isolation that parents feel, these groups cannot be expected to provide for all of parents' social support needs.

In order to have a more comprehensive base of social support as a buffer for their stress, parents of developmentally disabled individuals need to be able to relate effectively to other people who do not share their experience of parenting a handicapped child. If, as the research would indicate, they have significant difficulties in relating effectively to many of these persons (e.g., relatives, neighbors, co-workers, friends) they may not be able to avail themselves of the important types of support that only these individuals can provide. To date, however, no intervention for parents of the developmentally disabled has been designed to provide parents with the skills they may require to strengthen and broaden their social support networks.

This paper describes the results of a pilot study conducted to assess the degree to which the interpersonal problem solving skills of parents of developmentally disabled children may in fact be deficient and to assess their responsiveness to a training program designed to enhance their interpersonal problem solving competence. The decision to use this particular approach as a way to assist parents of developmentally disabled children was based on (1) the belief that interper-

sonal problem solving competence is essential for maintaining and nurturing relationships that can provide these parents with the support they need to cope more effectively with their significant life stress; (2) the indications that parents of developmentally disabled children may be deficient in interpersonal problem solving skills (Ro-Trock et al., 1981); and (3) the convincing evidence linking interpersonal problem-solving skill competence to overall personal adjustment (Larcen, Spivack, & Shure, 1972; Platt & Spivack, 1972; Shure, Newman, & Silver, 1970; Shure & Spivack, 1972.

Method

Setting

The setting for the pilot work of training parents in interpersonal problem solving skills was a Developmental Disabilities Service Office in Western New York. This office serves as a single point of entry for services in a four-county region and provides such services as initial intake and assessment of the child and family needs, information and referral, and assistance in obtaining residential as well as other support services (day programs, respite care).

Participants

The participants in this pilot effort were three single parents and one couple. In all, there were five developmentally disabled children living in the four family settings. They included two profoundly mentally retarded young girls (ages 6 and 8), one of whom had additional serious medical problems; two nonambulatory six-year old girls with cerebral palsy but no mental retardation; and one 18-year old girl with a severe seizure disorder and serious behavior problems. The parents ranged in age from their late twenties to their early forties and were all high school graduates.

Two other single parents initially indicated an interest in participating in the group but were unable to do so because of their inability to get respite care to enable them to attend. Before they agreed to participate, all participants were interviewed by the group leaders who explained the focus of the skills training group and indicated that participating would entail attending a two-hour training session once a week for a period of 10 weeks.

Measures

Given that the focus of the training program was to enhance participants' problem-solving skills, a measure was needed to assess their skill level in this area both prior to and following the training. The measure utilized was developed by Platt & Spivack (1975) and is called the Means-

Ends Problem Solving (MEPS) measure.

This instrument makes use of story stems portraying situations in which a need is aroused in the protagonist at the beginning of the story and is resolved by him at the end. The respondent is required to complete the story by filling in those events which might have occurred between the arousal and satisfaction of the hero's need (Platt & Spivack, 1975, p. 16).

The stories that respondents generate in completing the MEPS measure reflect the way that they typically think about and/or go about solving everyday problems with which they are confronted. The scoring procedure for the MEPS instrument was developed by Platt and Spivack (1975) and involves assessing the number and relevancy of means that the respondents indicate the protagonist uses in order to resolve the problem in each story. A relevant means is counted each time the protagonist engages in a discrete instrumental act that clearly enables him/her to move effectively toward or reach the resolution of the problem. Respondents' scores on this instrument have been shown to be significantly related to their real-life problem solving competence and to their overall level of mental health adjustment (Intagliata, 1978; Platt & Spivack, 1972; Shure, Newman, & Silver, 1970).

During the first training session each participant was asked to complete four separate stories. Two of the stories presented interpersonal problems (e.g., argument with spouse, disagreement with boss), another offered an intrapersonal problem (e.g., depression, nervous anxiety), and the final story presented a problem related to a handicapped child (e.g., arranging for respite care).

Following the tenth and final group session all participants were once again asked to complete four stories relating to two interpersonal problems, one intrapersonal problem and one problem associated with the care of a handicapped child. The first administration of the procedure involved the random selection of four stories from an eight-story MEPS protocol adapted from Platt and Spivack (1975). For the second administration, participants were asked to complete whichever four stories they had not previously been given. All stories, with the exception of those involving a handicapped child, were drawn directly from the standard MEPS protocol. The two stories involving a problem with a handicapped child were developed especially for this pilot study and were designed to carefully follow the format of the standard MEPS stories.

Description of Training

The package of ten training sessions developed for this parent group incorporated a variety of training materials developed by Platt, Spivack, & Swift (1973) as part of a program of interpersonal problem solving (IPS) group therapy for

adults and was modeled after a ten-session IPS training program that the first author had developed for use in an alcoholism treatment program (Intagliata, 1978; 1979). This program is highly structured, actively engages all participants in each session, makes extensive use of role playing and involves regular homework assignments between sessions. Specific didactic materials were also developed and added to the training program in order to better meet the particular needs of parents with developmentally disabled children.

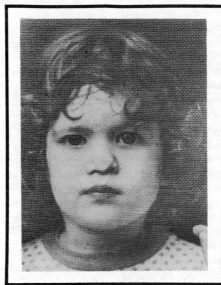

The ten training sessions were designed to teach participants a five-step process for dealing with interpersonal problems. These steps include (a) recognize that you have a problem, (b) define the problem, (c) generate several alternatives for dealing with it, (d) look ahead to the likely consequences of each, and (e) select and implement the alternative that best meets your goals. Specific issues dealt with in the sessions include understanding nonverbal cues about feelings, the importance of slowing down to avoid jumping to wrong conclusions, defining problems in such a way that they can be addressed, involving the "other" person in the problem-solving process, differences in interpersonal problem solving styles and the importance of deciding on your goal before attempting to resolve a problem.

Results

The Group Process

A major objective of this pilot study was to assess the responsiveness of parents of the developmentally disabled to training them in skills that, while useful in dealing with everyday problems, were not directly focused on helping them manage their disabled child more effectively. While the potential relevance of this type of intervention for this population is suggested in the literature, it clearly has not been a need articulated by parents in general, nor, at least initially, by the parents in our training group. Our experience in these sessions, however, confirmed for us that such training met a very real need, at least among the parents in our group.

During our first two group sessions, all of the participants spoke quite freely with each other about the significant grief, stress, and problems that having their handicapped child had created for them and their families. The single parents spoke of the conflicts and tensions that it had caused between them and their ex-spouses and how these conflicts had helped contribute to their divorces. The married couple spoke in some detail about the problems that their child created for them with their in-laws and other relatives. All group members spoke about the isolation they felt from others who could never really understand them because they did not also have a developmentally disabled child.

When asked to identify and list problems that they experienced daily, most of those listed involved their developmentally disabled child directly (e.g., the incredible amount of time, that he/she requires). Additional problems included marital conflict, depression, and anxiety and strained relations with friends or relatives. However, even for these additional problems the group members agreed unanimously that all were either caused by or could not be solved because of their disabled child. Further, they indicated that if they had not had their child to begin with, they doubted whether they would have any of these problems now. The parents then challenged the idea of our training group because it could not solve the only problem they really had; that is, to make their developmentally disabled child normal.

Over time, as we moved away from the relatively unstructured discussion that took place in the first two sessions and began to get the parents actively involved in interpersonal problem-solving exercises and homework assignments, their intensive focus on their child as their only problem diminished significantly. In fact, from Session 4 on, the vast majority of real life problems that group members volunteered for us to work with no longer involved or were attributed to their children. During one of the middle sessions, several of the group members got into a discussion about how they seemed to be a lot more competent at solving problems related to their handicapped child than they were with those involving other people. "That makes sense," said one of the parents, "we spend most of our time focusing on our kids. In fact, even when we go to parent association meetings all we ever seem to talk about is our kids. That's why this group is so important, here we're supposed to talk about us for a change."

One additional illustration of the change in orientation among most parents in the group

occurred in our final meeting. During this session, one of the participants got into an emotional discussion of a conflict she was presently involved in with one of her relatives. When one of the other participants commented that she probably would not have the problem if it were not for her handicapped child, the woman angrily retorted that this problem had nothing to do with her daughter. Other members in the group nodded their agreement.

Overall, the content and process of our training sessions confirmed a number of our initial hypotheses regarding the relevance of our approach. The parents in our group clearly had some very significant problems with managing conflicts with other individuals in their lives who could potentially offer much needed social support. The group also demonstrated, at least initially, their tendency as individuals to focus inordinate attention on the disabled child even to the point of blaming or attributing all the significant problems they had to their child. As the group members became gradually more aware of their own role in creating some of their problems, however, they came to appreciate how useful it was to have a training experience that focused attention on them for a change, instead of on their child.

Problem-Solving Skills

The measure utilized to assess participants' problem-solving skills was the MEPS (Platt & Spivack, 1975) described earlier. Despite the small sample size which precluded statistical tests of many relationships, a number of interesting findings seemed to have emerged from the MEPS results and deserve discussion.

On the MEPS stories completed by participants prior to their training, the group used an average of 1.5 relevant means in each story, with 65% of these means being rated as relevant. When the three categories of problems presented to group members were considered individually, participants demonstrated markedly greater proficiency with the problem related to a handicapped child as compared with either interpersonal problems or intrapersonal problems. Specifically, prior to training, the ideas generated by group members for dealing with problems involving their child were twice as likely to be rated as effective and relevant as were those they generated for resolving problems involving themselves or others. Given the very small sample size, the significance of this finding should not be overstated. However, it is consistent with what the group members independently acknowledged about themselves and is certainly a finding worth testing in subsequent studies.

When the group members' scores on the MEPS stories completed after training were calculated, the results indicated definite improvement. The average number of relevant means they used in each story increased from 1.5 to 2.3, and the proportion of these that were judged relevant and effective also increased noticeably. Such improvement clearly parallels that found when a similar training program was utilized in an alcoholic treatment program (Intagliata, 1978). While no control group was utilized in this study to rule out the possibility that subjects improved performance was simply a result of repeating the MEPS testing, use of a control group in the comparable study demonstrated no significant change from pre- to post-testing.

When the post-training MEPS scores were considered separately for the three problem categories, results indicated greater improvement in the interpersonal and intrapersonal problem categories compared with that for the problems related to a handicapped child. The average number of relevant means included in stories dealing with interpersonal problems increased from 1.0 to 2.5 and the relevancy ratio (proportion of all means generated that were relevant and effective) increased from 54% to 100%. For intrapersonal problems, the average number of relevant means per story increased from 1.0 to 2.2 with the relevancy ratio improving from 50% to 100%. Finally, for the problem related to a handicapped child, the average number of relevant means increased from 1.5 to 2.0 while the relevancy ratio remained at 100%. This suggests that the training may have had its effect where it was most needed.

Parent Follow-Up Reaction

Three months following completion of the training sessions, parents were contacted by letter and asked to complete a brief follow-up questionnaire evaluating the training. All participants felt that the sessions had been helpful for them. Particular ideas that participants felt had been most helpful included the importance of not making assumptions or jumping to conclusions when solving conflicts with others and the value of pushing yourself to bring a problem out into the open in order to discuss it with the other person. All participants also reported having consciously utilized the problem solving principles in dealing with problems they had encountered since training had ended. Further, all indicated they would recommend attending such a group to any parent who had a developmentally disabled child. Suggestions for improving the sessions included increasing the size of the group and perhaps running separate groups comprised exclusively of couples or single parents. While the results of most participant evaluations of service interventions tend to be overwhelmingly positive, these responses are nevertheless encouraging.

Discussion

The results of this pilot study indicate that a group designed to enhance the interpersonal problem-solving skills of parents with developmentally disabled children is a relevant and potentially helpful service intervention. While it was not an objective of this study, it will be important for subsequent research to assess the degree to which improved interpersonal problem solving competence actually facilitates the strengthening or broadening of parents' social support networks, insofar as it is this support that seems so essential to helping them cope with their significant stress.

It is hoped that the report of this study will lead those service providers involved with parents of the developmentally disabled to consider the need for interventions that focus on parents' needs, independent of their disabled child. The approach described here seems to be promising, but is only one such alternative. It is not our intention to suggest parent-focused interventions as a substitute for the many other services which help parents to better manage problems and caretaking burdens related specifically to their handicapped child. However, we do think that parent-focused interventions have been relatively neglected and should be considered an important component in any comprehensive package of supportive services made available to parents whose children are developmentally disabled or who suffer from other serious handicapping conditions.

References

Boggs, E. M. (1979). Economic factors in family care. In R. H. Bruininks & G. C. Krantz (Eds.), *Family care of developmentally disabled members: Conference proceedings.* Minneapolis: University of Minnesota.

Bricker, D., & Bricker, W. (1971). *Toddler research and intervention project: Report, Year I.* (IMRID Behavioral Science Monograph #21). Nashville.

Caplan, G. (1974). *Support systems and community mental health.* New York: Behavioral Publications.

Cassell, J. (1974). An epidemiological perspective of psychosocial factors in disease etiology. *American Journal of Public Health, 64,* 1040–1043.

Cobb, S. (1976). Social support as a moderator of life stress. *Psychosomatic Medicine, 38,* 300–314.

Cummings, S. T., & Stock, D. (1962). Brief group therapy of mothers of retarded children outside of the specialty clinic setting. *American Journal of Mental Deficiency, 66,* 739–748.

Davidson, B., & Dosser, D. (1982). A support system for families with developmentally disabled infants. *Family Relations, 31,* 295–299.

Dean, A., & Lin, N. (1977). The stress buffering role of social support: Problems and prospects for systematic investigation. *Journal of Nervous and Mental Disease, 165,* 403–417.

Drabek, P. E., & Boggs, K. S. (1968). Families in disaster: Reactions and relatives. *Journal of Marriage and the Family, 30,* 443–457.

Farber, B. (1959). Effects of a severely mentally retarded child on family integration. *Monographs of the*

Society for Research on Child Development, 24 (2, Series No. 71).

Farber, B. (1968). *Mental retardation: Its social context and social consequences.* Boston: Houghton.

Fotheringham, J. B., Skelton, M., & Hoddinott, B. A. (1972) The effects on the family of the presence of a mentally retarded child. *Canadian Psychiatric Association Journal,* 17, 283–290.

Frederickson, G. G. (1977) Life stress and marital conflict: A pilot study. *Journal of Marriage and Family Counseling,* 3, 41–47.

Hill, R. (1949). *Families under stress.* New York: Harper.

Hill, B. M., Raley, J. R., & Snyder, D. K. (1982). Group intervention with parents for psychiatrically hospitalized children. *Family Relations,* 31, 317–322.

Holt, K. (1958). Home of severely retarded children. *Pediatrics,* 22, 744–754.

Imig, D. R. (1981). Accumulated stress of life changes and interpersonal effectiveness in the family. *Family Relations,* 31, 367–371.

Intagliata, J. (1978). Increasing the interpersonal problem-solving skills of an alcoholic population. *Journal of Consulting and Clinical Psychology,* 3, 489–498.

Intagliata, J. (1979). Increasing the responsiveness of alcoholics to group therapy: An interpersonal problem-solving approach. *Group,* 3, 106–120.

Larcen, S., Spivack, G., & Shure, M. (1972). *Problem-solving thinking and adjustment among dependent neglected pre-adolescents.* Presented at Eastern Psychological Association Annual Meeting, Boston.

Matheny, A. D., & Vernick, J. (1969). Emotionally overwhelmed or unfortunately deprived? *Journal of Pediatrics,* 74, 953–954.

Mandelbaum, A. (1967). The group process in helping parents of retarded children. *Children,* 227–232.

McCubbin, H. (1979). Integrating coping behavior in family stress theory. *Journal of Marriage and the Family,* 41, 237–244.

Menolascino, F. J. (1977). *Challenges in mental retardation: Progressive ideology and service.* New York: Human Sciences Press.

Mercer, J. R. (1966). Patterns of family crisis related to reacceptance of the retardate. *American Journal of Mental Deficiency,* 71 19–32.

O'Connor, G. (1983). Social support ot retarded persons. *Mental Retardation,* 21, 187–196.

Platt, J., & Spivack, G. (1972). Problem-solving thinking of psychiatric patients. *Journal of Consulting and Clinical Psychology,* 39, 148–151.

Platt, J., & Spivack, G. (1975). *Manual for the Means-Ends Problem Solving procedure: A measure of interpersonal cognitive problem-solving skill.* Hahnemann Medical College and Hospital, Philadelphia, PA

Platt, G., Spivack, J., & Swift, M. (1973). Problem-solving therapy with maladjusted groups. *Research and Evaluation Report,* Hahnemann Medical College and Hospital, Philadelphia, Pa.

Polansky, N. A., Chalmers, M. A., Buttenweiser, C., & Williams, D. P. (1979). Isolation of the neglectful family. *American Journal of Orthopsychiatry, 49,* 149–152.

Porter, F. (1978). *Pilot Parents Program a design for developing a program for parents of handicapped children.* Omaha: Greater Omaha Association for Retarded Citizens.

Roos, P. (1972). Behavior modification and normalization. In W. Wolfensberger (Ed.), *Normalization.* Toronto: National Institute on Mental Retardation.

Ro-Trock, L. G., Kostoryz, J. L., Corrales, R., & Smith, B. (1981). *A study of characteristics of families with a severely handicapped child from a systems perspective.* Unpublished project report, Institute for Human Development, Inc., Kansas City, Mo.

Shure, M., Newman, S. & Silver, S. (1970). *Problem-solving among adjusted, impulsive and inhibited head-start children.* Presented at Eastern Psychological Association Annual Meeting, Atlantic City.

Shure, M., & Spivack, G. (1972). Means-ends thinking; adjustment and social class among elementary school-aged children. *Journal of Consulting and Clinical Psychology,* 38, 348–353.

Solnit, A. J., & Stark, M. H. (1961) Mourning and the birth of a defective child. *Psychoanalytic Study of the Child,* 16, 523–537.

Unger, D., & Powell, D. (1980). Supporting families under stress: The role of social networks. *Family Relations,* 29, 566–574.

Waisbren, S. (1980). Parents' reactions after the birth of a developmentally disabled child. *American Journal of Mental Deficiency, 84,* 345–351.

Weber, G. S., & Parker, T. (1980). A comparative study of family and professional views of the factors affecting positive family adaptation to a disabled child. *Building Family Strengths: Blueprints for Action, Vol. III,* University of Nebraska Press.

Weiss, R. S. (1974). The provisions of social relationships. In F. Rubin (Ed.), *Doing unto others.* Englewood Cliffs, N.J.: Prentice Hall.

Wikler, L. (1981). *Family relationships and stress.* Unpublished project report, University of Wisconsin, Madison, Wisconsin.

Wikler, L., Hanusa, D., & Stoychef, J. (1982). *The impact of home-based respite care on the developmentally disabled child and on family stress.* Unpublished manuscript.

Willer, B. S., Intagliata, J. C., & Atkinson, A. C. (1979). Crises for families of mentally retarded persons including the crisis of deinstitutionalization. *British Journal of Mental Subnormality,* 25, 38–49.

Wolfensberger, W. (1967). Counseling parents of the retarded. In A. Baumeister (Ed.), *Mental retardation: Appraisal, education, rehabilitation.* Chicago: Aldine Publishing Company.

Group home helps residents keep trying

By SUSAN A. LEWIS
Special to Saturday

Resident Heather Davis and Assistant Supervisor Joan Callaghan seem to enjoy making the salad for dinner.

EAST LYME -- In the span of a lifetime, eight months is but a passing moment. The time that has elapsed since last September, however, has been enough to change the lives of six Niantic residents.

It was in the early fall, that these adults moved into a ranch house at 126 Pennsylvania Avenue. On their own for the first time, they were apprehensive. All are mildly retarded and came from institutions and families where they were given little freedom. At that point in their lives, they talked with emotion and some bitterness about the priviledges that had always been denied them. The six had little confidence in themselves.

Yet these days there's something different about the four women and two men who rent rooms in the house. They talk about Easter Parties and walks to downtown Niantic on errands; they make coffee for visitors; and they treat each other to lunch at McDonalds.

They have independence. finally. What its done for them shows on their faces and in their attitudes about themselves.

Kim Marble, Allen Russo, Steven Kennedy, Heather Davis -- all in their 20s, as well as Janet Perrault, 43, and Patricia Sweeny, 46, are all part of a program that's changing the concept of care for the mentally retarded.

This "group home" near the town hall in Niantic was the first of a series begun by Sea Corp, a private, non-profit corporation established by the Southeastern Connecticut Association for the Retarded.

While the house and the staff (there's always a professional staff-member on duty) are the means by which these six are able to live on their own, the community has also made the difference in their lives.

"I'm grateful to the people in this town because they've unconditionally welcomed these people. For that reason, the adjustment has been really easy," says Kim Hurlock, full-time supervisor of the house.

The doorbell rings often at the house as relatives, friends and, volunteers stop in to visit. Teenagers who first met the residents through community service projects for church groups and the like, often come back just to hang-out. Whether they know it or not, these kids are teaching these six adults some valuable lessons.

As Hurlock explains, "Our basic goal is to teach these people to go out on their own, and social relationships with other people help them learn."

Both Hurlock and Assistant Supervisor Joan Callahan agree that, one day, these people will be ready to embark on their own. They're learning to shop for groceries and clothes, to do laundry, make telephone calls, and prepare food. They are also getting a chance to handle and budget their own money. Several residents can walk to the bank by themselves and cash their checks -- a monumental accomplishment to them.

The supervisors stress that no one has to move out until he or she feels ready.

The residents, gathered around the large dining room table, agree most emphatically that they are not for such a step. "We have to keep working on things and keep helping each other," explains Alan Russo. Several others nod in agreement.

In discussing the past eight months, they all agree they've made more progress than ever before in their lives. Phrases like "I learned how to...," "I was really proud of myself," and "I've really grown up" are offered. They talk about helping their peers at their jobs (they work at Seaside Reginal Center's workshops and at the Easter Seals Rehabilitation Center), and accepting assistance from others when they need help.

When one resident wants to buy greeting cards for her family, an employee in a local pharmacy reads the cards to her, as she's still learning how to read. Yet this is progress; a year ago, she wouldn't go into a store by herself.

Another resident who has cerebral palsy fell down in the bank and had trouble getting up, so a stranger rushed over and helped her to her feet. Yet, a year ago, she never dreamed she'd have the courage or skills to even walk into a bank.

Instead of others always doing for them, they're doing for themselves now -- and allowing others to help. Says Hurlock, "Before, when I tried to tell one of them they weren't doing something quite right, they'd say 'You're not giving me credit for trying.'"

Now, she says with a chuckle, the standard comment at 126 Pennsylvania Avenue is, "Well, I'm always trying."

"Group Home Helps Residents Keep Trying," Susan A. Lewis, *Clinton Recorder*, Vol. 3, No. 57, April 28, 1984. Copyright 1984 Capital Cities Communications, Inc.

Success of Niantic home paves the way for more

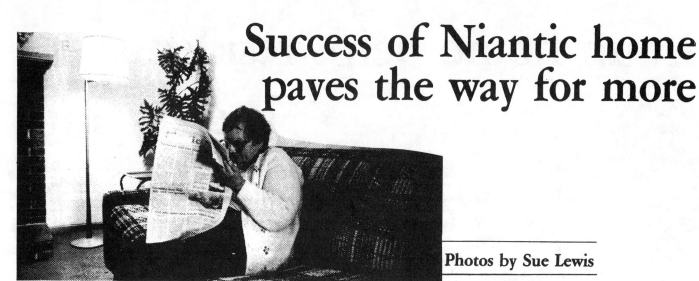

Photos by Sue Lewis

Enjoying a moment to herself is resident Pat Sweeny.

By SUSAN A. LEWIS
Special to Saturday

WATERFORD/EAST LYME -- Group homes for the mentally retarded, like the facility at 126 Pennsylvania Avenue in Niantic, will be the mode of care for the future, according to Thomas J. Sullivan, director of Seaside Regional Center.

Both the state legislature and the courts have played a part in this movement. In the past two years, lawmakers have supported group homes with state funding. In addition, a recent federal court ruling favoring smaller residential settings over large institutions, has mandated that Seaside and the state's other regional centers help place some of the residents of state institutions for the mentally retarded into smaller, group homes.

The ruling stemmed from a five-year suit against the state and Mansfield Training Center by the Connecticut Association for Retarded Citizens. The association claimed the retarded are better off in smaller homes than in large institutions.

Sullivan said that, while the future is not clear yet, both the court ruling and state funding will result in more group homes in the Seaside area which encompasses Southeastern Connecticut.

There are already six private group homes in the area, including the one in Niantic, together housing 32 people. Two more are expected to open by summer. In addition, the state is currently constructing two homes that will each house eight residents. One is being built in Waterford and the other in Groton. Existing state-owned group homes in the area house 41 people.

Sullivan believes that with the advent of individualized care offered by the group homes, things are "finally turning around for the mentally retarded." Part of the task, he said, involved dispelling some of the myths about the retarded.

The homes established so far have proven themselves. "The group homes unequivocably have been one hundred percent successful in terms of people adjusting to the community." The keys to these successes, he added, are the combined care provided by the staff and social workers in a less restrictive environment.

"Group homes are going to be the future for mental retardation care, with the enthusiasm and support from the legislature. The direction is there, and the communities have been very receptive."

Heather Davis, who seems to be in charge of salad-making detail on this day, gets a hand from resident Stephen Kennedy.

"Success of Niantic Home Paves The Way For More," Susan A. Lewis, *Clinton Recorder*, Vol. 3, No. 57, April 28, 1984. Copyright 1984 Capital Cities Communications, Inc.

PARENTAL PARTICIPATION IN A VOLUNTARY ORGANISATION FOR INTELLECTUALLY HANDICAPPED PERSONS

RON K. PENNEY

School of Behavioural Science
Western Australian Institute of Technology

A qualitative analysis was made into the parental participation of parents of a voluntary organisation concerned with the intellectually handicapped. The voluntary organisation requested the research as a result of the lack of participation in recent years that affected attendance at branch meetings, case conferences and general support for activities.

Theme analysis revealed concern about the services being offered by the organisation and their fulfilment of the needs, particularly of the younger parents with the major theme being benefit.

Several recommendations were made to the voluntary organisation based on the results of the theme analysis.

The necessity of parental involvement is acknowledged by many professionals working with young intellectually handicapped people. The assistance and education of parents by early interventionists and the inclusion of parents in the intervention programme are accepted as necessary activities if the child is to make maximum developmental progress (Bricker et. al., 1976; Bricker and Casuso, 1979; Tymchuk, 1975).

The support and active involvement of parents does not stop at early intervention. Parents continuing involvement when their intellectually handicapped child is in special education and later in vocational preparation is vital if these programmes are to be effective (Brolin, 1976; Reynolds and Birch, 1977; Whelan and Speake, 1977). Moreover, the benefits derived from parental involvement are reciprocal. Not only is parental involvement helpful to programme specialists and the intellectually handicapped person, but it is also beneficial to the parents. Kroth and Scholl (1978) suggest that parents derive a sense of being useful and productive in assisting in programmes and it allows the parent to achieve a closer and perhaps more positive perspective on the child's education.

As is the case with individual programmes for the intellectually handicapped person, it is also necessary for active parental involvement in voluntary organisations if the organisation is to meet its objectives and if parents are to benefit from membership. According to Telford and Sawrey (1977) the benefits for parents involved in self-help organisations are multiple. These authors suggest that voluntary organisations allow for an exchange of information about ameliorative and coping devices, provide for mutual motivation and support and perhaps most importantly facilitate group identification which reduces feelings of isolation and alienation. Likewise the benefits from the organisation's perspective are multiple as well and include assistance in fund raising, support for the organisation's policies and programmes (e.g. advocacy, human relations training), and aid/support in setting objectives.

But what happens if active participation in a voluntary organisation is minimal? According to Wolfensberger (1973) the lack of participation in a voluntary organisation is not uncommon and is associated with success in obtaining services as well as expanding in its provision of services. "Obtaining services" is defined by Wolfensberger as a decision by the organisation to get other bodies to fund and operate services while "providing services" is defined as a decision by the organisation to run its own services regardless of the source of funds, e.g. government or private/charitable funds. Wolfensberger argues that voluntary organisations who have been successful in obtaining and expanding the provision of services face problems such as a loss of active membership, or even membership itself, bureaucratisation, stagnation or all of these. The reasons for these problems result from loss of identity in the case of obtaining services and professionalization of an organisation in the case of expansion of the provision of services.

The problem of parental participation in a voluntary organisation for the intellectually handicapped as viewed by parent members is the subject of this evaluation.

A large voluntary organisation was concerned over recent years with the lack of parental participation in branch meetings, case conferences, and parental assistance in providing effective services. In particular, the organisation wished to determine from the parents' perspective why they did not participate in a variety of areas and what changes in the organisation would lead to more active participation.

The history of the organisation is a model of the history of voluntary organisations referred to by Wolfensberger (1973). This particular organisation was founded in 1951 and, as in the Wolfensberger description, the formation was based on the lack of services for intellectually handicapped persons and professional neglect.

In 1951 the Department of Education decided to close a demonstration/special class for 11 boys and girls with I.Qs. below 75. The parents and friends objected to the closure and formed a voluntary organisation who within the first six months organised a summer camp and formed their first branch in 1951.

During the remaining years of the 1950s, additional branches were formed, a diagnostic clinic opened and residential and activity centres were developed with the aid of the State government and the Lotteries Commission.

Using Wolfensberger's definitions of provision of services, the organisation was very successful in expanding the provision of services during the early 1960s. But in 1964 the diagnostic centre was subsumed under the State government's Department of Mental Health and the first incursion into taking responsibility for direct services was made by the State government.

Perhaps the success of the organisation can be reflected by the following statement made in 1970 by the organisation:

"In 19 years from a Parents Group of some 20 or so people, the organisation has expanded to provide facilities for children and adults who are mentally retarded. In addition to the Day Activity Centres and Workshops, the organisation operates 4 metropolitan hostels and 2 hostels in the country and provides a transport service with its fleet of 30 vehicles."

Methodology

A qualitative analysis approach was utilized in the present research. The qualitative approach to social life utilizes a mechanistic and static assumption following the natural sciences' positivistic paradigm (Filstead, 1979). However, qualitative analysis subscribes to a phenomenological, inductive, holistic, process-oriented view of the world (Cook and Reichardt, 1979). Patton (1980) expands on this distinction by arguing that the qualitative approach captures what people have to say in their own words and describes the experiences of people in depth. The qualitative approach seeks to determine what experiences and interactions mean to people and is an attempt to understand people in their own terms.

The researcher in the qualitative paradigm negotiates the research questions with both data providers and those who will utilize the results. The former are involved because as consumers they are most helpful in focusing the questions to be asked in the research while the latter are the users of the information and if they are to utilize the information, they must have input. Too often evaluation research is not used for rational decision-making (Patton, 1978) and the involvement of decision-makers from the very beginning increases the probability that the results will be utilized.

In the present research, the involvement of the decision-makers and some of the consumers was incorporated into the research by the participation of the Executive Director of the voluntary organisation as well as some of the senior staff and parents. This group suggested and discussed with the researchers questions that should be asked to the data providers. A series of meetings led to the production of a number of questions. These questions were then focused and placed in the following categories:

1. Knowledge about the organisation (7 questions)

2. Involvement with the organisation (6 questions)

3. Communication in the organisation (3 questions)

4. Services provided and not provided (2 questions)

5. Adequacy of case conferences (5 questions)

6. Other information related to the topic (3 questions).

The questions were then submitted to the organisation's Board of Management who made several suggestions that were incorporated.

Sample

A total of 79 parents were randomly selected from the current membership list of the organisation. As some of the randomly selected parents were unable to participate due to work schedules, ill-health, transportation problems, and care-taking responsibilities, the next parent on the list immediately following the randomly selected parent was contacted. If this parent was unable to participate the next name was contacted and so on down the list until the next randomized parent's name was indicated. A total of 31 parents were chosen by this procedure while 48 parents were the originally designated random numbered parents.

An additional 39 parents (volunteers) in two country areas were included. These parents were not chosen at random as it was difficult to obtain participation in these regions as a result of the short period (one day each) during which the research was conducted in the country.

The original intent was to interview all the parents in groups but this procedure was not possible as many of the parents had problems that did not allow them to be interviewed outside their home.

The participants ranged in age from 28 to 68 years of age. Of the 118 participants approximately 29 per cent were new members (less than two years) while the remaining were established members (more than two years).

condition with the majority (78%) being in the moderate to severe area of classification. All of the participant's children/adults were either in Special Schools, Activity Centres, Hostels *or* Workshops.

Scoring

The interviews were transcribed and theme analysis applied to the data. The initial task was to examine the transcripts for convergence, i.e. determining what things fit together, and from this convergence a classification system was established. Two researchers separately determined their own theme classification system, and these themes were discussed/compared by the two researchers. From this latter list of themes priorities were applied to determine which category system was more satisfactory than another. Some of the criteria for "satisfactory" were taken from Guba (1978) and included the following:

1. The themes should relate to the mandate given by the client.

2. The data on which the themes are based should hold together *or* integrate in a meaningful way.

3. The differences among the themes should be marked and clear. "The existence of a large number of unassignable or overlapping data items is good evidence of some basic fault in the category system" (Guba, 1978: 53).

4. The themes should be reproducable by another judge.

Once the themes were categorized on the basis of 1 to 3 above, another experienced/competent researcher was asked to develop the themes from the data provided and those themes that did not agree with this researcher's judgement were discarded.

The next step was to determine the validity of utilizing these themes. Two researchers applied the theme analysis to the first two questions for each of the six interview categories described earlier and a consensual validity based on the following ratio was applied:

$$\text{Consensual validity} = \frac{\text{agreements}}{\text{agreements} + \text{disagreements}}$$

The consensual validity was .89 for interview category 1, .78 for interview category 2, .94 for interview category 3, .76 for interview category 4, .82 for interview category 5, and .79 for interview category 6. These consensual coefficients indicate a high degree of consistency in applying the themes to the interview data by two researchers.

Results

Although a typical theme analysis avoids placing percentages on the themes derived from the results section, this report analyzed the percentage of the sample that expressed the theme in order to demonstrate to the organisation the seriousness of the themes.

Seven major themes were identified. The first theme can best be described as a benefit

The children/adults of the participants were perceived by their parents as educable to moderate to severe in their handicapping theme as applied to the organisation and its programmes. This theme is exemplified by:

1. Dissatisfaction with the bureaucratic nature of the organisation (72% of total sample). More particularly, the organisation in its business role has lost its meaning to younger members in that they cannot see the benefits of belonging to the organisation and being actively involved (92% of younger sample).

2. The need for innovative programmes that directly *benefit* the *younger* parents (68% of total sample).

Presently, the State government agency for the Intellectually Handicapped and Special Education Department are providing services and particularly younger parents view these services as beneficial. This is not to state that these parents are completely satisfied with the quality of these services but nevertheless they are services presently benefiting the younger parents. On the other hand, the organisation's current services are adult/oriented and of little or no use to the younger parents at this point in time.

A second predominant theme is the charity role of the organisation. There is some confusion in this theme in that some parents (55% of total sample) believe the organisation should not seek charity from the public but should obtain more funds from government. On the other hand, some parents (25% of total sample) wished the organisation to be more independent from the government so that they could advocate/monitor government services.

The communication theme suggested communication was poor with *younger parents* (78% of younger sample) not knowing what the services of the organisation are and how they could benefit from them. The organisation's newsletter apparently did not facilitate communication for either older or younger parents (72% of total sample).

Related to the communication theme was the theme that the organisation's goals and objectives were unknown (69% of total sample). Younger parents in particular wished for more information on the organisation's aims and objectives and its future direction (89%).

As is the case in the benefit theme referred to earlier, *beneficial* services were emphasized in a support theme. Services that received favourable mention were parent-to-parent, baby-sitting, recreation (including the Discovery Club). A service that did not receive completely favourable mention from either older or younger members was the Hostel service in that some parents (68% of total sample) felt that there was poor

communication between themselves and the Hostels and the staff were inadequately trained.

The support needed by *younger* parents appeared to be services that would aid the day-to-day living of these parents, e.g. counselling, advocacy/support, relief (64% of younger sample).

The case conference theme was equivocal. Many parents (69% of total sample) believed that they were beneficial in that they outlined the progress of their children/ adults. Other parents (31% of total sample) felt intimidated and maintained that since their in-put was not sought, the conferences were useless.

Under the theme of change the predominant reaction to Branch meetings was that they should be less formal/business oriented and more informal/social oriented (82% of total sample). Few parents (92% of total sample) received benefit from attending Branch meetings. The business side of these meetings was above their heads and boring (78% of total sample). Moreover, the stress as perceived by the parents (72% of total sample) on fund raising was objectionable unless this fund raising had direct benefit to the Branch.

In general, the common theme was benefit. Both younger and older parents sampled, but more generally younger parents, could not see the benefits derived from belonging to the organisation. This state of affairs may be due to (1) poor communication as was suggested by some parents, (2) services not relevant to younger parents, (3) bureaucratic nature of the organisation, (4) perceived intimidation by the older parents preventing younger parents from lobbying for more relevant services and (5) lack of stated aims and objectives of the organisation.

The above listed themes are summarized in Table I.

Conclusions

The parents interviewed gave some very sound suggestions to the organisation for how to get people to attend, join up, speak out, work on committees and lend support.

Although the benefit theme was only one suggestion, the concept of benefit is supported by other researchers. In particular Rothman, Erlich and Teresa (1979) conclude that the findings of recent research on participation can be summarized as follows:

"The amount of voluntary participation in an organisation depends on the benefits gained from participation, and the degree to which the benefits are shown to result directly from participation" (p. 385).

Under the heading of benefits the follow-

TABLE I.

Summary of themes with percentages

Themes	Percentage of Sample
I. Benefit Themes	
Dissatisfaction with Bureaucratic Nature	72% (total)
Need for Innovative Programmes	68% (total)
II. Charity Role	
More Government support for Organisation	55% (total)
Less Government support for Organisation/	
Advocacy Roles	25% (total)
III. Communication Theme	
Poor	78% (younger)
Dissatisfaction with Newsletter	72% (total)
IV. Goals and Objectives	
Unknown, poorly defined	69% (total)
V. Support Services	
Poor Communication in Hostels	68% (total)
Need for Counselling, Support, Relief	64% (younger)
VI. Case Conference	
Beneficial	69% (total)
Useless	31% (total)
VII. Suggestions for Change to Branch Meetings	
Informal/Social	82% (total)

ing recommendations were made to the organisation:

1. The organisation give consideration to its advocacy/support role. There appears to be a concern that the organisation is not fulfilling this role presently although the parent-to-parent programme is a step in this direction. Special attention could be given to providing for short-term placements in Hostels to provide relief support.

2. Fund raising and the charity image be examined. Many parents resent these activities unless they can see direct benefit to their handicapped person. This issue may be one of communication and the stressing of the benefits of fund raising. Also, consideration could be given to funding in Regions for specific purposes related to the Region.

3. Innovative/demonstration projects be examined with the aim of establishing such projects, e.g. a travelling bus library.

4. Liaison persons be designated (employees of the Organisation or volunteers) for a given area for information dissemination and membership enlistment.

The suggestion for a needs analysis was also recommended to the organisation as the research was not designed to assess needs but in order to take into consideration benefits, this type of analysis is required. More specifically the recommendation was —

A needs analysis be performed with members of the organisation to determine their current needs as they relate to the organisation. It is apparent that the organisation is not meeting some of the needs of its younger parents. The question of benefits would be addressed by this process. The present report suggests that the members needs are not being met in such areas as counselling, support and advocacy (see item 1 above).

In order to address the other themes described in the results section, the following recommendations were submitted:

1. The organisation give consideration to restructuring its organisation. The country regions in particular suggested a more decentralised organisation with autonomy given to Regional Boards of Management on the basis of some Central division of funds and policy. Perhaps, a regionalisation in the central area could be considered at the same time because regionalisation, decentralisation and autonomy may increase involvement and lead to less perception of the organisation as 'bureaucratic".

2. Communication be improved through a reorganisation of the Newsletter publicising the aims and objectives and future directions of the organisation and include articles (in lay terms) on day-to-day problems faced by members. Communication can also be improved through greater utilisation of the media and better

staff to parent communication in the organisation's facilities. Perhaps the public relations section needs to be kept separate from fund raising so that all efforts can be channelled into public relations. Special attention could also be given to the orientation literature (Welcome To The Organisation) where goals/objectives, benefits are specified.

3. Branch meetings be made more informal/social and less business oriented with age-related groups being formed at different Branches/Regions under the auspices of the organisation. Perhaps these informal structures could be organised around

facilities (e.g. Workshops, Hostels) rather than Branches/Regions.

4. Review of case conferences is needed and perhaps uniform guideline procedures developed with special attention to parent input and professional "intimidation"

5. The results and recommendations of this report be fed-back to the members through meetings/workshops, written communication or any other means so as to highlight the organisation's concern for the problem and its interest in discovering

ways to bring about better participation for the benefit of intellectually handicapped persons.

Although the research was concerned with a voluntary organisation for intellectually handicapped, the results and conclusions need not be restricted to organisations for intellectually handicapped nor to voluntary organisations. In particular the concept of benefit could be applied to any human service where parental participation is a goal. Indeed, one of the first steps is for organisations to recognize the goal of participation and further to recognize that benefits for members must derive from participation.

Extending this analysis to special education, one of the goals of such programmes must be parental participation. Too often, teachers of special education view parents as a hindrance. Barsch (1969) notes that special education teachers are well trained in meeting the needs of the child but poorly trained in meeting the needs of the parents. Perhaps, training in special education should include parental participation as a significant goal and examine the benefits for teachers, parents and children as they relate to participation.

References

BARSCH, R. L. *The Parent Teacher Partnership*. Arlington Council for Exceptional Children, 1969.

BRICKER, D., BRICKER, W., IACINO, R. and DENNISON, L. Intervention strategies for profoundly retarded children. In N. Haring and L. Brown (Eds.), *Teaching the Severely Handicapped* (Vol. 1), New York: Grune & Stratton, 1976.

BRICKER, D. and CASUSO, V. A critical component of early intervention. *Exceptional Children*, 1979, 46, 108-117.

BROLIN, D. *Vocational Preparation of Retarded Citizens*. Ohio: Merril Publishing, 1976.

COOK, T. D. and REICHARDT, C. S. *Qualitative and Quantitative Methods in Evaluation Research*. London: Sage Publications, 1979.

FILSTEAD, W. J. Qualitative methods a needed perspective in evaluation research. In T. D. Cook and C. S. Reichardt (eds.). *Qualitative and Quantitative Methods in Evaluation Research*. London: Sage Publications, 1979.

GUBA, E. Towards a methodology of naturalistic enquiry in educational evaluation. *CSE Monographs Series in Evaluation*. Los Angeles: Center for the Study of Evaluation, 1978.

KROTH, R. L. and SCHOLL, G. T. *Getting*

Schools Involved With Parents. The Council for Exceptional Children, 1978.

PATTON, M. Q. *Utilization Focused Evaluation*. Beverly Hills: Sage Publishing, 1978.

PATTON, M. Q. *Qualitative Evaluation Methods*. Beverly Hills: Sage Publishing, 1980.

REYNOLDS, M. C. and BIRCH, J. W. Teaching exceptional children. In V. Reston (ed.) *All America's Schools*, Council for Exceptional Children, 1977.

ROTHMAN, J., ERLICH, J. L. and TERESA, J. G. Fostering participation. In F. Cox, J. Erlich, J. Rothman and J. Tropman (eds.) *Strategies of Community Organisation*. Itasca, Illinois: Peacock Publishers, 1979.

TELFORD, C. W. and SAWREY, J. M. *The Exceptional Individual*. Englewood Cliffs: Prentice-Hall, 1977.

TYMCHUK, A. J. Training parent therapists, *Mental Retardation*, 1975, 19-22.

WHELAN, E. and SPEAKE, B. *Adult Training Centres in England and Wales*. National Association of Teachers of the Mentally Handicapped, 1977.

WOLFENSBERGER, E. W. *The Third Stage in the Evolution of Voluntary Associations for the Mentally Retarded*. Toronto: National Institute on Mental Retardation, 1973.

A Grandparent's View

by JOAN M. GERVER

Daniel with his family.

Joan M. Gerver, Ph.D., is a psychologist on the staff of the Lifeline Center for Child Development, Queens Village, N.Y.

Anticipating the arrival of a first grandchild is a special experience. Our initial joy when our son telephoned to announce the birth of his son was followed two days later by despair and depression, when he called again to tell us that the baby had Down syndrome. An alert pediatrician had suspected what the obstetrician and nurse had missed. Several characteristics were present, an X-ray showed a displacement in the hip joint (characteristic of the syndrome), and chromosomal tests confirmed the diagnosis of Trisomy 21.

The only associations I had toward Down syndrome were negative. I recalled a protesting child making unrecognizable sounds, being pulled by an exhausted mother in a playground. Scenes from Letchworth Village—a state institution for the "feeble-minded" where I spent several days during my clinical internship in the 1940s—emerged from the recesses of memory: hydrocephalics, unable to lift their grossly disproportionate heads; mildly retarded women feeding profoundly retarded inmates; rows of adult-size cribs housing a population of idiots and imbeciles, as they were labeled then. It was such a grotesque world that I pushed it far back in the depths of memory, preferring to work with the gifted, or at least those of normal intelligence.

Now it was here, in my family, knocking at the door of my heart. Emotions flooded me. Elizabeth Kübler-Ross has described the stages that one goes through when confronting imminent death. Here, too, one may experience anger, denial (mistaken diagnosis—maybe those features that typify Down syndrome are only a throwback to some ancestor?) and a kind of bargaining or rationalization (since the parents are gifted, retardation will mean the baby is merely normal) as one attempts to deal with unexpected tragedy.

Amid all of this inner turmoil, there was concern over my son and daughter-in-law, compounded by the fact that they were living literally halfway around the world from us. After a week of crying, I pulled myself together. The situation existed,

the baby was real, what *could* and *should* be done?

For me, the first step was to get information. There was never any hesitation in telling relatives, friends, even colleagues. Their responses were positive and supportive. They provided newspaper clippings, popular magazine articles and anecdotes. But I wanted more scientific information. A hunger for accurate information seems to be an early reaction to the diagnosis, and the need to be up-to-date on the latest research is continuous.

Our local public library has a good selection of books, and I was fortunate in my initial choice: *Children of Dreams, Children of Hope* by Raymundo Veras (Henry Regnery, 1975).* I say "fortunate" because the book expressed great hope for what could be done with children formerly given up as "hopeless." The author, a Brazilian physician, described his personal encounter with discouraging professionals after his son's tragic accident and how, through persistence, patience and hope, the child made remarkable strides. Even though the methods of patterning he advocated are not applicable and do not work for everyone, the underlying theme of hope provided an emotional and cognitive *set* that was, and continues to be, extremely helpful.

I also searched for material in the professional journals and current medical and psychological texts. (Some still use the term Mongoloid!)

My first advice to other grandparents would be to start with a hopeful book. One couple, faced with a similar need to acquire "instant information," told me of their visit to a small local library in the area where they were vacationing when the news arrived that their grandchild was born with Down syndrome. The only available books referred to Mongolism as hopeless and advocated institutionalization as the only recourse. The initial impact of this obsolete information was negative and only exacerbated the conflict, especially when there was no rejection of the baby by the family.

In addition to the desire for accurate information—a cognitive need—I wanted to meet and talk with others who were affected by Down syndrome, and I especially wanted to see babies with the disorder. A friend who was a social worker told me of an organization that visited new mothers of Down syndrome infants in the hospital. Another friend gave me the name of a social worker connected with a medical institution serving our area. A series of telephone calls—networking—provided the names of the Parents' Assistance Committee for Down syndrome liaison persons in our county. Both were parents of children with the disorder.

I will never forget the warmth and understanding that permeated my initial contacts with Barbara Levitz and Emily Kingsley. Barbara offered me the opportunity to speak with other grandparents (her own parents), since my concern also involved my children—the parents of our new grandchild. Emily volunteered to bring her son, Jason, to our house, so I could see a real, live, functioning child with Down syndrome. I did want to see the child, but I wanted to see him in his own home, on his territory.

My 23-year-old daughter offered to come with me, and I, who rarely ventured on the road after dark, drove on unfamiliar highways at night to reach the Kingsleys' home. The motivation to see and learn overcame my fear and discomfort. Finding unknown strengths in oneself is another thing one experiences. When you have to do something, you go ahead and do it. One rises to the demands of the situation of the moment.

We were welcomed into the house, and a little boy insisted on hanging our coats in the closet. Although he was a trifle clumsy, he knew what to do for visitors. We were amazed. We had expected to find a living vegetable; instead, we spent an enjoyable time with an alert youngster.

The anticipation and fear of the unknown are worse than the reality. Seeing and being with a Down syndrome child assuaged our dread of the unknown. The problems were real, but they were tangible, and it is easier to cope with the known.

I would encourage other new grandparents to look—feel—handle—a child with Down syndrome as soon as possible. If one is geographically close, one can see the new grandchild, but if the baby is miles away, as in our case, get in touch with a support group and visit a child with the disorder living at home.

I eventually met my new grandson—three visits to Hawaii in two years, once with my daughter and twice with my husband—always laden with presents and warm wishes from our friends to the baby and his parents. My first glimpse of the baby was after an exhausting 12-hour airplane trip. My son and his wife were waiting at our hotel, carrying a tiny, embryonic-looking creature. Their love for their baby was obvious, and soon we were involved with watching his responses and reactions. The first 24 hours of each visit were depressing and sad for me, partly due to the long intervals between visits. But after being with the baby and observing him closely, we saw evidence of curiosity and experimentation. The depression was replaced with delight and pride in his accomplishments.

I would urge grandparents to accept the fact that their grandchild will develop in a different time frame, using a different clock. This is not easy; one cannot refrain from ever comparing, or wishing "What if . . . .?" It is normal to have such thoughts, as long as they don't immobilize you, or keep you from loving and enjoying the child that is, not the child that might have been.

What else can grandparents of a Down syndrome child do? Some of the same things a grandparent would do for any new parents. Offer them respite, if possible, a few hours "off" to go to a movie—or services, such as help with shopping and cooking. Give them "another pair of arms," as one grandfather described it. The help might also be financial, if you are able to give and they are willing to receive. If nothing else, there is always a need for psychological support. We have rejoiced with each new milestone our grandson has attained and showed our concern over problems that arise.

Realizing the importance of early intensive stimulation in raising Down syndrome children at home, we have made and bought things we felt would be helpful in his development—records, books, puppets, talking clocks, a sturdy wagon, puzzles, an anatomically correct boy doll, a shirt with his name across the front.

The rewards are unexpected. They occur when he gives us a sweet smile of recognition, or spontaneously "sings" several verses of a school song using sign language, or recognizes words printed on cards.

Despite some similarities in physical characteristics of Down syndrome children, it is important for grandparents to realize that each child will be different physically and mentally and should be treated as an individual with different strengths and weaknesses. By developing a positive and hopeful outlook, grandparents can do much to encourage their grandchild to reach his or her full potential, whatever it may be.